Mike Davis (1946–2022) was a writer, political activist, urban theorist, and historian. He is best known for his investigations of power and class in works such as *City of Quartz*, *Late Victorian Holocausts*, and *Planet of Slums*. His last two nonfiction books are *Set the Night on Fire: L.A. in the Sixties*, co-authored by Jon Wiener, and *The Monster Enters: COVID-19, Avian Flu, and the Plagues of Capitalism*. He was the recipient of the MacArthur Fellowship and the Lannan Literary Award.

Praise for *Old Gods, New Enigmas*

"Mike Davis's guiding vision is clear and bold: a reinvigorated and politically charged Marxism, brimming with original insights and suffused with historical depth."

—Nancy Fraser, author of *Cannibal Capitalism*

"A formidable intellectual, and this collection contains many gems."

—Troy Vettese, *Boston Review*

Praise for Mike Davis

"Davis remains our penman of lost souls and lost scenarios: He culls nuggets of avarice and depredation the way miners chisel coal."

—*Nation*

"A rare combination of an author, Rachel Carson, and Upton Sinclair all in one."

—Susan Faludi

"The thread that runs through his work is the cruel and perpetual folly of the ruling elites."

—*New York Times*

Praise for *City of Quartz*

"Absolutely fascinating."

—William Gibson

"As central to the L.A. canon as anything that Carey McWilliams wrote in the forties or Joan Didion wrote in the seventies."

—Dana Goodyear, *New Yorker*

"A history as fascinating as it is instructive."

—Peter Ackroyd, *The Times*

OLD GODS, NEW ENIGMAS

Marx's Lost Theory

MIKE DAVIS

VERSO

London • New York

This paperback edition first published by Verso 2025
First published by Verso 2018
© Mike Davis 2018

Earlier versions of chapters 2, 3, and 4 appeared in *New Left Review*, published in
the following issues: II/90, May–June 2015; II/97, January–February 2016; II/61,
January–February 2010

1 3 5 7 9 10 8 6 4 2

Verso
UK: 6 Meard Street, London W1F 0EG
US: 207 East 32nd Street, New York, NY 10016
versobooks.com

Verso is the imprint of New Left Books

ISBN-13: 978-1-80429-820-6
ISBN-13: 978-1-78873-219-2 (US EBK)
ISBN-13: 978-1-78873-218-5 (UK EBK)

British Library Cataloguing in Publication Data
A catalogue record for this book is available from the British Library

The Library of Congress Has Cataloged the Hardback Edition as Follows:

Names: Davis, Mike, 1946– author.
Title: Old gods, new enigmas : Marx's lost theory / Mike Davis.
Description: London ; New York : Verso, 2018. | Includes bibliographical
  references and index.
Identifiers: LCCN 2018012478| ISBN 9781786631107 | ISBN 9781788732192
(US
  e-book) | ISBN 9781788732185 (UK e-book)
Subjects: LCSH: Marx, Karl, 1818–1883—Criticism and interpretation.
Classification: LCC HX39.5 .D337 2018 | DDC 335.4/1—dc23
LC record available at https://lccn.loc.gov/2018012478

Typeset in Fournier by MJ & N Gavan, Truro, Cornwall, UK
Printed and bound by CPI Group (UK) Ltd, Croydon, CR0 4YY

It is when you have done your work honestly, when you have contributed your share to the common fund, that you begin to live. Then, as Whitman said, you can take out your soul.

Eugene Debs

Contents

Preface

Marx at the Chicken Shack[1]

READ MARX!

Lee Gregovich's injunction has been rattling around my brain for more than half a century. A good friend of my dad, he was, I suppose, my "red godfather." His family, like many others from the Dalmatian coast, had emigrated to the copper mines of the American Southwest before the First World War. There they were embroiled in epic labor conflicts. Lee told rousing stories about his days as an IWW paper boy, selling the *Industrial Worker* in saloons and cathouses, and then watching as his father and 1,300 other striking miners, mostly Mexican and south Slav, were arrested by Phelps-Dodge vigilantes, put in manure-floored cattle cars, and "deported" to a bleak stretch of desert in New Mexico. In the 1930s he became active in the Cooks Union in San Diego and joined the Communist Party. The House Committee on Un-American Activities brought its inquisition to San Diego in 1954 and Lee was subpoenaed and then blacklisted by employers. He finally found a job cooking at the Chicken Shack, an old-style roadhouse near the picturesque mountain town of Julian.

When my father had a catastrophic heart attack in my junior year, I quit high school for a semester to drive a delivery truck for my uncle's wholesale meat company. The Chicken Shack was our most distant customer and once every week or so, after delivering to country restaurants with names like the Lariat and the Lazy J, I'd scuttle up the long road to Julian. On such days Lee and I had a ritual. After the order had been put in the walk-in, he'd pour me a small glass of red wine, we'd talk briefly about my dad's health or the Civil Rights movement (he was proud that I had become active in San Diego CORE), then, as I got up to leave, he'd slap me on the back and say, "Read Marx!" (I've always liked telling this story and was not surprised when a garbled version of it, insinuating that Lee was a mysterious Soviet agent, appeared in my FBI file.)

Lee himself, like millions of other rank-and-file socialists and communists, had read little or no Marx. *Wage, Labor and Capital*, perhaps, and certainly some Lenin, whose *The Teachings of Karl Marx* was a popular substitute for reading the old man himself. Most ordinary readers, however, cowered in face of that Everest of theory, *Capital*. The few who attempted it usually fell into one of the early crevasses of the first chapter and never returned for a second try. This only added, of course, to the mystique of Marx's genius and the prestige of party intellectuals who claimed to have reached the summit. A study of workers' libraries in Wilhelmine Germany found that serious proletarian readers were especially interested in Darwinism and materialist interpretations of natural history, not the critique of political economy. Kautsky's *Economic Doctrines of Karl Marx* was "more borrowed than actually read."[2] In 1936, the Menshevik authors of *Karl Marx: Man and Fighter*—a biography that admirably focused on the thinker as revolutionist—estimated that "perhaps one socialist in a thousand has ever read any of Marx's economic writings, and of a thousand anti-Marxists not even one."[3]

Little had changed when I joined the Southern California Communist Party in 1968 in solidarity with their stand against the

Russian suppression of the Prague Spring. I was flabbergasted that new members' political education consisted solely of reading Julius Fucik's *Notes from the Gallows*—the stirring last testament of a young Czech Communist executed in 1943, but hardly an introduction to Marxism. My own knowledge was limited to the *Paris Notebooks* and bits of *The German Ideology*, recommended in a popular book that I had read on Marx and alienation. The only member of the L.A. Party, young or old, who seemed to have a serious understanding of Marx, and indeed was reading the *Werke* in German, was newly recruited Angela Davis, and she was fighting too many important battles to have time to tutor the rest of us.

What made Marx a stranger to Marxist movements, however, was not simply the difficulty of certain key works and passages, but a series of other obstacles. Where to begin, for example? If you began at the beginning with dialectics, you had to endure Hegel scowling at you while you became increasingly befuddled—at least, that was my experience while trying to digest Marcuse's *Reason and Revolution* during lunch and supper breaks at work. I was delighted years later to discover an epigram in which the young Marx registered his own frustration with the Master and his interpreters:

"On Hegel"

> Words I teach all mixed up into a devilish muddle,
> Anyone may think just what he chooses to think;
> Each may for himself suck wisdom's nourishing nectar;
> Now you know all, since I've said plenty of nothing to you![4]

If you gave G. W. F. a detour, you might discover, with the aid of interpretations by the Marxist Humanists then in vogue, the inspiring Marx of the Paris and Brussels years. (*The Holy Family* [1845], however, never made my reading list since the only person that I've ever known who read it was on acid at the time.) But then, once you thought that you had learned to walk, Althusser came along and the Young Marx suddenly became the Wrong Marx.

With few exceptions, however, the Marx of the Rue Elm and other seminars was disembodied from the "man and fighter." The works most infused with the passion of the barricades, the extraordinary political analyses of the 1848–50 cycle, were usually ignored by the philosophers. In my unsuccessful autodidact years, Marx seemed either emulsified in incompatible doctrines imposed by party ideologists (Diamat, for instance) or hidden away in mysterious untranslated manuscripts. In addition, it was almost impossible to gain an overview of the *oeuvre* since the publication of the English version of the collected works was still years in the future. Martin Nicolaus's translation of the legendary *Grundrisse* in 1973—a milestone of the New Left Review/Penguin Books collaboration—considerably leveled the playing field for non-German readers, but it also added 900 pages of required study to the several thousand pages of the four volumes of *Capital*.

That same year, after losing a coveted niche in the trucking industry, I started UCLA as an adult freshman, attracted by rumors of a high-powered seminar on *Capital* led by Bob Brenner in the History Department. Brenner and his gang (Richard Smith, Jan Breidenbach, Maria Ramos, and others) were reading *Capital* in the context of debates within British Marxism on agrarian class struggles and the transition from feudalism to capitalism. Later the seminar moved on to crisis theory and twentieth-century economic history. It was an exhilarating experience and gave me the intellectual confidence to pursue my own agenda of eclectic interests in political economy, labor history, and urban ecology. Apart from Hal Draper's *Karl Marx's Theory of Revolution* and Michael Löwy's *The Theory of*

Revolution in the Young Marx, both indispensable, I lost interest in Marx studies as it turned from the modes-of-production debate to intensely microscopic battles over the value form, the transformation problem, and the role of Hegelian logic in *Capital*. "Theory" in general, as it became disconnected from real-life battles and big historical questions alike, seemed to take a monstrously obscurantist turn toward the end of the century. I could never imagine Lee Gregovich imploring anyone to "read Jameson, read Derrida," much less to wade through the morass of *Empire*.

SURFING THE COLLECTED WORKS

Over the years my Marxism became rusty, to say the least. But there comes a time when every old student must decide whether or not to renew their driver's license. And reading Daniel Bensaïd's *Marx for Our Times*, a spectacularly imaginative reinterpretation that breaks free of talmudic chains, whetted my appetite for a fresh look at the "non-linear Marx" that Bensaïd proposes.[5] Retirement from teaching, then a long illness finally gave me the leisure to browse through the *Collected Works of Marx and Engels* now in English and, in a pirated version, available for free online.[6] Amongst recent writers who have made brilliant use of the *Collected Works* are John Bellamy Foster, the editor of *Monthly Review,* who has carefully reconstructed Marx's powerful ecological critique of capitalism—a new and exciting topic, particularly in light of later socialism's fetishism of large-scale agriculture; and Erica Benner, whose invaluable recovery of Marx's usually misrepresented views on nationalism is discussed in Chapter 2 ("Marx's Lost Theory"). And the mother lode has hardly been mined out: for example, Marx and Engels's hundreds of pages of acerbic commentaries on the deep games of

nineteenth-century European politics, especially the geopolitical chess match between the British and Russian empires, clearly
warrant a major new interpretation. Likewise, it would be illuminating to compare his theoretical writings on political economy with
his concrete analyses of contemporary economic crises such as 1857
and 1866, topics usually assigned to the footnotes. More generally, I
suspect, "Marx on the conjuncture" should become the new slogan
of Marxologists.

The panoramic view of the *oeuvre* now available also makes it
easier to recognize the blind spots and misdirections in the collaboration of Marx and Engels. The former, for instance, never wrote *a
single word* about cities, and his passionate interests in ethnography,
geology, and mathematics were never matched by a comparable
concern with geography (later the forte of anarchists such as Élisée
Reclus and Peter Kropotkin). He was relatively untraveled, and
only at the very end of his life, desperately sick and seeking the sun,
did he venture outside Western Europe. His letters from Algiers,
praising the culture and dignity of the Arabs, indicated his capacity
to transcend Eurocentric categories and revel in the newness of
other worlds. (Alas, if only he hadn't been so wracked by illness and
family tragedy.) The United States was another paradox. Its protean
future was often on his mind—he was after all a correspondent
for the *New York Tribune*—and he and Engels worked mightily to
win support for Lincoln and Emancipation within the British labor
movement. Yet, despite having read Tocqueville, he never focused
on the unique features of its political system, especially the impact
of early white-manhood suffrage on the development of its labor
movement.

There can be no question that Marx saw far beyond the horizon
of his century and that *Capital*, as the *Economist* (which Marx
read faithfully) pointed out a few years back, remains startlingly

contemporary even in the age of Walmart and Google. But in other cases Marx's vision was limited by the anomalous character of his chronological niche: arguably the most peaceful period of European history in a thousand years. Colonial interventions aside, liberal London-centered capitalism did not seem *structurally* to require large-scale inter-state warfare as a condition of its reproduction or as the inevitable result of its contradictions. He died, of course, before the new imperialism of the late 1880s and 1890s led to zero-sum conflicts amongst the major powers for shares of the world market. Nor could Marx, even after the massacre of the Communards, have possibly foreseen the horrific price that counter-revolution in the next century, including Thermidorean Stalinism, would exact from rank-and-file anarchists, socialists, and communists: at least 7–8 million dead.[7] Since the youngest and most politically conscious tended always to be in the front lines, these repeated decimations of the vanguard entailed incalculable consequences—ones that have been almost entirely ignored by historians.

Likewise, all signs in Marx's day pointed to the continued erosion of belief and the secularization of industrial society. After the early writings, religion was quite understandably not a topic on his agenda. By the end of the century, however, the trends reversed, and political Catholicism, along a spectrum from embryonic Christian Democracy to the *Zentrum* to fascism, became the main competitor with socialism/communism in much of Europe, and the major obstacle to left electoral majorities in the 1910s–20s and 1950s–70s. This surprising Catholic resurgence, almost a second counter-reformation, owed much to the spread of Mariolatry and the church's aggressive appeal to proletarian mothers. The patriarchal character of the workers' movement, which Marx and Engels never challenged, made it blind to the forces at work. Despite a household full of strong, radical women, including three daughters who became prominent revolutionists in their own right, Marx never wavered as *pater familias*, and the movements built in his name, as Barbara Taylor and others have pointed out, actually registered a retrogression from the striking feminism of many utopian socialist sects.[8] Indeed, between Flora Tristan and Clara Zetkin, no woman was able to claim leadership in any of the major labor or socialist formations.

The point, even if initially difficult to swallow, is that socialists, if incomparably armored by Marx's critique of capitalism, also have something to learn from the critique of Marx and his Victorian extrapolations. I say "critique of Marx" rather than "critics of Marx" since, even in the case of those who were noble revolutionary figures in their own right, such as Bakunin and Kropotkin, the mischaracterizations of Marx's ideas were quite fantastic (as were his calumnies against them). The cult of Marx, preceded in the German workers' movement by the cult of Lassalle, justly honored a life of almost sacrificial dedication to human liberation, but otherwise did what all cults do—it petrified his living thoughts and critical method. He, of course, was aware of this danger, which is why he famously said of Jules Guesde and his "orthodox Marxist" wing of the French Workers Party: "Ce qu'il y a de certain c'est que moi, je ne suis pas marxiste" ("What is certain is that [if they are Marxists] I myself am not a Marxist"). How many more times would he have had to say that in the twentieth century?

THE CHAPTERS

In the epilogue to my 2006 book *Planet of Slums*, I asked: To what extent does the informal proletariat, the most rapidly growing global class, possess that most potent of Marxist talismans, "historical agency"? Although I was not aware of it at the time, Eric Hobsbawm had asked exactly the same question in an interview given in 1995. (He is quoted at the beginning of the next chapter.) Neoliberal globalization over the last generation has recharged the meaning of the "wretched of the earth." Hobsbawm's "gray area of the informal economy" has expanded by almost 1 billion people since his interview, and we should probably subsume the "informal proletariat" within a broader category that includes all of those who eke out survival by day labor, "micro-entrepreneurship," and subsistence crime; who toil unprotected by laws, unions, or job contracts; who work outside of socialized complexes such as factories, hospitals, schools, ports, and the like; or simply wander lost in the desert of structural unemployment. There are three crucial questions: (1) What are the possibilities for class consciousness in these informal or peripheral sectors of economies? (2) How can movements, say, of slum-dwellers, the technologically deskilled, or the unemployed find power resources—equivalent, for example, to the ability of formal workers to shut down large units of production—that might allow them to struggle successfully for social transformation? and (3) What kinds of united action are possible between traditional working-class organization and the diverse humanity of the "gray area"? However, in thinking about a sequel to *Planet of Slums*, based on comparative histories and case studies of contemporary activism in the informal economy, I realized that I first needed to clarify how "agency" was construed in the era of classical socialism—that is to say, from Marx's lifetime down to the isolation of the young Soviet state after 1921.

Although everyone agrees that proletarian agency is at the very core of revolutionary doctrine, one searches in vain for any expanded definition, much less canonical treatment. For this reason, **Chapter 1** adopts an indirect strategy: a parallel reading of Marx's

Collected Works and dozens of studies of European and U.S. Labor history in the nineteenth and early twentieth century. The goal has been to find accounts of how *class capacities* and consciousness arose on the principal terrains of social conflict; in the socialized factory and the battles within it for dignity and wages; through sometimes invisible struggles over the labor process; out of the battles of working-class families against landlordism and the high cost of living; from crusades for universal suffrage and against war; in campaigns of solidarity with workers and political prisoners in other countries; and in movements to build alternative socialist and anarchist cultures in the very heart of industrial capitalism. The result, presented as a series of theses, is something like a historical sociology of how the Western working classes acquired consciousness and power. A persistent theme that emerges from these case studies is that class capacity on larger scales arises conjuncturally, as activists reconciled both in practice and in theory different partial demands and interests. In other words, it was precisely at the confluence of struggles (wages and suffrage; neighborhood and factory; industrial and agricultural, and so on)—and sometimes intra-class antagonisms (skilled versus semi-skilled)—that the creative work of organizing became most important and radically transformative. Historical agency, in other words, derived from the capacity to unite and strategically synthesize the entire universe of proletarian grievances and aspirations as presented in specific conjunctures and crises. And, it is necessary to add, to respond successfully to the innovations of employers' offensives and counter-revolutions.

Years ago, Robin Blackburn made the surprising claim that the "real originality of Marx and Engels was in the field of politics, not in economics or philosophy." I would amend this to say "both in politics and economics."[9] **Chapter 2**, "Marx's Lost Theory," influenced by Erica Benner's work on the politics of nationalism in Marx, argues that Marx's requiem for the failed revolution in France (*The Eighteenth Brumaire* and *Class Struggles in France*) stands second only to *Capital* as an intellectual achievement; moreover, it is one grounded completely in the urgency of revolutionary activism. Marx, so to speak, opens up the engine compartment of contemporary events to reveal what Antonio Labriola would later call the "inner social gearing" of economic interests, as well as the autonomous role of the executive state, in a situation where no class was able to form a political majority or lead the way out of the national crisis. The French essays, heralds of a materialist theory of politics, explore a middle landscape, usually unrecognized by Marx interpreters, where "secondary class struggles" over taxes, credit, and money are typically the immediate organizers of the political field. They are also the relays whereby global economic forces often influence political conflict and differential class capacities. (The theory of hegemony, in other words, starts here, with the underlying-interest structure of politics, which is doubly determined by the relations of production, at least in the long run, and the artful activity of leaders, organizers, and brokers.) In any future revolution, Marx argued, the workers' movement must be adept at addressing all forms of exploitation (such as over-taxation of the peasantry and the credit squeeze on small business) and, in the event of a foreign intervention—which he saw almost as a precondition for proletarian hegemony—to lead resistance in the name of the *nation*. These essays, finally, signaled a radical innovation: the retrospective "balance-sheet" method of strategic critique at which Lenin and Trotsky would become so masterful.

Chapter 3 focuses on Marx's critic, Kropotkin, who in his scientific persona instigated a great international debate on climate change. The prince, of course, was the most congenial and charming of late-Victorian anarchists, at least as encountered in the parlors of

London's middle-class radicals and savants, usually hand in hand with his stunningly beautiful daughter Sophia. But the Okhrana, which kept him perpetually under surveillance, regarded this turncoat noble and former explorer as one of the world's most dangerous revolutionists. His intellectual interests, like those of Marx and Engels, were omnivorous; but whereas Marx admired scientists from afar, Kropotkin was one: an outstanding physical geographer whose explorations of Manchuria and the Amur watershed rank in importance and daring with those of contemporaries such as John Wesley Powell and Ferdinand Hayden in the American West. Although he wrote frequently for *Nature* in later years, and his book *Mutual Aid* brilliantly anticipated the "symbiotic turn" in modern biology, his major scientific work on glacial geology and the recession of the ice sheets (the first installment finished in a dungeon) has never been translated, and has only recently been republished in Russian.

From his fieldwork in Siberia and Scandinavia he made a number of deductions about climate change that were popularized decades later in a 1904 article in the *Geographical Journal*. The significance of this article, and the chief topic of Chapter 3, is that Kropotkin was the first scientist to identify *natural* climate change as a major driver of human history. This might not seem terribly original, but in fact it was. In contrast to the current reign of denialism in the White House, educated opinion in the nineteenth century widely embraced the idea that human activity, especially deforestation and industrial pollution, was changing the climate in ways that might threaten agriculture, or even human survival. What was missing until Kropotkin was any observationally grounded case for important cyclical or secular trends in natural climate processes, and evidence that they had shaped history in consequential ways. In his *Geographical Journal* piece he argued that the ending of the Ice Age was a still ongoing process, and that the resulting effects of progressive desiccation were visible across

Eurasia and had produced a series of catastrophic events, including the episodic onslaughts of Asian nomads upon Europe.

Unfortunately, his research became immediately annexed to the debate about a "dying civilization" on Mars, as revealed by the elaborate system of "canals" supposedly observed on the Red Planet. Perceval Lowell, the most zealous proponent of these canals, wrote a book claiming that Mars merely rehearsed the future of the Earth, citing Kropotkin and others on the progressive aridification of Eurasia. But Kropotkin's real Frankenstein monster, shocked to life by the *Geographical Journal* debate, was the American geographer and former missionary Ellsworth Huntington, a tireless self-promoter, who reinterpreted linear desiccation as a natural cycle, the famous "Pulse of Asia." Huntington's belief in climatic determination, whether of civilizations' rise and fall, or simply of human moods, soon morphed into a bizarre racial theory of history, poisoning the well for research on historical climates for almost two generations.

When I wrote **Chapter 4**, "Who Will Build the Ark?," debate about the "Anthropocene," a proposed geological epoch without previous analogue, defined by the biogeochemical impacts of industrial capitalism, was still largely confined to earth science circles. Since then the term has expanded at meme speed to encompass not only these debates but virtually everything else. A quick perusal of recent and forthcoming books under the heading "Anthropocene" reveals titles like *World Politics in …; Learning to Die in …; Love in …; Bats in …; Virtue in …; Poetry in …; Hope and Grief in …; Coral Reefs in…;* and so on. The Anthropocene, in other words, has morphed far beyond the original parameters of earth-system processes and stratigraphical markers to become post-modernism's successor in the double sense of a vast and at times meaningless blanket thrown over everything novel and a permit for wild and undisciplined speculations about "post-natural" ontologies. Radical critics have justifiably focused on the false universals conflated in promiscuous discussions of the Anthropocene: "Man as geological agent" (instead of capitalism); "the threat to human survival" (the rich will assuredly survive; the existential threat is to the poor majority); "the human fossil fuel footprint" ("What did you say, kemosabe?"); and so on.

"Ark" is an argument with myself. In the first half, I make the case for pessimism: there is no historical precedent or rational-actor logic that would lead rich countries (or classes) to repay their "ecological debts" to the poor countries that will suffer the greater part of the catastrophic consequences of rich counties' historic emissions. Likewise, the chaos of the Anthropocene is indissolubly linked to the broader civilizational crisis of capitalism. A large portion of the labor-power of the planet, for example, needs to be devoted to the unmet housing and environmental needs of poor cities and their adaptation to extreme climate events. But global capitalism is no longer a job machine; quite the contrary, the fastest-growing social classes on earth are the unemployed and the informally employed. There is no realistic scenario in which market forces would mobilize this vast reservoir of labor to meet the challenge of the Anthropocene, nor is there any likelihood of adopting the kind of policies that would accommodate the human migrations necessitated by mega-droughts and rising sea levels. That would require a revolution from below of a scope far beyond anything imagined by Marx and Engels.

In the second half of "Ark," I focus on the false choice defined by environmentalists who argue that there is no hope of reconciling a universally high standard of living with the requirements of sustainability. If capitalist urbanization is in so many ways the chief problem, responsible for the majority of emissions, groundwater deficits, and major pollutant flows, I propose the city as its own possible solution. We must transform private into public affluence with a zero carbon footprint. There is no planetary shortage of "carrying capacity" if we are willing to make democratic public space, rather than modular, private consumption, the engine of sustainable equality. We need to ignite our imaginations by rediscovering those extraordinary discussions—and in some cases concrete experiments—in utopian urbanism that shaped socialist and anarchist thinking between the 1880s and the early 1930s. The *alter monde* that we all believe is the only possible alternative to the new Dark Ages requires us to dream old dreams anew.

1

Old Gods, New Enigmas

Notes on Revolutionary Agency

In a 1995 interview shortly after the publication of *The Age of Extremes*, Eric Hobsbawm was asked about the future currency of socialist ideas. It depended, he answered, on whether or not a "historic force" would still exist to support the socialist project. "It seems to me the historic force rested not necessarily on the ideas but on a particular material situation ... the major problem of the Left being that of *agency*." In face of the declining ratio of variable capital in modern production and thus of the social weight of the industrial proletariat,

> we may well find ourselves back in a different pattern to a society like the one of the pre-capitalist society, in which the largest number of people will not be wage workers—they will be something else, either, as you can see in the large part of the Third World, people who are operating in the gray area of the informal economy, who cannot be simply classed as wage workers or in some other way. Now, under those circumstances, clearly the question is, how can this body of people be mobilized in order to realize the aims which unquestionably are still there and to some extent are now more urgent in form?[1]

Hobsbawm, of course, didn't factor in the shift of global manufacturing to coastal East Asia and the almost exponential growth of the Chinese industrial working class (231 million in 2011) over the last generation, but otherwise the reduction of traditional working-class economic and political power—now including stricken BRICS like Brazil and South Africa—has been indeed epochal.[2] In Europe as well as the United States, the erosion of industrial employment through wage arbitrage, outsourcing, and automation has gone hand in hand with the precaritization of service work, the digital industrialization of white-collar jobs, and the stagnation or decline of unionized public employment.[3] Revolutionary increases in productivity that a half-century ago, when union contracts regulated the macro-economy, might have been shared with workers as higher wages and reduced hours now simply augur further deterioration of the economic security of the majority. According to the Bureau of Labor Statistics, the American economy in 2013 produced 42 percent more goods and services than in 1998, yet the total hours worked (194 billion) were exactly the same in 2013 as in 1998.[4] Looking at manufacturing per se, its output share of the *real* GDP has remained surprisingly stable since 1960 while its share of employment has plunged since the inauguration of Ronald Reagan. In absolute size, the production workforce, approximately 20 million in 1980, fell to 12 million in 2010, with almost 6 million jobs lost in the 2000s.[5]

"A new system," André Gorz warned twenty years ago, "has been established which is abolishing 'work' on a massive scale. It is restoring the worst forms of domination, subjugation and exploitation by forcing each to fight against all in order to obtain the 'work' it is abolishing."[6] This increased competition for jobs (or at least the perception of such competition) has inflamed working-class resentment against the new credentialed elites and the high-tech rich, but equally it has narrowed and poisoned traditional cultures

2

of solidarity, transforming the revolt against globalization into a virulent anti-immigrant backlash.[7] Traditional social-democratic and center-left parties have universally failed to project alternatives to neoliberal globalization or popularize strategies for creating compensatory high-wage jobs in rust belt regions. Even if the hurricane of neoliberalism were to pass—and there is yet little sign this will happen—the automation, not just of production and routine management, but potentially of half or more of all jobs in the OECD bloc, will threaten the last vestiges of job security in core economies.[8]

Automation, of course, has been an approaching death star for generations, with major debates about technological unemployment in every modern decade. The Cassandras have included Stuart Chase and the Technocracy movement in the early 1930s; Norbert Wiener and Ben Seligman in the 1950s; the Ad Hoc Committee on the Triple Revolution and its prestigious progeny, the National Commission on Technology, Automation and Economic Progress, in the 1960s; and over the following half-century, hundreds of studies, books, and articles.[9] On the left, Herbert Marcuse and André Gorz argued that since automation was inevitable, it was time to abandon "work-based" Marxism and bid adieu to the proletariat (the title of the latter's 1980 book). But until recently the employment impacts of labor-saving technology have been blunted by new products and industries (typically financed by military spending), the growth of administrative and public-sector jobs, and the relentless expansion of consumer credit and household debt. All evidence, however, now points to the (robo-)wolf actually at the door, especially the doors of low-income workers. The 2016 *Annual Report of the Council of Economic Advisers* warned that fully 83 percent of jobs paying less than $20 per hour face the threat of automation in the near future.[10] As a direct corollary, the "precariat" has a brilliant future.

3

The replacement of human labor-power by the next generation of artificial-intelligence systems and robots, the so-called "Third Wave" of digital technology, will not exempt industrial East Asia.[11] Indeed, the job killers have already arrived. Foxconn, the world's largest manufacturer, responsible for an estimated 50 percent of all electronic products, is currently replacing assembly workers at its huge Shenzhen complex and elsewhere with a million robots (they don't commit suicide in despair at working conditions).[12] Philips Electronics, for its part, has advertised the debut of robotic production systems that "can make any consumer device in the world," replacing the need for cheap Asian labor. Their prototype is a fully automated plant in Friesland that will eventually replace its sister factory in Zhuhai, near Macau, which employs ten times as many workers.[13] GE, likewise, is pouring billions into the development of an industrial internet or "internet of things" to integrate machines and manufacturing systems with networked sensors and automated design processes using cheap data clouds. Ultimately it hopes to build "virtual twins" of all of its products, allowing engineers to test products before they are built and also letting them feed the virtual model with real-world data to improve performance. In this manufacturing mirror-world, computer-aided design would be replaced by computer-directed design, resulting in further attrition of both engineering and assembly-line jobs in Asia, as well as Europe and North America.[14]

Table 1.1 The Global Job Crisis[15]

Active global labor force (2015)	3 billion
"Vulnerable workers" (informal/unwaged)	1.5 billion
Workers earning less than $5 per day	1.3 billion
Working-age people not in labor market	2.0 billion
Inactive youth (not working or studying)	500 million
Child workers	168 million

In much of the global South, meanwhile, structural trends since 1980 have overthrown textbook ideas about "stages of economic growth," as urbanization has become decoupled from industrialization and subsistence from waged employment.[16] Even in countries with high recent rates of GDP growth, such as India and Nigeria, joblessness and poverty have soared instead of declining, which is why "jobless growth" joined income inequality at the top of the agenda at the 2015 World Economic Forum.[17] Meanwhile rural poverty, especially in Africa, is being rapidly urbanized—or perhaps "warehoused" is the better term—with little prospect that migrants will ever be reincorporated into modern relations of production. Their destinations are the squalid refugee camps and jobless peripheral slums, where their children can dream of becoming prostitutes or car bombers.

The summation of these transformations, in rich as well as poor regions, is an unprecedented crisis of proletarianization—or, if you prefer, of the "real subordination of labor to capital," embodied by subjects whose consciousness and capacity to effect change are still largely enigmas. Neilson and Stubbs, using the terminology of Chapter 25 of *Capital*, contend that "the uneven unfolding of capitalism's long-term contradictory labour-market dynamic is generating a massive relative surplus population, distributed in deeply unequal forms and sizes across the countries of the world. It is already larger than the active army, and is set to grow further in the medium-term future."[18] Everywhere we look, we are reminded of Marx's warning: "Since the purpose of productive labour is not the existence of the worker but the production of surplus value, all necessary labour which produces no surplus labour is superfluous and worthless to capitalist production."[19]

Whether as contingent or uncollectivized labor, as micro-entrepreneurs or subsistence criminals, or simply as the permanently unemployed, the fate of this "superfluous" humanity has become the core problem for twentieth-first-century Marxism. Do the old categories of common sentiment and shared destiny, asks Olivier Schwartz, still define an idea of "the popular classes?"[20] Socialism, as Hobsbawm warned, will have little future unless large sections of this informal working class find sources of collective strength, levers of power, and platforms for participating in an international class struggle. From the standpoint of classical socialism, there could be no greater historical catastrophe than the disappearance of proletarian agency. "[If] the conception of proletariat as the motive force of the coming social revolution were abandoned," Karl Kautsky wrote in 1906, "then I would have to admit that I was through, that my life no longer had any meaning."[21]

It would be a gigantic mistake, however, to conclude, as the post-Marxists have, that the starting point for theoretical renewal must be a funeral for the "old working class."("As it stands today, the classical revolutionary subject no longer exists," declare Srnicek and Williams, and many others.)[22] To put it crudely, it has been demoted in agency, not fired from history. Machinists, nurses, truck drivers, and school teachers remain the organized social base defending the historical legacy of labor in Western Europe, North America, and Japan.[23] Trade unions, however weakened or dispirited, continue to articulate a way of life "based around a coherent sense of the dignity of others and of a place in the world."[24] But the ranks of traditional workers and their unions are no longer growing, and the major increments to the global workforce are increasingly unwaged or jobless.[25] As Christian Marazzi complained recently, it is no longer easy to use a category like "class composition" "to analyze a situation that is increasingly characterized by the fragmentation of the subjects constituted in the world of employment and non-employment."[26]

At a high level of abstraction, the current period of globalization is defined by a trilogy of ideal-typical economies: super-industrial (coastal East Asia), financial/tertiary (North Atlantic), and hyper-urbanizing/extractive (West Africa). "Jobless growth" is incipient in the first, chronic in the second, and virtually absolute in the third. We might add a fourth ideal-type of disintegrating societies, caught in a vice of war and climate change, whose chief trend is the export of refugees and migrant labor. In any event, we can no longer rely on a single paradigmatic society or class to model the critical vectors of historical development. Imprudent coronations of abstractions like "the multitude" as historical subjects simply dramatize a poverty of empirical research. Contemporary Marxism must be able to scan the future from the simultaneous perspectives of Shenzhen, Los Angeles, and Lagos if it wants to solve the puzzle of how heterodox social categories might be fitted together in a single resistance to capitalism.

THE UNIVERSAL CLASS

Even the most preliminary tasks are daunting. A new theory of revolution, to begin with, begs benchmarks in the old, starting with clarification of "proletarian agency" in classical socialist thought. In the first instance, of course, self-consciousness of agency preceded theory. The faith that "labor will inherit the earth" and that "the International will be the human race" did not rest on doctrine but arose volcanically from struggles for bread and dignity. Workers' belief in their collective power to effect radical change, whose deep roots were located in the democratic revolutions of the late eighteenth century, was amply ratified by the fears and nightmares of the Victorian bourgeoisie. (Although this is an obvious fact, not a small number of Marx's critics have charged at one time or another that revolutionary agency was nothing more than a metaphysical invention, a Hegelian hobgoblin, foisted upon working masses whose actions were actually dictated by simple utilitarian calculation.)

Summarizing the general view amongst Marxists, Ellen Wood succinctly characterized agency as "the possession of strategic power and a capacity for collective action founded in the specific conditions of material life." I would add that "capacity" is a developable potential for conscious and consequent activity, for *self-making*, not a disposition that arises automatically and inevitably from social conditions. Nor in the case of the proletariat is capacity synonymous with *endowment*, such as the power to hire and fire that a capitalist receives from simple ownership of means of production. Agency in the classical socialist sense also imputed hegemony: the political and cultural ability of a class to institute a transformational project that recruits broad sections of society. "Only in the name of the general rights of society," wrote the young Marx, "can a particular class lay claim to general domination."[27]

Marx's model, of course, was the revolutionary middle class of 1789 whose historical vocation had been so famously heralded by the Abbé Sieyès: "What is the Third Estate? Everything. What has it been hitherto in the political order? Nothing."[28] By equating the rights of man to the rights of property, and political equality to free economic competition, the great ideologues of revolutionary France translated class interests into a stunning vision of universal freedom. The explicit identification of the bourgeoisie as a revolutionary class, the unique architect of progress and human emancipation, was consequently enshrined in the histories written by the celebrated trio of Restoration liberals—Augustin Thierry, François-August Mignet, and François Guizot ("the bourgeoisie's Lenin").[29] Their interpretation of 1789 as a bourgeois revolution against feudalism, the culmination of centuries of conflict between the nobility and the rising Third Estate, framed contemporary thinking about those events as well as providing a powerful ideological justification for the attenuated liberal revolution of 1830.[30] "As Marx himself freely acknowledged," emphasizes Hobsbawm, "these were the men from whom he derived the idea of the class struggle in history."[31] In effect they had already taken all the preliminary conceptual measurements for a theory of revolutionary agency.

A new Third Estate

Marx's own itinerary can be briefly described. As German idealist philosophy was largely a complex response to 1789, his final break from that philosophy entailed a return to the Revolution and the ongoing battle over its meaning and ultimate destination. The political alignments of the Revolution continued to constitute through the 1840s the principal horizon of the European political imagination, including the Young Hegelians' opposition to Prussian autocracy. As Leopold von Ranke once complained, "the Revolution, which has often been pronounced at an end, seems never to be finished. It reappears in ever new and antagonistic forms."[32] In the case of Marx, he had already in his final days as crusading editor of *Rheinische Zeitung*—the voice of Rhenish liberalism—crossed the line from democratic reformism to a social republicanism in the mode of Jacques Roux and *Les Enragés* of 1793. "Faced with the social question," says Stathis Kouvelakis, "Marx place[d] himself in the tradition of the French Revolution and the project of a 'popular political economy' defended by the Robespierreans, the urban *sans-culottes*, and the most radical wing of the peasant movement: a project centred on subordinating property rights to the right to existence."[33]

9

From his honeymoon summer of 1843 with Jenny Marx in Spa Kreuznach through spring 1844, after their move to Paris, Marx immersed himself in an intense study of the historiography of the Revolution, especially the monumental collection of documents annotated and published in forty volumes by the former Saint-Simonians P.-J.-B. Buchez and P. C. Roux.[34] (A portion of his reading notes have been preserved as the *Kreuznach Notebooks*.) His collaborator Arnold Ruge wrote to a friend: "Marx wants to write a history of the Convention and has already done an enormous amount of reading."[35] Although he eventually abandoned the book, his research on revolutionary history was integral to his first important cycle of theoretical work, from the "Introduction to the Critique of Hegel's Theory of Right" (1843–44) to *The Poverty of Philosophy* (1847). "Setting out to be the Feuerbach of politics [i.e. the critic of Hegel's conception of the state], the young Marx instead wound up sketching the outlines of a critical theory of the French Revolution."[36] This became self-critique to the extent that he now confronted the contradictions in the Jacobin model of "purely political revolution" and radical democracy that he had recently advocated in the Rhineland.

Although everywhere on the continent the unfinished work of 1789 begged resumption, Marx recognized that neither the destruction of absolutism nor the victory of universal suffrage would any longer achieve that egalitarian society of small producers that was the true goal of popular republicanism, much less overcome the alienation of labor and human "species-being" that was the essence of a liberal order based on competition and possessive individualism. Moreover, having enthroned its own special interests in the July Monarchy, the French bourgeoisie "abdicated henceforth the pretension of incarnating a universal ideal of the state, charged with realizing the ultimate ends of humanity."[37] Instead, the rising power of industrial and commercial capital, growing out of the expropriation of small producers by large, confirmed the prescience of the original *sans-culotte* communists, Gracchus Babeuf and Sylvain Maréchal, who had argued that *liberté* could be realized as *égalité* only within a system of common property.

The evidence was ominous and ubiquitous. Warren Breckman, in his highly regarded study of Marx and the Young Hegelians, emphasized that their "receptiveness to French socialism in the early 1840s" was not "merely an expression of their own ideological impasse" but a response to the worsening "pauperism crisis" in Western Europe: "by 1842, many German intellectuals were acutely aware of the plight of the poor."[38] But Lorenz von Stein, whose detailed account of contemporary French socialist and communist sects excited vivid interest amongst young German radicals like Marx, pointed out that there were really two different species of poverty, one familiar, the other confoundingly novel.

> It is not only the poverty of part of the laboring class, not only impoverishment which hits large sections of the population through industrial changes, but it is the poverty reproduced by industrial conditions from generation to generation within the family which characterizes industrial pauperism. The great differences between mere poverty and pauperism can be clearly seen. Lack of work and income result in poverty, but pauperism is brought about by work and wages. In industrial society, poverty can be coped with through charity; in order to fight pauperism the whole industrial working- and wage-system has to be changed … It is pauperism that has led practical people … to adopt the ideas of socialism.[39]

In other words, only a social revolution that transformed civil society could redress this central paradox of the Victorian age: the radical new misery—Marx called it "artificial poverty"—associated with the growth of unprecedented productive powers. But who would constitute the Steam Age's new Third Estate, its "universal class"?

By the time that Marx and Jenny had moved into 38 rue Vaneau on the Left Bank, there was little doubt about the answer. Like other young radical intellectuals, Marx was electrified by the Chartist movement in Britain, the contemporary revolt of the Silesian weavers, and the dramatic ferment of communist and socialist ideas amongst Parisian artisans and laborers. A new social power was awakening, and Marx, following in the footsteps of Moses Hess, Flora Tristan, and von Stein, nominated the property-less proletariat —a group excluded from, and with no stake in, the traditional system of estates and private property—as the successor to the revolutionary bourgeoisie. Of course, in its original Hegelian swaddling clothes, Marx's proletariat was an abstraction—or, rather, an abstract solution—that emerged from his parallel critiques of French revolutionary history and Hegel's theory of the state. In his Paris writings he simultaneously confronted his former "philosophical conscience" and drew up a balance-sheet of the recent failure of German liberalism. As Kouvelakis points out, "Marx encounters the proletariat at the theoretical and symbolic level before making contact with the real (specifically, the Parisian) workers' movement, because he is looking (literally) for an answer to a pre-existing *political* question (how to conceive the imminent transformation of the crisis into a German revolution)."

The "philosophical proletariat" quickly acquired flesh and blood as Marx engaged with revolutionary artisans in Paris, especially the German tailors and cabinetmakers in the underground League of the Just. (His next-door neighbor was one of its leaders.) "The social text of Paris," observes Lloyd Kramer, "significantly extended his understanding of the other texts that he had read before he went to

France."[40] By spring 1844, Marx was openly identifying himself as a communist, and later that summer he broke with Ruge, his co-editor on the ill-fated *Deutsch-Französische Jahrbücher,* over the latter's disparagement of the June uprising of weavers in Silesia as a primitive act of desperation with no larger significance. "The German poor," Ruge claimed, "are no wiser than the poor Germans, i.e., nowhere do they see beyond their own hearth and home." Marx answered in a fiery polemic ("Critical Marginal Notes on the article 'The King of Prussia and Social Reform by a Prussian'") that contrasted the "dynamic capabilities" of the proletariat—especially its sophisticated ability to formulate general interests and act upon them—to the "political impotence" of the bourgeoisie:

> Recall the *song of the weavers*, that bold *call* to struggle, in which there is not even a mention of hearth and home, factory or district, but in which the proletariat at once, in a striking, sharp, unrestrained and powerful manner, proclaims its opposition to the society of private property. The Silesian uprising *begins* precisely with what the French and English workers' uprisings *end*, consciousness of the nature of the proletariat ... Not only machines, these rivals of the workers, are destroyed, but also *ledgers,* the titles to property. And while all other movements were aimed primarily only against the *owner of the industrial enterprise*, the visible enemy, this movement is at the same time directed against the banker, the hidden enemy.[41]

Marx's intense education in the communist circles of Paris was soon followed by a six-week expedition to Manchester and London in the summer of 1845 (July 12–August 21) with his new collaborator Friedrich Engels, whose *Condition of the English Working Class* was a burning bush on Marx's road to communism. "Engels," Neil

Davidson points out, "was among the first commentators to see beyond the existential misery of the British working class—a subject that had already exercised such notably non-revolutionary figures as Thomas Carlyle—to the *potential power* it possessed, and in this he was in advance of Marx himself."[42] Lancashire, of course, was the hearth of the First Industrial Revolution as well as the epicenter of the great movement for the Peoples' Charter. "The Chartist movement," Dorothy Thompson reminds us, "was the movement above all on which Marx and Engels based their analysis of class consciousness."[43] (Marx's knowledge of Manchester would become increasingly intimate: over the course of his lifetime, according to the *Marx-Engels Chronicle,* he visited Engels twenty-five times, spending a year and a half in the industrial metropolis.)[44]

By 1847 at the latest, his rapidly maturing conception of the proletariat as a revolutionary force differed from that of the utopian or "bourgeois socialists" (Engels's term) in at least three major regards. *First,* as Hal Draper and Michael Löwy have shown in their detailed exegeses of his early writings, Marx eschewed the premise of *instrumental agency*: the workers as mere constituency and brute means for achieving a new society designed by some reformer. Instead, he embraced, as had Flora Tristan even earlier, the interpretation of agency as self-reliance and *self-emancipation* that was advocated in radical artisan circles by the so-called "materialist communists." The most eloquent and fiery exponent of this viewpoint was Théodore Dézamy, a school teacher, former comrade-in-arms of Blanqui, and the chief organizer of the legendary Communist Banquet in Belleville in 1840. In polemics that influenced Marx, Dézamy rejected the Icarian fantasy of reconciliation between the rich and poor, made proletarian unity the highest priority, and scorned his former associate Étienne Cabet for not attending the banquet because "the proletarians were allowing themselves to raise the communist flag on their own, without having at their head some *bourgeois*, some *well-known name*."[45]

Löwy, in his reconstruction of this period, proposes two milestones in Marx's reworking of the idea of self-emancipation. In his "singularly underestimated" *Vorwärts* article, "The King of Prussia and Social Reform" (August 1844), Marx celebrated the uprising of the Silesian weavers and revised his earlier left-Hegelian distinction (in the "Introduction") between philosophy as the active and the proletariat as the receptive force. "Socialism is no longer presented as pure theory, an idea 'born in the philosopher's head,' but as a *praxis* [and] the proletariat now plainly becomes the *active* element in emancipation." A year later, shortly after his expulsion from France, Marx penned *The Theses on Feuerbach*, which Löwy characterizes, following Engels, as "the first of Marx's 'Marxist' writings." The third thesis in particular banishes "condescending saviors" by making the self-education of the proletariat through its own revolutionary struggle the "theoretical foundation" of auto-emancipation. "The coincidence of the changing of circumstances and of human activity or self-changing can be conceived and rationally understood only as *revolutionary practice*." This formulation, Löwy argues, represents nothing less than "the transcendence, the sublation (*Aufhebung*) of the antithesis between 18th-century materialism (changing of circumstances) and Young Hegelianism (changing of consciousness)."[46]

Second, the proletariat—even in its immature or transitional incarnations such as poor artisans and hand workers in unmechanized manufactories—was now the only class with both the political will and radical needs to pursue the struggle for democracy to its conclusion. Marx's stormy experiences as editor of the *Rheinische Zeitung*—whose bourgeois sponsorship collapsed under the first blows of the Prussian censor—had shattered any illusion that the

German liberal middle class was capable of leading the movement against the *ancien régime* in the resolute manner of the Third Estate in 1789. Already in the 1844 "Introduction," as Draper, Löwy, and others have emphasized, is the kernel of the theory of "permanent revolution": the German bourgeoisie, deradicalized by its apprehension of the emergent threat of the proletariat, abdicates the battle for a democratic republic; the proletariat, which takes its place en bloc with sections of the petty bourgeoisie and the peasantry, will not halt the revolutionary process with mere achievement of a constitution. In 1848, after his return to the Rhineland as a leader of the Communist League and editor of the *Neue Rheinische Zeitung*, Marx refined his ideas about proletarian leadership in the daily battles to keep the German democratic revolt alive; his subsequent reflections in exile on the German and French events then codified these experiences.

Third, Marx was uniquely pessimistic about contemporary prospects for resisting proletarianization or building an alternative society on artisan—cooperative principles such as advocated by Proudhon and his many followers.[47] The Industrial Revolution, although lived as a catastrophe by millions of contemporary artisans and peasants, was not only creating a property-less class of industrial workers but also developing the productive forces that they would someday seize in order to free all of humanity. History could not be rewound or stopped, but it could be fast-forwarded. The eventual fusion of the proletariat's material interest in common property with the Promethean productive powers created by its labor is the implicit formula in all of Marx's references to emancipatory agency. It clarifies his famous claim that the proletariat was charged not only with its own liberation but with "the categorical imperative to overturn all circumstances in which man is a degraded, a subjugated, a forsaken, a contemptible being."[48]

The missing links

It has always been odd, to put it mildly, that so many critics, beginning with Heidegger's student Karl Löwith, have explained Marx's embrace of proletarian agency as evidence of a stealth Judeo-Christian eschatology underlying his theory of history, rather than the straightforward result of his growing engagement with a workers' movement already infused with the conviction that it could build a new world. Certainly, many of the Paris socialist sects of the 1840s, especially the Icarians, were awash in messianic slogans and evocations of a proletarian Christ, but this was a specifically French reaction to the liberal bourgeoisie's embrace of materialism. There were in fact two camps on the left: the communists, like Dézamy and the neo-Babouvists, who were proud heirs to materialism, and a larger group who rejected the materialist tradition because they identified it with the Directory and the ideology of liberalism. Louis Blanc, the father of the "social workshop" movement and an influential figure in the first stages of the 1848 Revolution, was a particularly ardent advocate of the "religious model." "The secular materialism of the eighteenth-century French *philosophes*," Blanc argued, "produced individualist theories to justify bourgeois rule during and after the French Revolution. French democracy, on the other hand, grew out of a Rousseauistic legacy that opposed the materialistic (individualist) *philosophe* tradition and favored unity, liberty, and the fraternal principles of the Christian gospels."[49]

But whether preached from the gospels or presented as the arduous result of a "critique of the critique," the general figure of *proletarian agency* arose from a substitution of subjects in the classic paradigm of democratic revolution as broadly understood by liberals and radicals alike. Judeo-Christian concepts of emancipation were influential only at the popular level and primarily amongst artisans and poor peasants. But revolutionary socialists became accustomed to moving back and forth between materialist and popular–millenarian representations of revolutionary subjectivity. As Zinoviev, while chairman of the Communist International, once explained:

> The economist critics would say, "So what, in your opinion, is the working class, a Messiah?" To this we answered and answer now: Messiah and messianism are not our language and we do not like such words; but we accept the concept that is contained in them: yes, the working class is in a certain sense a Messiah and its role is a messianic one, for this is the class which will liberate the whole world .... We avoid semi-mystical terms like Messiah and messianism and prefer the scientific one: the *hegemonic proletariat*.[50]

The three crucial elements of revolutionary agency—organizational capacity, structural power, and hegemonic politics—received their most careful if non-systematic treatment from Marx in his writings on 1848, discussed in Chapter 2. Thereafter he bade adieu for the most part to French revolutionary history in order to concentrate on his monumental analysis of English capitalism. Although *Capital*, as Bensaïd has emphasized, analyzes structural determinations or preconditions of class consciousness at the level of production (*Volume 1*) and circulation (*Volume 2*), there is no canonical text from his "mature period" that directly addresses agency at the level of concrete social formations.[51] As Lukács famously lamented:

> Marx's chief work breaks off just as he is about to embark on the definition of class [Chapter 52 of *Capital Volume III*]. This omission was to have serious consequences both for the theory and the practice of the proletariat. For on this vital point the later movement was forced to base itself on interpretations, on the collation

of occasional utterances by Marx and Engels, and the independent extrapolation and application of their method.[52]

Since Lukács first attempted to rectify this "omission" in *History and Class Consciousness* (1923), a trove of Marx's unpublished works and drafts, including *The 1844 Manuscripts*, *The German Ideology*, *The Grundrisse*, the *1861–63 Economic Manuscripts*, the important fragment "Results of the Immediate Process of Production" (Chapter 7 of *Capital Volume I*), and the original manuscript of *Capital Volume III*, have been recovered, interpreted, and debated; but the itinerary of the key macro-concepts—class, historical agency, the state, modes of production, and so on—still requires careful exploitation of three very different kinds of sources: explicit philosophical statements (what Étienne Balibar aptly calls "programme texts"), mainly from 1843–47; the politico-strategic narratives written in 1848–1850; and gleanings from the economic manuscripts that extend or modify earlier ideas.[53] But such a reconstruction from fragmentary sources, no matter how exegetically rigorous, should not be construed as the "true Marx." It is simply a plausible, or better, a useful Marx.

Marcello Musto has proposed that Marx's failure to update and systematize his ideas was not just a result of debilitating illness and the constant revision of *Capital*, but an inevitable consequence of "his intrinsic aversion" to schematization: his "inextinguishable passion for knowledge, not altered by the passing of the years, leading him time and again to new studies; and, finally the awareness he attained in his later years of the difficulty of confining the complexity of history within a theoretical project; these made incompleteness [his] faithful companion."[54] In the same vein, Balibar observes:

More than other writers, Marx *wrote in the conjuncture*. Such an option did not exclude either the "patience of the concept" of which

Hegel spoke, or the rigorous weighing of logical consequences. But it was certainly incompatible with stable conclusions: Marx is the philosopher of eternal new beginnings, leaving behind him *many* uncompleted drafts and projects … The content of his thought is not separable from his shifts of position. That is why, in studying him, one cannot abstractly reconstruct his system. One has to retrace his development, with its breaks and bifurcations.[55]

The most costly of Marx's silences, according to Michael Lebowitz, was the proposed but never written *Wage-Labor*—volume three in the original 1857 plan for "The Critique of Political Economy." "Its absence is at the root of the one-sidedness in the system elaborated in *Capital*," which focuses on "*capital* as a whole." The theory of "*Capitalism* as a whole," however, presumes a counterpart focus "on the worker as a subject who develops through her struggles," which is only weakly developed in *Capital Volume I*. The missing volume, in other words, would presumably have adumbrated a theory of proletarian agency as an integral aspect of this self-making of labor as antagonist of capital. Although sections of Marx's intended volume were incorporated into *Capital Volume I*, and Lebowitz has made a heroic effort to piece together fragments of a two-sided theory of capital and labor, *Wage-Labour* is reconstructible only in part.[56]

Bearing this in mind, the present chapter makes no pretense of being an orthodox exercise in Marxology or a rigorous attempt to deduce the determinations of agency from the unfinished opus of *Capital*—something I regard as impossible. Rather, I make sweeping, even promiscuous use of Lukácsian extrapolation to propose a *historical sociology* conforming to the ideal-type of a socialist working class in the eras of the First and Second Internationals. In particular, I mine our current understanding of nineteenth- and early twentieth-century working-class history—the fruit of hundreds if not thousands of studies since 1960—to highlight the conditions and forms of struggle through which class capacities were created and the socialist project organized itself. Against the simplistic idea (not held by Marx) that socialist consciousness and the power to change history principally emerge from the economic class struggle, I stress the *overdeterminations* (for instance, of wage struggles by movements for suffrage and vice versa) that Rosa Luxemburg, in her brilliant analyses of the "mass strike," identified as the most potent generators of class consciousness and revolutionary will.

This reconstruction, moreover, is designed primarily as a comparative matrix for thinking about agency in the radically changed conditions of contemporary class conflict, and it saves for a future work any consideration of the classical counter-arguments against revolutionary agency, the most compelling of which were probably Werner Sombart's *Why There Is No Socialism in the United States* (1906) and Robert Michels's *Political Parties: A Sociological Study of the Oligarchical Tendencies of Modern Democracy* (1911).[57] I propose, in other words, an idealized, *maximum* argument—presented in the form of theses—for the traditional working class as the gravedigger of capitalism. Imagine, if you will, the proletariat being asked by the World Spirit for a résumé of its qualifications for the job of Universal Emancipator.[58]

Such an enumeration of *capacities* might be amended or extended in various ways, but Marx's central premise remains: that the sum of these capacities acquired in struggle is a realistic potential for self-emancipation and revolution. The conditions which confer capacity, we should recall, can be either *structural* or *conjunctural*. The first arise from the proletariat's position in the mode of production; for example the possibility, if nothing more, of organizing mass strikes that shut down production in entire cities, industries, and even nations. The second is limited to historical stages or episodes, and is ultimately transient: as, for example, the stubborn maintenance of informal control over the labor process by late-Victorian engineering workers and ship-builders which survived until the First World War and the adoption of new production methods. The conjunctural can also denote the intersection of unsynchronized histories, such as the persistence of absolutism in the middle period of industrialization, which led in Europe to the potent convergence of suffrage struggles and industrial conflict—not the case in North America.

Moreover, as the careful student of Marx eventually discovers, capitalism's "laws of motion" come with a lot of fine print. There are few pure determinations or simple secular trends in his historical analyses and economic manuscripts. Indeed, one is tempted to apply Newton's Second Law to the accumulation process, since its dynamics often produce tendencies and counter-tendencies at the same time. "The form of the factory," for example, "embodies and therefore teaches capitalist notions of property relations. But, as Marx points out, it can also teach the necessarily social and collective character of production and thereby undermine the capitalist notion of private property."[59] Likewise in *Capital*, the increasing organic composition (capital intensity) of production is indeterminately offset in value terms by the cheapening of capital goods. Similarly, resources can be deployed for alternative, even opposite ends. A thirst for technical and scientific knowledge, for example, is a precondition for workers' control of production, but also serves the ambitions of an aristocracy of labor that hopes one day to become managers or owners. Self-organized proletarian civil society likewise can reinforce class identity in either a subordinate, corporatist sense, as a *subculture* in orbit around bourgeois institutions, or in a hegemonic, anticipatory sense, as an antagonistic *counterculture*.

Furthermore, in focusing on *resources for self-organization and*

22

action, as well as the interests that mobilize them and the historical tasks that demand them, I side-step more abstract debates about social ontology and consciousness as well as recent agency/ structure controversies amongst social theorists and historians that Alex Callinicos addresses so well in *Making History.*[60] I also skirt the thorny thickets of crisis theory, although agency is ultimately conditioned by the dynamics of accumulation and inter-capitalist competition. Indeed, it was Marx's brilliant insight that the spiral of the business cycle periodically opens and closes the possibilities for proletarian advance. For example, the boom of the 1850s, ignited by the California gold rush and the opening of the eastern Pacific to global commerce, quieted labor conflict in Britain while inflation and falling real wages in the 1909–13 period kindled class struggle on an international scale.[61] *Capital* gave the "objective conditions" of revolution a new and more powerful meaning in terms of inevitable crises of production and exchange, with balances of class power regulated by unemployment levels. But Marx, whose political and intellectual life spanned the most peaceful era in European history, did not discuss the political economy of war or its role in accumulation on a world scale. This was a major if understandable caesura in the master-plan of *Capital.* It was left to Luxemburg, in her writing on primitive accumulation as an ongoing requirement of valorization, and Lenin, in his articles on state capitalism as exemplified by Ludendorff's German war economy, to visualize intra-imperialist war as a forcing house of structural change and/or revolutionary opportunity comparable to the greatest financial and trade crises.[62]

Finally, how do we characterize the actual gravediggers? The "classical" proletariat, for the purposes of these notes, is the European and North American working classes, considered in the period 1838–1921.[63] The world of labor, of course, was structurally and socially heterogeneous, including many transitional and contradictory class locations. A crude typology of the metropolitan working classes would include the *formal proletariat* (all property-less wage workers); a *paleo-proletariat* of pauperized artisans; *semi-servile labor*, often regulated by statute, including servants, prisoners and unwaged family workers; the *agricultural proletariat*, many of whom were also poor peasants or farm tenants; and the *core industrial proletariat* (factory workers, miners, and transport workers) The last was objectively socialized by mechanized production—what Marx calls the "real subsumption of labor"—and did not become the true backbone of the labor movement until the 1880s, or even later. The whole class (the formal working class) might be envisioned as a huge power grid, with the core as the chief dynamo, generating resistance to capital and leveraging the weak economic power of other sectors.

It was common in revolutionary literature to speak of "avant-garde detachments" of the proletariat, but the term can be applied in two different ways: (1) those portions of the core working class wielding the most economic power and capable of sustained militancy over long cycles; and (2) specific occupational groups, even with slight economic power, that were distinguished by the prevalence of socialist and anarchist ideas. Until the First World War, printers, bakers, tailors, stone-cutters, cigar-makers, and maritime workers were most likely to incorporate explicitly revolutionary ideologies into their work-group subcultures.[64] In areas like the Pale and Sicily, moreover, village artisans remained a crucial transmission belt between urban radicalism and agrarian discontent well into the twentieth century, and from the 1890s casualized or seasonal workers like dockers, lumberjacks, harvest hands, and building laborers became major constituencies for syndicalism and anarchism.[65] Only after 1916 did revolutionary metalworkers take the helm of the class struggle, and only in the great strikes of the 1930s did the assembly-line proletariat in "Fordist" factories assume a central role.

THE AGE OF CLASS WAR

Although this chapter is thematically organized, it obviously assumes specific historical patterns of class formation and conflict. "Classes," Daniel Bensaïd wrote, "do not exist as separable entities, but only in the dialectic of their struggle."[66] Thus my notional chronological bookends are the Peoples' Charter of 1838 (a debut) and the so-called March Action of 1921 (a finale). During this short century, artisanal resistance to proletarianization laid the ideological foundations for the movements of their grandchildren, the factory proletariat, while the early dream of a social republic of small producers was transformed into a vision of an industrial republic of workers' councils. Both futures had brief existences: the first as the radical artisanal communes of Paris in 1848 and 1871; the second as the various "soviet" city-states of 1917–19. (Just as the Paris Commune was in many ways the final act of 1848, the anarcho-syndicalist revolution in Barcelona in 1936–37 can be viewed as the encore to Petrograd 1917.) With the failure of the ill-prepared communist insurrection in Saxony in 1921 and general repression of the labor movement in most countries, the Soviet Union was fatally isolated and besieged for a full generation, morphing into an authoritarian social formation unlike anything envisioned in Smolny in October 1917. At the same time, the polarization within the European labor movement between old Socialist and new Communist parties became a permanent barrier to united action. Comintern Marxism, as a result, turned toward historical subjects—anti-colonial movements, "surrogate" proletariats, peasants, the unemployed, Muslims, even American farmers—not encompassed within the original theoretical vision of Marx and Engels.

Periodizing the Class Struggle: 1838–1921

(1) 1838–48: The hothouse proliferation of socialist and communist doctrines amidst mass revolts against proletarianization and industrial poverty. On the continent the typical revolutionary subject was a self-educated artisan fighting for survival in the mass handicrafts on the eve of mechanization. But this was also the decade of Chartism: the first modern working people's movement on a national scale that included large numbers of Northern factory workers. The period ended in June 1848, less than four months after the publication of *The Communist Manifesto*, with the defeat of the "socialist" insurrection in Paris that followed the closure of the national workshops. Mass emigration of revolutionaries from Europe gave utopian socialism a second life in the American West.

(2) 1849–64: The great mid-Victorian boom, led by railroad and steamship construction, urban renewal, and cotton textile exports, was a recession for class consciousness and social revolution. In Britain most traditional handicrafts (but not the construction trades) continued their decline, but a new elite of metalworkers was consolidated at the expense of the broad solidarity of the Chartist period. In the United States the young labor movement was divided by the "Know Nothing" backlash against Catholic immigrants from Ireland and southern Germany. In France, the vast financial bubble engineered by the Péreire brothers, the former acolytes of Saint-Simon who founded the Credit Mobilier, produced an Indian summer of artisan prosperity amidst the delirium of the Second Empire. With revolution nowhere visible on the horizon, Marx retreated to the British Library, Blanqui languished in a dungeon, and Communist émigrés divided into embittered and increasingly obscure factions. Even Garibaldi, the Che Guevara of the nineteenth century, was temporarily forced to lay down his sword and

pay off his debts by captaining a shipload of bird guano from Peru to Canton.

(3) 1865–77: The rise and fall of the First International. The American Civil War and the 1863 Uprising in Poland elicited powerful expressions of working-class solidarity in Britain and France that eventually brought trade-union leaders together from both countries to form the International Working Men's Association in September 1864. Within two years, both the New World and the Old were in the grip of what Hobsbawm characterized as "the first international upsurge of labor struggles," a strike wave that continued even after the reactionary backlash that followed the defeat of the Paris Commune, but then collapsed with the Depression of 1873. The composition of the labor movement was rapidly changing. "The Commune's defeat," Roger Magraw emphasizes, "decimated the artisan vanguard," and in France, although even more so in Britain and the United States, coal miners and railroad workers moved to the fore.[67] When the Baltimore and Ohio Railroad began to slash wages in the summer of 1877 it ignited a forty-five-day-long labor revolt across the North that quickly took the form of bloody street battles (100 dead) that pitted railroad strikers and their worker allies against police, militias, and federal troops. In St Louis the socialist Workingmen's Party, largely composed of German-American followers of Marx and Lassalle, helped organize the first municipal general strike in U.S. history. Class war had crossed the Atlantic.

(4) 1878–89: This was the *Sturm-und-Drang* decade of the workers' movement in Europe and North America. Economic recovery and organizational growth, of both unions and worker parties, was followed by downturn and repression, and then the cycle was

repeated. The factory system, once confined to textiles and shoes, now expanded to machine building and capital goods, with the new Bessemer process allowing U.S. and German steelmakers to catch up and then surpass their British masters. Modern large-scale production methods in France and the United States often went hand in hand with the "new industrial feudalism" practiced in company towns like Le Creusot and Pullman.[68] May Day and the eight-hours movement were born in Chicago under the leadership of anarcho-communist immigrants, seven of whom were quickly marched to the gallows (the Haymarket Martyrs). The non-revolutionary Knights of Labor, appealing particularly to the Catholic working class, grew to almost a million members then rapidly declined, leaving the field open to the new American Federation of Labor and its continuing campaign for the eight-hour day. In the rapidly industrializing German Empire, the dramatic growth of the SPD (newly formed at Gotha in 1875) led Bismarck, who had once flirted with Lassalle, to ban it along with most forms of trade unionism. During these "heroic years" of underground organizing, "persecution not only failed to destroy the party but radicalized its membership, and led to a process of theoretical clarification which culminated in the adopting at the Erfurt party congress of 1891 of a program written by Karl Kautsky that was avowedly Marxist." In Britain, the New Unionism, organizing unskilled, sweated, and casual labor, made a stunning debut during the 1889 dockers' strike—an uprising of the entire East End that sent shock waves through the bourgeois West End.

(5) 1890–1906: This was socialism's long spring. Urbanization and industrialization reached peak velocity in Europe, dramatically increasing the social weight and potential voting power of the factory working class. In Germany the expiration of Bismarck's

Anti-Socialist laws in 1890 opened the way for the explosive growth of Social Democracy and its allied Free Unions. Socialist groups from across Europe gathered at the 1889 Exposition in Paris to celebrate the centenary of the French Revolution, and founded the Second International. They also adopted May Day as the universal day of struggle for the eight-hour day—and in Belgium, Austria, and Sweden, for universal suffrage. Unions became more genuinely national in scope with the creation of federations such as the CGT in France (1895) and the LO in Sweden (1898), while collective bargaining gradually spread, especially in the skilled trades and crafts. In heavy industries, however, employers—with the partial exception of the British—still fiercely resisted unionization and collective bargaining. Genuine industrial unions were still very rare, and in the United States the AFL unions, with few exceptions, refused to organize the new immigrants flooding into factories and mines. The global economy, meanwhile, swayed violently between depression (the Panic of 1893) and fervid expansion (the Belle Époque boom), but unions for the first time weathered the periods of high unemployment.

The Revolution of 1905 in the Russian Empire, with its general strikes, naval mutinies, urban insurrections, national uprisings, and rural jacqueries, reset all the clocks in Europe. Although the explosion was not entirely unexpected, the central role of urban workers and the parties of the left was a rude shock not only to Europe's other monarchies but also to the revisionist wing of the labor movement. It immediately spurred monster demonstrations for equal suffrage in Germany and Austro-Hungary, and put the "mass strike," as exemplified in Russia, at the center of the debate on socialist transition. The spectacle of workers taking over factories and the popular classes governing through direct democracy (the *soviets*) especially energized the left wing of European labor:

revolutionary syndicalists in France and Scandinavia; anarchists in Spain and Italy; and the left opposition in the SPD.

(6) 1907–14: In the wake of the Russian Revolution and the great suffrage strikes, there was a general hardening of the class struggle, marked by greater employer unity, industrial lockouts, widespread use of troops to suppress strikes, and the breakdown of electoral alliances between liberal middle-class parties and social democracy. Workers fought back in a series of general strikes across Europe, but all were defeated. The year 1907 was the turning point: Russian Prime Minister Stolypin dissolved the Second Duma, and launched a reign of terror against radical workers and peasants. In Germany, Chancellor von Bulow's so-called "Hottentot election," essentially a plebiscite on imperialism, united all the middle-class parties against the SPD, which consequently lost half of its seats in the Reichstag: a bitter refutation of the belief that the Socialists' progress was unstoppable. In Paris, 50,000 troops crushed a May Day strike for the eight-hour day, and in the fall Clémenceau took the helm of government, vowing to keep an iron heel on the neck of the CGT. On May Day 1909, three-quarters of the Ottoman Empire's 100,000 or so industrial workers, mainly in Salonika, defied the police and walked off the job.[69] In August, 300,000 Swedish workers launched an unsuccessful month-long general strike in response to a wave of employer lockouts. Meanwhile working-class resistance to colonial wars in North Africa led to the rioting and massacres of the Semana Trágica in Barcelona 1909 and Settimana Rossa in Romagna in 1914. For the first time since Chartism, the British army (and navy) was deployed on a large scale to suppress strikes in Wales (the Tonypandy riots), Merseyside ("Bloody Sunday"), and Dublin (the "Dublin Lockout").

Reformist leadership of the workers' movement was challenged both from the left and from below. Growing disillusionment with the parliamentary path and increasingly bureaucratized unions produced a powerful surge of worker support for revolutionary syndicalism as represented by the IWW (1905) in the United States, the CGT (1906 Amiens Congress) in France, the CNT (1910) in Spain, and the USI (1912) in Italy. Their common goal was the creation of all-grades industrial or general unions that would aggressively fight capital and eventually act as organs of industrial self-government. Syndicalists also believed that the widening of the strike movement to include previously unorganized groups such as immigrant laborers, female garment workers, and sailors would make an ultimate general strike invincible. Even in Britain and Germany, where syndicalism was only a minor current, a wave of wildcat strikes and rank-and-file revolts in 1910–13 demonstrated labor leaders' shocking loss of control over militant sectors of the class—especially miners, waterfront workers, and railroadmen. Before Sarajevo, all signs pointed toward larger and more violent collisions between labor and capital, if not the *lutte final*, during the next economic downturn.

(7) 1916–21 (The Third European Revolution). The European proletariat did not gleefully rush to slaughter in 1914, as it has been caricatured as doing in so many accounts of "war euphoria." Nor, according to Kevin Callahan, "were socialists overwhelmed by a wave of nationalism engulfing their rank-and-file members ... Close to one million antiwar activists took to the streets in the waning days of July in France and Germany alone, and the vast majority of workers met the fate of the war with resignation, not jubilation."[70] But after the war began, the only parties of the Second International to organize significant opposition were either in neutral nations (including Italy until 1915 and the United States until 1917) or

represented underground antiwar minorities of larger parties (as in Russia, Austria, and Germany). Two events prepared the groundwork for the re-emergence of the class struggle on an epic scale in 1917: first, the great massacres of 1916 at Verdun (700,000 casualties), the Somme (1.1 million), and during the Brusilov offensive in the western Ukraine (2.3 million); second, the deterioration of working and living conditions in the major industrial centers and national capitals. As military-age workers, except for the most skilled and irreplaceable, were conscripted for the slaughter, several million new workers, mainly young women but also teenagers and foreign migrants, were recruited to the grueling, dangerous conditions of labor in the munitions industry. (The scale of production was mind-boggling: an estimated *1.5 billion* high-explosive shells were fired on the Western Front alone between 1914 and 1918.) The new workers brought with them acute concerns about the high cost of living and the food shortages that were emaciating their children. Following the mutiny of 40,000 French troops, widespread bread riots in Germany and Russia, and huge metalworkers' walkouts in Berlin and elsewhere, the chain of industrialized murder broke at its weakest link, in Petrograd, in February 1917. Henceforth the Entente and the Central Powers struggled not only to defeat each other, but also to keep the fronts from collapsing into revolution.

A year after Russian workers seized power from the pro-war Provisional Government, a great mutiny in the German Navy in November 1918, led by sailors inspired by the Russian example, forced an abrupt end to fighting on the Western Front. A socialist republic, backed by the might of Berlin's revolutionary metalworkers, was declared in Germany, while other socialist parties took power in Finland and Hungary, and briefly in Austria. The countrysides as well as the cities were in revolt from the Volga to the Danube. The Third International was born in 1918 with the impossible hope of coordinating the new European revolution; but the old reactionary landed elites, allied in Germany with a powerful industrial bourgeoisie, quickly struck back with political sanction and military support from the victor powers gathered in Versailles. Civil war engulfed Russia, and then central and eastern Europe, while in France, Italy, Spain, Britain, Canada, and the United States industrial conflict reached all-time heights in 1918–20. But everywhere apart from Russia, where 1.25 million Red Army soldiers perished to save socialism, the European Counter-Revolution, backed by Entente armies, *Freikorps*, and other paramilitary formations, was successful.[71] "By the end of 1920 and early 1921," wrote Charles Maier, "the left was in retreat everywhere … a world-wide Thermidor."[72]

THESES

I. Radical Chains
The modern proletariat, in the words of the "1844 Introduction," wears "radical chains." Its emancipation requires the abolition of private property and the eventual disappearance of classes.

However, it is essential to distinguish between the chains worn by Marx's "philosophical proletariat" in the 1843–45 writings and those that later fettered the industrial working class in Volume 1 of *Capital*.[73] The first were forged by absolute destitution, exploitation, and exclusion, creating "a class of civil society which is not a class of civil society, an estate which is the dissolution of all estates, a sphere which has a universal character by its universal suffering." Its existence, according to the young Marx, was not only a "negation" of humanity but a condition whose own negation requires a "radical revolution," the overthrow of the "hitherto existing world order."[74]

33

Marx, here writing in the "1844 Introduction," echoed Lorenz von Stein who, as we have seen, in his 1842 book, *Socialism and Communism in Contemporary France*, had contrasted the preindustrial poor "whose destitution resulted from their inability to work" with the contemporary proletariat, pauperized by its non-ownership of the means of production. Von Stein argued (as paraphrased by the Singelmanns) that "being locked into an inherent structural contradiction with capital, the proletariat now becomes the first class in history to recognize the source of human bondage at its roots; its struggle for freedom thus is not only directed against the ruling classes of their period but against the structural conditions of bondage as such."[75] Both Marx and von Stein believed that the contemporary French experience demonstrated that class consciousness would arise almost automatically and syllogistically from the proletarian condition. As the former put it in *The Holy Family* (1845):

> When socialist writers ascribe this world-historic role to the proletariat, it is not at all, as Critical Criticism [left Hegelianism] pretends to believe, because they regard the proletarians as *gods*. Rather the contrary. Since in the fully-formed proletariat the abstraction of all humanity, even of the *semblance* of humanity, is practically complete; since the conditions of life of the proletariat sum up all the conditions of life of society today in their most inhuman form; since man has lost himself in the proletariat, yet at the same time has not only gained theoretical consciousness of that loss, but through urgent, no longer removable, no longer disguisable, absolutely imperative *need*—the practical expression of *necessity*—is driven directly to revolt against this inhumanity, it follows that the proletariat can and must emancipate itself. But it cannot emancipate itself without abolishing the conditions of its own life.[76]

But the contemporary proletarian subject of von Stein and the young Marx, who gave social weight to socialist and communist ideas, was not really the modern industrial worker, but rather the *semi-proletarianized* artisan, whom the Germans called a *Handwerksproletarien*: the consumptive tailor crowded with a dozen others into a Parisian garret, the doomed handloom weaver in Lancashire or the Erzgebirge competing against Cartwright's infernal power looms, and the Ruhr peasant–miner stripped of his elite status and protection by the Prussian state. Paradoxically, as Karl Kautsky emphasized in his commentary on the Erfurt Program of 1892, "the private ownership of the means of production increases not only the material misery but also the dependence of the small man … There is no more miserable, wretched existence than that of the petty industrialist or the small farmer who is struggling hard against overwhelming capital."[77] Accordingly, craftsmen such as the famed *canuts* of Lyon and the shoemakers of New England dreaded above all being "forced into the abyss of the proletariat."[78] Socialism in the first instance was a revolt against proletarianization and the separation of the artisan from the means of production. Its original ideal was society as a cooperative workshop.

In *Capital*, on the other hand, structural *position* and the potential power it confers became as important as existential *condition* in defining the essence of the proletariat. Marx demonstrated that the poverty of the factory hands, while less extreme than that of the starving countryside, was more *radical* in nature since it arose from their role as producers of unprecedented wealth. "Only in the mode of production based on capital does pauperism appear as the result of labor itself, of the development of the productive forces of labor."[79] In contrast to the obsolete artisans, the poor peasants, or even slaves, industrial workers do not look backward through Jeffersonian or Proudhonist nostalgia to a utopian restoration of petty production, natural economy, and egalitarian competition. As Marc Mulholland summarizes Marx: "The human instinct for control of oneself and one's immediate environment, which for previous classes meant essentially a drive towards perfecting private control of the means of personal subsistence and wealth creation, for the proletariat is converted into a desire for collective control and ownership of the means of production."[80] The proletarian accepts that the massacre of small property by Capital is irreversible and that economic democracy must be built upon the abolition of the wages system rather than of large-scale industry per se. Unlike rebellious slaves or serfs, who could burn down the big house and then distribute the land amongst themselves, industrial workers cannot simply divide up the machines and take them home. Alone of all subalterns and exploited producers, the proletarian has no vestigial stake in the preservation of private ownership of the means of production or the reproduction of economic inequality.

Marx makes a central but often overlooked distinction between wage-labor in the broadest sense and highly socialized factory labor employed in machine-dominated production. The labor movement in the nineteenth century was the protest of the stricken world of the hand worker as much as the brave new world of the factory proletariat.

The *formal relations of production* (wage-labor and capital) arising from the expropriation of small producers by agricultural and merchant capital shaped the broad boundaries of a property-less, commodity-producing working class. But the "wages system," David Montgomery reminds us, "has historically *not* been coextensive with industrial society."[81] Indeed, the commodification of labor generally preceded industrialization, and Marx considered wage-labor to be "completely realized in form in England ... at the end of the eighteenth century with the repeal of the law of apprenticeship."[82]

By then, the merchant-controlled putting-out system (rural "proto-industrialism") had reached staggering proportions, while in urban manufacture, especially in lines like ready-to-wear clothing and cheap furniture, de-skilled journeymen were becoming mere detail workers.[83] Their tools did not have to be transformed into machines in order for craftsmen themselves to become little more than moving parts of the manufacturing system. Writing about the great Lyon silk workers' uprising of 1834, Sanford Elwitt stresses that "artisans can and do become proletarians without leaving their workshop for the factory and without any transformation in the structure of work. What does change, and the change is momentous, is the system of social production into which they enter more or less involuntarily."[84]

The artisans forcibly subjugated to the capitalist mode of production, however, were not a simple, unitary class. "The class interests of many nineteenth-century French Republican socialist artisans," writes Ronald Aminzade, "were contradictory. As small master artisans, their positions within production made them employers intent on resisting the demands of the workers they employed. As producers engaging in manual labor alongside their apprentices and journeymen, however, they had an interest in resisting the innovations of capitalist merchants and manufacturers whose activities threatened the demise of their small workshops."[85]

Moreover, as Jacques Rancière emphasizes in his discussion of the French case, the axe of capitalism—merchant or industrial—did not fall equally on the heads of all "artisans"—a category that he argues has been reified or at least used too generically by labor historians. It was not the corporately powerful luxury crafts in Paris that embraced utopian socialism and marched doomed to the barricades in June 1848, but their "poor relations": "the tailors but not the hatters ... the shoemakers but not the curriers ... the woodworkers but not the carpenters ... the typographers who, in their relation to the intellectual world, are outcasts as well. Workers' militant identity would seem to go in the opposite direction from collective professional identity … The militant worker population was situated within the poorest of the world of organic professional collectivities."[86] (Should we not see early socialism, then, especially Icarian Communism, as the Ghost Dance of the tailors and cobblers?)

In The Poverty of Philosophy *(1847), Marx used the examples of England and Chartism to portray the homogenization of proletarian life under industrial capital, and, parallel with this, the development through struggle of an increasingly united and class-conscious labor movement. The picture of class formation in* Capital, *however, is far more complex, with economic growth producing a heterogeneous working class whose modern core of factory workers and miners is surrounded by a penumbra of construction and transport laborers, farm and sweatshop workers, service and office employees, and staggering numbers of domestic servants.*

Contrary to legend, Marx did *not* believe that industrial workers would inevitably become the majority of society: instead, "the extraordinary increase in the productivity of large-scale industry, accompanied as it is by both a more intensive and a more extensive exploitation of labour-power in all other spheres of production, permits a larger and larger part of the working class to be employed unproductively."[87] He clearly recognized the "double meaning of proletarianization" that Adam Przeworski, in an otherwise illuminating essay, erroneously claimed eluded him. "In terms of the destruction of places in pre- and early-capitalist organization of production it means separation from the ownership of the means of production and from the capacity to transform nature independently. But in terms of creation of new places within the structure of advancing capitalism it does not necessarily denote creation of new places of productive, manual labor."[88]

The most telling example—*as a direct consequence of the Industrial Revolution*—is that there were more servants in Britain in 1861 than workers in textile factories and metal industries.[89] Marx called them "modern domestic slaves" for a good reason: the Law of Master and Servant made disobedience under contract to employers an offense punishable by imprisonment.[90] (The attempt, in both Britain and the early American republic, to apply such statutes to miners, artisans, or trade unionists in general provoked violent reactions from workers and led to several epic court battles.)[91] Similarly, in Bismarckian Germany "the servants' law (*Gesindeordnung*) required unqualified obedience to one's employer, forbade organization, and excluded domestics [almost 1 million] as well as farm servants from protective legislation and social insurance programs."[92] (The bourgeoisie, which like the aristocracy measured its status by staff, inherited and defended this intimate power of servile oppression, while the workers' movement, with few exceptions, disdained the servant caste for its submissive obedience.)

Meanwhile the mass craft occupations and the out-work economy continued to flourish alongside the factory system for most of the nineteenth century and into the next. The Great Exhibition of 1851, Raphael Samuel once pointed out, may have glorified the age of steam-powered machinery, but the sixteen acres of glass (300,000 panes) that clothed the Crystal Palace were blown by hand. Indeed, as factory production and imported grain displaced artisans and farm laborers, the "superabundance of labour … encouraged capitalists to engage in capital-saving rather than labour-saving investment"—a negative feedback loop that slowed the pace of mechanization while vastly expanding the ranks of sweated and casual labor.[93] The development of the labor process under capital followed a logic of uneven and combined development even in the most advanced societies.

It was also the case, as Marx emphasized in *Capital*, that certain key mechanical inventions led away from, rather than toward, the socialization of labor in the factory system. Some peasant–artisans may have marched straight from the weaver's cottage to the cotton mill, but others exchanged their hand-looms for sewing machines, usually within a new production unit, simultaneously alternative and complementary to the factory, the *slum*. Following Marx, Gareth Stedman Jones, in *Outcast London,* cited the examples of the sewing machine and the bandsaw, which from the 1850s were rapidly adopted throughout the apparel, shoe, and furniture industries. Removing the bottleneck of hand-sewing or sawing allowed ready-to-wear goods and furniture to be produced in vast quantities without fundamental transformations of the old divisions of labor. These inventions, Jones emphasized, "strengthened a supposed pre-industrial pattern of manufacture based upon sub-contract and the 'vertical disintegration of production' carried to its furthest extent."[94]

Unlike domestic and agricultural workers, who were almost never successful in making claims against their employers, sweat-shop workers, although lacking the economic centrality and clout of metalworkers, dockers, and miners, had the advantages of urban concentration and neighborhood solidarity. They eventually produced some of the most renowned fighters in the international labor movement. Although many immigrant groups, starting with the Irish and Italians, followed in the footsteps of the expatriate German artisans of the 1840s and 1850s (60,000 in Paris alone!), "sweatshop socialism" was largely the creation of Jewish immigrants in the East End of London and the East Side of New York, as well as their counterparts in Antwerp, Salonika, Chicago, and Montreal. From the great tailors' strike of 1889 in London, which Eleanor Marx so passionately supported, to the general uprising of Manhattan's garment trades from 1909 to 1915, Yiddish became a major dialect of class struggle.[95]

The Industrial Revolution and its subordination of the producer to the machine created a new historical subject, the "collective worker"; a new form of exploitation, relative surplus extraction; and a new terrain of class struggle, mass production.

The separation of the wage worker from the means of production took on a new, revolutionary meaning inside the steam-powered factory. Although the manufacture system, based on hand labor and oriented to export goods like textiles and china, raised productivity (and thus relative surplus value) to a limited extent through economies of scale and a more intricate division of labor, "it never attains a complete technical unity on its own foundation."[96] In contrast, "the modern workshop, which is based on the application of machinery ... is a [distinctive] *social production relation*" characterized by the "constant, continuous and repeated revolution in the mode of production itself, in the productivity of labour and in the relations between capitalist and worker."[97] (Later Marx would make a subtle but key revision to this definition: "The productive powers of directly ... *socialized* (common) labour are developed through cooperation, through the division of labour within the workshop, and the employment of machinery, *and in general through the transformation of the production process into a conscious application of the natural sciences.*")[98]

Like the artisan–proletarians and common laborers, industrial workers sell their labor-power individually, but unlike their predecessors they produce value only as a *collective worker*. (The German term *Gesamtarbeiter* can also be translated as "total" or "global" worker.) As Balibar emphasizes in *Reading Capital*, "this collective worker in a relationship with the unity of the means of production is now a completely different individual from the one who formed the characteristic unity of artisan-manufacturing labour with different means of labour."[99] This is a decisive distinction. The industrialist, says Marx, "pays for their individual labour capacities, not for their combination, not for the social power of labour." The productive capacity that arises from the factory collectivity, a higher species of labor, he appropriates for free.[100] Moreover as the workforce is increasingly subordinated to a machine-dominated and machine-integrated labor process, the power of capital is "imposed *inside* the production process and no longer only outside it."[101] "The technical subordination of the workman to the uniform motion of the instruments of labour … give[s] rise to a barrack discipline." This is the "real subjection [or subsumption] of labor to capital."[102]

Ultimately, Marx predicts, "the *living connection* of the whole workshop no longer lies here in cooperation; instead, the system of machinery forms a unity, set in motion by the PRIME MOTOR and comprising the whole workshop, to which the living workshop is subordinated, in so far as it consists of workers. Their *unity* has thus taken on a form which is tangibly autonomous and independent of them."[103]

This development of the productive power of *socialised labour*, as opposed to the more or less isolated labour of the individual, etc. and, alongside it, the *application of science*, that *general* product of social development, to the *direct production process*, has the appearance of a *productive power of capital*, not of labour. The mystification which lies in the capital-relation in general is now much more developed than it was, or could be, in the case of the merely formal subsumption of labour under capital.[104]

But these same monolithic productive powers could be turned against capital if proletarians organize industrially and on a large scale. Indeed, for the workers' movement to acquire a universal form, inclusive of all varieties of wage-labor, it had to accumulate power above all in the *advancing* industrial sectors: textiles, iron and steel, coal, ship-building, railroads, and so on. They alone, in the words of the *Manifesto*, possess "historical initiative." Accordingly, industrial workers (including miners and transport workers) formed the powerful core of the labor movement and the political left for a century, roughly from 1880 to 1980. The inflection point at which factory workers rather than artisans and hand-workers began to dominate the labor movement obviously depended on the level of economic development: Friedrich Lenger suggests the end of Chartism in England, the Civil War in the United States, the Commune in France, and the anti-socialist laws in Germany.[105] But by 1865 even Proudhon, whose "petty bourgeois point of view" Marx never tired of deriding, came around in his last book (*De la Capacité politique des classes ouvrières* [1865]) to a very similar understanding of the leading role of industrial workers, "especially those in large enterprises."[106]

If poverty, as André Gorz claimed, is the "natural basis" of the struggle for socialism, it is the "unnatural poverty" of the industrial working class, which grows in lockstep with the productive powers of collective labor.[107] Workers, especially in boom periods, may win significant wage improvements that foster the growth of new "necessities," but they are likely to be reversed during downturns. It is not progressive impoverishment—the so-called "law of absolute immiseration"—that usually generates revolutionary impulses but mass unemployment and the sudden loss of hard-won and apparently permanent gains.

It is important to understand that, when Marx talks about the poverty that drives revolt, he truly means *misery,* not just relative deprivation or a high Gini coefficient. It is worth quoting Herbert Marcuse on this point:

> One must insist on the inner connection between the Marxian concepts of exploitation and impoverishment in spite of later redefinitions, in which impoverishment becomes a cultural aspect, or relative to such an extent that it applies also to the suburban home with automobile, television, etc. "Impoverishment" connotes the *absolute need and necessity* of subverting *intolerable* conditions of existence, and such absolute need appears at the beginnings of all revolutions against the basic social institutions.[108]

Certainly, Marx acknowledged a "historical and moral element" in the constitution of wages, as well as victories for the "political economy of the working class such as the ten-hour day." Likewise, the level of "necessary needs," as Michael Lebowitz rightly insists, is "the product of class struggle," not a fixed physiological minimum; and, in turn, the qualitative growth of the "standard of necessity" helps drive the economic class struggle forward.[109] But Marx believed that such gains and the new needs they created would be cyclically eroded by crises, whose tendency was to become more general and destructive over time.

A sub-section of *Capital Volume I* ("Effect of Crises on the best paid part of the Working Class") illustrates this thesis with the plight of London's elite iron shipbuilders following the collapse of the huge Millwall Iron Works during the financial panic of 1866.[110] These "aristocrats of labor" soon faced starvation, and Marx quotes at length a description of their fallen condition reported in Cobden and Bright's newspaper, the *Morning Star*:

In the East End districts of Poplar, Millwall, Greenwich, Deptford, Limehouse and Canning Town, at least 15,000 workmen and their families were in a state of utter destitution, and 3,000 skilled mechanics were breaking stones in the workhouse yard (after distress of over half a year's duration) … I had great difficulty in reaching the workhouse door, for a hungry crowd besieged it. They were waiting for their tickets, but the time had not yet arrived for the distribution.[111]

This *episodic* immiseration, from which Marx believed no group of workers were exempt, was in fact a fairly accurate forecast of the behavior of the business cycle from 1870 to 1938. "The burden of adjustment in the classical era," writes economic historian Jeffry Frieden, "was on labor. If business conditions worsened, wages were cut [and] under the gold standard, wages had to be cut in order to restore a country's competitiveness in export and import markets."[112] Although the deflation of consumer goods offset wage depression to some extent, the general experience of industrial workers was the instability of employment and income. Marx emphasized this in his famous 1865 report (reprinted as *Value, Price and Profit*) to the General Council of the International Workingmen's Association: "During the phase of sinking market prices and the phases of crisis and stagnation, the working man, if not thrown out of employment altogether, is *sure* to have his wages lowered."[113] Such was the case in France and Britain between 1899 and 1913, when, as Hobsbawm points out, capital transferred higher costs of production, largely due to rising agricultural prices, onto the working classes in the form of falling real wages.[114] Unions, whose role Marx conceived as almost totally defensive, could protect wage standards in some instances during mild economic slowdowns, but not during full-scale recessions, when unemployment swelled the ranks of potential replacement workers and strike-breakers. In general, then, periods of fast growth and blind faith in progress were inevitably punctuated by abrupt slowdowns and predictions of war and collapse. As a result, European perspectives on contemporary history violently shifted back and forth between the Belle Epoque[115] and the "Decline of the West," from Eduard Bernstein's incremental road to socialism to Trotsky's armored train.

In the "Manifesto" that he wrote for the Communist International, Trotsky reviewed the outcome of the debate about immiseration from the perspective of that *annus horribilis,* 1919:

> As a result of the war the contradictions of the capitalist system confronted mankind in the shape of pangs of hunger, exhaustion from cold, epidemics and moral savagery. This settled once and for all the academic controversy within the Socialist movement over the theory of impoverishment and the gradual transition from capitalism to socialism. Statisticians and pedants of the theory that contradictions were being blunted, had for decades fished out from all the corners of the globe real or mythical facts testifying to the rising well-being of various groups and categories of the working class. The theory of mass impoverishment was regarded as buried, amid contemptuous jeers from the eunuchs of bourgeois professordom and mandarins of Socialist opportunism. At the present time this impoverishment, no longer only of a social but also of a physiological and biological kind, rises before us in all its shocking reality.[116]

II. Factories and Unions
The factory system organizes the workforce as interdependent collectivities that, through struggle and conscious organization, can become communities of solidarity. Moreover, factories and other large industrial enterprises such as shipyards and railroad repair shops are miniature political systems.

In the *Eighteenth Brumaire*, Marx famously compared the backward strata of the French peasantry to a "sack of potatoes." "Their mode of production," he wrote, "isolates them from one another, instead of bringing them into complex interactions."[117] As a result, Hobsbawm adds, peasant consciousness tends to be entirely localized or constituted in abstract opposition to the city, often in the language of millenarian religion: "The unit of their organized action is either the parish pump or the universe. There is nothing in between."[118] The industrial proletariat (Marx includes factory hands, building laborers, miners, workers in capitalist agriculture, and transport workers) on the other hand, is only constituted *en ensemble*, as integral collectivities within the social division of labor. The French socialist Constantin Pecqueur, in his 1839 book on the revolutionary character of the steam age, had already extolled the factory, in words that strikingly prefigured those of Marx, for its "progressive socialization" of the labor force and its creation of a "proletarian public life."[119]

But solidarity, as noted earlier, is not directly endowed by factory relations of production; equally, class consciousness, as David Montgromery reminds us, "is always a project." Workers in new industries or plants are initially atomized: a competitive situation that capitalists attempt to prolong through favoritism, piecework wages, and gender/ethnic divisions of labor. In the cases, common in nineteenth-century iron works and shipyards, where bosses "contracted in"—that is to say, allowed groups of skilled workers to bid on jobs and hire their own laborers—craft autonomy included a managerial dimension, leading at the extreme to co-exploitation of laborers and the unskilled. The Hobbesian factory or mill, as sociologist Katherine Archibald memorably argued in *Wartime Shipyard: A Study in Social Disunity* (1947), might even be considered the default condition of industrial life.[120] Accordingly, even the most elementary forms of solidarity must be consciously constructed, beginning with the informal work groups, defined by common tasks or skills, that are the nuclei out of which a plant society, or rather counter-society, is built.

As Ralph Darlington emphasizes, "the transformation of a set of individuals into a collective actor is normally the work of a small but critical mass of workplace activists whose role in industrial relations has been seriously understated."[121] These activists, whether or not members of an outside union or political organization, utilized work-group solidarities as building blocks of unionization, while constantly struggling to overcome the hurdles of ethnic, gender, and regional differences that were so often embodied in the division of labor.[122] Unlike the broad-chested heroes of proletarian novels or Eisenstein films, rousing their workmates to rebellion with a single fiery speech, the classical rank-and-file organizer was more like a patient gardener constantly weeding daily plant life of its inevitable dissensions and jealousies. A large plant was often a fractious congeries that recapitulated the ethnic and geographical rivalries of the larger society.

In the case of the famed Moscow Metalworks, for example, each production department was recruited from a particular village or region which "fostered shop-loyalty (*tsekhovshchuna*) … [that] transcended craft divisions because former peasants maintained strong ties between specific shops and particular villages." Overcoming these petty patriotisms and shop rivalries was a heroic task for Social Democrat activists. Even after the Revolution, according to Kevin Murphy, "shop loyalty prevailed" and Old Bolsheviks liked to squabble over whose department (and by implication village) was the most revolutionary.[123] Similarly, in a groundbreaking study of the creation of a UAW local in 1930s Detroit, Peter Friedlander recounted the intricate diplomacy that was necessary to unite a dozen ethnically segmented plant departments, each with its own distinctive "social personality" and set of grievances. The turning point came when a previously disinterested group of young workers in the press department—members of a feared Polish street gang— decisively rallied to the union.[124] Militant workplace society, in other words, was the product of a *synthesis of partial group interests* around a common resistance to exploitation and employer despotism. Organization was anything but spontaneous and always risked the possibility that one or another workplace interest group might take control of the local union or organizing campaign for its own purposes.

Organizing campaigns and strikes have a politico-moral *momentum that necessarily exceeds the economic demands that were their first cause. Marx was insistent on this point. Moreover, "as schools of war," Engels added, "the Unions are unexcelled."*[125]

In the classical era, the first steps toward inclusive organization were almost always defensive in character—to protest, for instance, a sudden reduction in wages or piece rates, the firing of a popular shopmate, the introduction of dangerous machinery, or some other egregious grievance. But as Marx emphasized in *The Poverty of Philosophy,* the union (or in some cases the clandestine workplace organization) quickly became a goal in itself, as irreducible to its purely utilitarian functions as, say, a church or village. "This is so true," Marx wrote, "that English economists are amazed to see the workers sacrifice a good part of their wages in favor of associations, which, in the eyes of these economists, are established solely in favor of wages."[126]

This collective moral transcendence of what might be called game-theoretical economic calculation was regularly and vividly illustrated in strikes. "The public rituals of a strike forge an esprit de corps among workers, a feeling of belonging to a group struggling for a common end; they make brothers (or sisters) in arms. Strike action establishes bonds of debt and mutual obligation. It is on strike that workers become a working class."[127] Prolonged strikes often enlarged the circumference of struggle to include whole communities—leading to the classic confrontation, recounted in innumerable labor narratives, of women demanding of men an active, more equal part in the struggle. Likewise, the life or death of a strike typically depended on its lateral extension into other shops and related industries; in this sense every strike might be the seed of a general strike. Thus the 1888 walkout of 1,500 girls and young women in a Bow phosphorus-match factory electrified the entire unorganized working class of East London, setting in motion the events that led to the successful 1889 strike of 100,000 dockworkers and the advent of the "New Unionism." Such explosions of popular militancy, even if defeated, could carve out a legend, define the character of a community, and be templates for industrial militancy a century later. They were milestones in the cultural memory of the working class.

A poorly organized strike, on the other hand, could leave a long trail of recrimination, division, and despair: a negative inoculation to further militancy. In either case, the rank and file paid a high price for their unions. In addition to massacres, imprisonments, deportations, and exile, former strikers were blacklisted by the tens of thousands. A grim example was the fate of militant members of the American Railway Union, the first great U.S. industrial union, who walked out in support of the Pullman strikers in 1894. As Nick Salvatore explains in his biography of the ARU's leader, Eugene Debs,

> the railroad corporations inaugurated an extensive and severe blacklist. When a worker asked for a recommendation from his pre-strike employer, he would receive the usual assessment of his

technical abilities. A prospective employer then held the letter to the light after the applicant left the room. If the watermark showed a crane with its head cut off, the man had been active during the strikes and was not to be hired. The decapitated crane caused untold suffering throughout the western half of the country.[128]

In an era of family upheaval and household recomposition, gender equality was often the most difficult solidarity to achieve inside factories and other modern workplaces. Together with white supremacy, patriarchy was the true Achilles' heel of the labor movement.

The super-exploitation of women and children in the textile industries quite rightly was the scandal of the Victorian era; but too often the response of the male working class was to demand the expulsion of women from the factories, rather than to seek the improvement of their working conditions. Indeed, the wage of a male "bread-earner"—the material basis for a household that emulated the middle-class nuclear family with a stay-at-home mother—was a fundamental demand of early trade unionism, especially amongst the better-paid crafts. The "modern Hercules" viewed the single working woman, not as a sister and comrade, but as a strike-breaker and enemy of the family. "The workers' movement," writes Michelle Perrot, "which based its identity on the exaltation of production and the great virile trades—the brave miner, the physically strong construction worker, the technically clever mechanic, heroes who brought about the second industrial revolution and would change the world—denigrated feminism as 'bourgeois.'"[129] In reality, patriarchy never brought home all the bacon: a true "family wage" was rarely achieved, much less servants for craftsmen, and "respectable working-class wives" were forced to take in laundry, sew at home, or engage in part-time domestic service. But women remained essential to capitalist production even if in increasingly segregated departments and industries: food-processing, industrial laundries, matches, textiles, ribbon-making, millinery, and garment production. Prominent in early Victorian factory struggles, younger women workers again took center stage in the great industrial struggles in the United States, Britain, and Russia that immediately preceded the First World War. (New York's glorious shirtwaist strikers—young Jewish and Italian women arm in arm—were one celebrated example.) In this period, and again in the later phases of the war and then revolution, women's struggles for decent wages, affordable rents, and safe workplaces often combined with demands for full citizenship—not only the right to vote but access to public employment, the professions, and political office—to generate pyrotechnic moments of exceptional militancy: prefigurations, as it were, of the gender-equal liberating force that the socialist movement had to become, yet largely failed to be.

"Was Fourier wrong," asks Marx rhetorically in Capital, *"when he called factories 'mitigated jails'?"*[130] *Resistance to workplace despotism (i.e. disciplinary codes, arbitrary power of overseers, firings without cause, sexual harassment, and so on) has always been the pilot light of the modern class struggle. By fighting to establish* rights *on the factory floor, workers challenged not merely "managerial prerogative," but implicitly the principle of wage-labor itself.*

One of the most shocking aspects of the early factory system in Lancashire was the corporal punishment routinely meted out to the children and adolescents who formed about 40 percent of the workforce in cotton and 50 percent or more in the flax, silk, woolen, and worsted industries.[131] Adult workers, in turn, were sanctioned by demotion, dismissal, or fines, although beatings and sexual assaults were not uncommon. Indeed, some foremen and supervisors seemed to regard rape as a feudal prerogative of their jobs. Kathleen Canning, in her work on women workers in Germany, finds that they

> frequently engaged in collective action to enforce and defend their own code of morality. In 1905, male and female workers in a Bocholt mill went on strike to demand the firing of an overseer who had raped several female employees. The issue of rape also led to a turbulent confrontation in the government district of Düsseldorf in 1902 when an angry crowd of both male and female workers assembled in front of the home of a master weaver who had assaulted a female subordinate. One worker was killed in the resulting melee, and four others received jail sentences.[132]

Foremen, even those promoted directly from the shopfloor, relished arbitrary despotism, and owners usually rewarded them for its practice. In the Ruhr steel mills, studied by Barrington Moore and others, "a worker could be fired for just about any reason that occurred to a foreman. Many foremen apparently used their authority to vent on the workers all sorts of hatred, envy, and personal dislike." One of the most outrageous and bitterly resented practices, widespread at Krupp plants, was "to fire workers after long years of service just before the time when they could collect their pensions."[133]

The unilateral power of employers, especially when it was used to speed up production, introduce deskilling technologies, or demand higher quotas, was robustly contested by workers across a spectrum of resistance that ranged from subtle "soldiering" (conscious restriction of output) to machine sabotage, spontaneous strikes, and even "industrial jacqueries" like that led by young miners and glassworkers in Belgium's Charleroi Basin in

March 1886 (twenty-eight killed).[134] Guerrilla warfare was even an option. In the Wyoming Valley of Pennsylvania, immigrant Irish anthracite miners drew upon their experiences in anti-landlord secret societies in their homeland to create the "Molly Maguires" to take revenge against despotic supervisors and mine bosses. The great 1905 miners' strike in the Ruhr was largely nonviolent, but the grievances of a heavily immigrant workforce, in this case Polish, were again focused, as in Pennsylvania, on a "general atmosphere of arbitrary authority combined with personal abuse." Moreover, as Barrington Moore emphasizes, the strike was literally forced on the unions by angry miners, including the previously unorganized. "Dignity," as always, was the transcendent demand.[135] Likewise, in Russia during the great strike wave of that year, "workers were especially infuriated at foremen and supervisors who refused to treat them civilly. In one factory after another, workers demanded that the supervisors responsible for 'insults to human dignity' be required to change their conduct or else be dismissed." When management refused to comply, "workers would subject the despised men to ridicule by carting them on wheelbarrows outside the gates of the factory and dumping them on the street." In his history of the 1905 Revolution, Abraham Ascher cites twenty of these "cartings" in Petersburg factories in March alone.[136]

Paternalism might soften abuse on the shopfloor, even create a façade of the "works family," but it was usually accompanied by obnoxious intrusions into workers' family lives and private habits. For instance, the famous Waltham-Lowell system in early industrial New England, which advertised itself as a kind of finishing school for poor farm girls, was a model of puritanical moral regulation as well as relentless exploitation. The United States was indeed a test-bed for some of the most radical experiments in the control of industrialized workforces, especially in its many privately policed company towns, such as Pullman, Illinois, or Hershey, Pennsylvania, where the appellation "semi-feudal" was usually well deserved. (Although at the extreme of this type, it should be recalled that Auschwitz was quite literally an I. G. Farben company town.) Even Henry Ford, that most "visionary" and modern of employers, maintained a brutal internal police agency, the Ford Service Department, under the infamous thug Harry Bennett, which enforced speedup on the assembly lines by intimidating and often beating workers—and, in the 1930s, murdering strikers.

On the eve of the First World War, a few industrial corporations began to experiment with "functional foremanship" as part of the larger movement to implement scientific management. The idea was to depersonalize shopfloor supervision through formalizing instructions in detailed codes and standard procedures. "One *person* should not give orders to another *person*, but both should agree to take their orders from the situation." But this Taylorization of management and the correlate fetishization of standard operating procedures only made foremen and line supervisors more despotic.[137] And numerous. "In 1900 the ratio of workers to foremen [in the United States] was 16:1. By 1910 it had declined to 14:1, and by 1920, strikingly, to 10:1."[138] The great 1930s uprising of U.S. workers in mass-production industries would be inspired, first and above all, by the quest to limit arbitrary authority through grievance procedures and the shop-steward system: seeds of the dangerous idea of industrial democracy.

The path from the anomic, internally divided factory to workforce solidarity and the successful exercise of shopfloor power did not always follow the narrative of heroic union-building. Where workers were less replaceable because of special demographic or labor-market conditions, conflict inside the factory might be more informally, even invisibly organized.

France under the Third Republic, Alain Cottereau argues, was a case in point, with militant workers but relatively weak unions, and a more or less permanent "disjunction between the labor movement and labor organizations." The "silent class struggle," as he calls it, of pervasive and successful restriction of output, whether by slowdowns or actual sabotage, assumed unusual dimensions in France, in part because the countryside did not empty out into the cities, as occurred elsewhere, under the impact of agricultural imports after 1880, and thus French employers had a smaller pool of strikebreakers and replacement workers. "Considered in purely economic terms as a 'labor market,' France was characterized from 1852 on by a permanent relative shortage of rural and industrial wage labor." This "configuration of the labor market enabled French workers to defend themselves effectively without relying on legally recognized formal organizations." Occupational heredity was more common than in Germany or the United States, and workplace cultures of resistance more entrenched, with 1848 and the Commune as unifying memories and myths. "In their correspondence," Cottereau continues, "employers complained about the strict rules imposed by workers against the productivist race [rationalization, deskilling, speedup], sanctioned by anonymous sabotage, which could not be repressed in an authoritarian manner." When capitalists did attempt to crack down on labor, strikes often took on a volcanic form, requiring army intervention. Until the 1890s and the emergence of the *bourse* movement, strikes were typically organized by clandestine committees, and misinterpreted by outsiders as primitively "spontaneous" or "irrational" outbursts.[139]

"It was always by way of sudden actions and outbursts, unexpected by political observers, that the French labor movement

achieved its most 'concrete' economic and political successes."
French working-class tradition, in other words, preceded and prefigured the articulation of syndicalist doctrine.

> Even before the institutionalization of "direct-action syndicalism,"
> there was at work in the culture of the workers what might be called
> a "pragmatic of direct action," whose tenets can be expressed as
> follows: avoid separating action on behalf of specific demands
> from the development of parallel worker power; reject the com-
> partmentalization between the public sphere (the state, elected
> representatives, public opinion) and the economic or "private"
> sphere proposed by parliamentary democracy; emphasize at all
> levels of the movement the illegitimacy of established social rela-
> tionships and propose a different legitimacy, to be acknowledged
> by other social classes.[140]

Proletarianization in late-developing nations was sometimes an explosive
process that transferred the raw countryside to the factory without any
urban acclimation. Russia was the classic case of such "non-linear" pro-
letarianization, and its young peasant workers often combined impressive
shopfloor militancy with the most backward rural prejudices.

As Trotsky explained in "Peculiarities of Russia's Development,"

> the reservoir from which the Russian working class formed itself
> was not the craft-guild but agriculture, not the city, but the country.
> Moreover, in Russia the proletariat did not arise gradually through
> the ages, carrying with itself the burden of the past as in England,
> but in leaps involving sharp changes of environment, ties, relations,
> a sharp break with the past ... [It] was forever repeating the short
> history of its origin. While in the metal industry, especially in
> Petrograd, a layer of hereditary proletarians was crystallized out,

in the Urals the prevailing type was *half-proletarian, half peasant.*
A yearly inflow of fresh labor forces from the country in all the
industrial districts kept renewing the bonds of the proletariat with
its fundamental social reservoir.[141]

Trotsky cites this lack of industrial tradition, together with the
"concentrated oppression of tsarism," as what "made the Russian
workers hospitable to the boldest conclusions of revolutionary
thought." But there was also a darker side to the "mixed consciousness" of the peasant worker, which Charters Wynn explored in his
important study of Russia's Ruhr, the Donbass. In the first decade of
the twentieth century, the fastest-growing working class in Europe
was mining coal and making steel in the treeless steppes between
the Dnepr and Donets rivers. The Donbass was an extraordinary
example of Trotsky's law of "uneven and combined development."
It was developed by American, French, and Belgian capital and its
steel plants were the most modern in Europe; indeed, one state-
of-the-art pipe plant was shipped directly from the United States.
But the region's advanced technology and giant plants contrasted
with its squalid labor camps and instant slums. Ukrainians for the
most part eschewed the dangerous labor of the mills and mines, so
employers looked to young Russian peasants from different regions
and Jews from the Pale of Settlement. To master the ultra-modern
technology, a small cadre of skilled and well-paid metallurgical
workers was also recruited, but a "vast gulf separated those workers
whose skills had been acquired in a few weeks or months from those
who had undergone years of apprenticeship." The "ruffian" rank
and file, as Wynn calls it, was riven by internal divisions. "These
regional differences within the industrial labor force ... and more
importantly, ethnic differences between workers and artisans—
proved to be a source of violent intraclass conflict." In struggles

against their foreign bosses, the Donbass workers were superbly militant and, as Trotsky maintained, unpolluted by reformism and receptive to the agitation of Social Democrats and Left Social Revolutionaries. But in periods of defeat, such as 1907–10, regional rivalries and anti-Semitism quickly rose to the surface. "In many cases, workers who participated in radical strike activity with the support and praise of the radical party *intelligentsiya* also engaged in the brutal, destructive violence of pogroms. Radical activists' attempts to constrain workers' ethnic violence repeatedly proved futile." In this case, the most militant and the most backward sections of the proletariat-in-formation were the same.[142]

III. Mass Strikes and Workers' Control

As industrial capitalism grew both domestically and through world markets, strategically emplaced workers gained unprecedented power to non-violently disrupt economic activity, and even to hold hostage the means of production. Neither capital nor labor, however, knew the limits of this power, or, on the part of the latter, to what extremes of force owners might resort when confronted with its full exercise. The general strike was the late Victorian and Edwardian proletariat's "atomic bomb."

The mass strike, pioneered by 0.5 million British miners and textile workers in 1842 (the Plug Riots), was rare in Marx's time but increasingly common toward the end of the century, with the Belgian General Strike (for suffrage) in 1893 and the U.S. Pullman Strike in 1894, just a few months before Engels's death. Workers' leaders and radical theorists differed sharply over the value of such strikes as weapons of class war. Was the general strike the ultimate revolutionary act, a useful tool for pressing reform and defending suffrage, or a provocation that would lead to the military repression of the entire workers' movement? The ensuing debate directly addressed fundamental questions of agency and class power, especially the relationship between parliamentary and non-parliamentary modes of struggle.

Shortly before his death in 1895, Engels penned a new introduction to the German edition of Marx's *The Class Struggles in France*, in which he counterposed the dramatic electoral progress of the SPD to what he called the "Belgian idiocy" of the general strike as advocated within the French, Belgian, and Austrian socialist parties. Such strikes, he argued, risked becoming suicidal insurrections: "The powers-that-be positively want to get us to go where the guns shoot and the sabers slash." In face of the revolutionary firepower commanded by modern armies, "the mode of struggle of 1848 is today obsolete in every respect"; no barricade could stand up to modern high-explosive shells, nor could a workers' militia hope to obtain arms comparable to the breech-loading repeating rifles of regular troops.[143] In countries such as Germany, where universal suffrage in some form had been won, "an entirely new method of proletarian struggle came into operation," and peaceful political campaigns had shown that they were a far more powerful organizing tool than agitation for mass strikes.

> The workers took part in elections to particular diets, to municipal councils and to trades courts; they contested with the bourgeoisie every post in the occupation of which a sufficient part of the proletariat had a say. And so it happened that the bourgeoisie and the government came to be much more afraid of the legal than of the illegal action of the workers' party, of the results of elections than of those of rebellion.[144]

Mass strikes, whether general or not, risked becoming out-of-control conflicts that allowed the bourgeoisie to unleash their military might to crush unions and roll back electoral gains. The threat of self-immolation was greatest in Germany, since it was the largest, most advanced and successful socialist movement in the world.

"There was only one means by which the steady rise of the socialist fighting forces in Germany could be temporarily halted, and even thrown back for some time: a clash on a grand scale with the military, a blood-letting like that of 1871 in Paris."[145] For this reason, Engels and Bebel, chairman of the SPD, opposed general strikes on May Day, as vigorously advocated by other major socialist parties, preferring instead to set aside the first Sunday in May as a festive celebration that avoided any confrontation with employers or the state. This undermined the original hope of the majority of delegates who had gathered in Paris in 1889 that May Day would be a revolutionary day of struggle. Resolutions in favor of May Day work stoppages at later congresses of the Second International were also circumvented by the SPD and the Free Unions.

Although he went along with the SPD's policy on May Day, Eduard Bernstein, soon to become the leader of the "Revisionists" in the party, had a more favorable opinion of the defensive role of general strikes: union power, disciplined and well-organized, might be the best assurance that a peaceful road to socialism remained open. Invited by Kautsky over Engels's objections to contribute an article on the topic to *Neue Zeit*, Bernstein argued that a general strike or its credible threat could ensure the implemention of reforms passed by a socialist majority in parliament. It was a necessary deterrent to counter-revolution and the suspension of democracy.[146]

This position was echoed in later years by Rudolf Hilferding, the Austro-Marxist economist who was also a major SPD leader, who declared that "behind universal suffrage must stand the will to the general strike." But Hilferding stressed that the general strike could be no more than this—a defensive weapon. It could not be used to hinder war, advance trade union struggles or make the revolution.[147]

Meanwhile other moderate or right-wing socialist leaders saw the general strike primarily as a useful safety valve for mass anger and romanticized militancy. Thus the reformist Socialist leadership under Vandervelde in Belgium twice defused pre-revolutionary crises by cleverly manipulating and prematurely ending general strikes for suffrage in 1902 and 1913. "The Belgians," observes Janet Polasky,

> stretched Marxist theories of class struggle and of revolution in their definition of a new social democratic practice ... To other members of the Second International, the three Belgian general strikes [including 1893] had shown the potential of controlled demonstrations. General strikes did not have to result in a bloodbath; they could be peaceful and orderly. They also did not necessarily lead to revolution.[148]

Likewise, the head of the Swedish LO, Herman Linqvist, who had previously denounced the use of the general strike as "tantamount to suicide," ultimately endorsed the 1909 action because it would "most likely dampen syndicalist and other leftist radical options."[149]

Table 1.2: General Strikes after 1890

1890	France: May Day (after Formies massacre)
	Belgium (led by Walloon miners)
1893	Belgium (spontaneous strikes over suffrage coalesce into national strike)
1902	Barcelona
	Belgium (suffrage)
	Buenos Aires
	Sweden (suffrage)

1903	Holland (two successive strikes led by dock and railroad workers)
	Rio de Janeiro (solidarity strike)
1904	Buenos Aires
	Italy (soldiers as strike breakers)
	St Petersburg
1905	Finland
	Russia (several)
1906	Hamburg (electoral reform)
	Italy
	Porto Alegre (Brazil)
1907	Italy
1908	France (after cavalry attack on Draveil strikers)
	Parma (rising of agricultural workers)
1909	Barcelona (Semana Trágica)
	Buenos Aires
	Salonika
	Sweden (against wage cuts)
1911	Liverpool
	Montevideo
1912	Brisbane (union rights)
1913	Belgium (electoral reform)
	Dublin (general lockout)
	New Zealand
1914	Petrograd
1917	Australia (solidarity with railroad workers)
	Barcelona (insurrectionary)
	Russia
	São Paulo
1918	Austria
	Germany (various cities)

1919 Buenos Aires (Semana Trágica—50,000 imprisoned)
Barcelona
Belfast
Glasgow
Seattle
Winnipeg
1920 France (great railroad strike)
1921 Argentina

For anarcho-syndicalists, in contrast, mass strikes were rehearsals —"revolutionary gymnastics"—for the ultimate general strike that would unleash militant spontaneity and revolutionary initiative on a scale beyond the capacity of socialist politicians and trade-union bosses to channel and control. Engels's nightmare was their dream. Syndicalist theorists like Fernand Pelloutier, the secretary of the National Federation of Bourses du Travail in France, Hubert Lagardelle, the editor of the influential journal *Mouvement Socialiste*, and the fiery Émile Pouget, after Pelloutier's death the editor of the CGT's newspaper, envisioned a revolutionary general strike that would establish workers' control of production, with the Bourses as centers of social administration. Meanwhile, that famous camp follower of extremist movements of all kinds, Georges Sorel, theorized the general strike as both the apocalyptic door to a new world and the necessary "myth in which Socialism is wholly comprised."[150]

Rosa Luxemburg, however, rejected both the Revisionist (especially the Belgian) and syndicalist interpretations of the great strike waves of the early twentieth century. Analyzing the first Russian Revolution, as well as the huge contemporary socialist demonstrations for suffrage in Central Europe, she wrote that the mass strike was "not an isolated act but a whole period of the class struggle," in which "the ceaseless reciprocal action of the political and economic struggles" created explosively unpredictable scenarios that elicited extraordinary rank-and-file ingenuity. She was one of the first socialist intellectuals to pay careful attention to the grassroots processes of proletarian radicalization—what Trotsky would later call "the molecular work of revolutionary thought." In particular, she pointed to the sudden activation of previously unorganized strata in Germany such as Silesian textile workers and Ruhr miners (who later, in 1918–19, would famously organize their own "Red Army"). Far from building a cargo cult to spontaneity, as she was often accused of doing, her crucial insights about working-class self-activity (that is to say, of unauthorized but not unled militancy) were part of a withering critique of the SPD leadership's "parade ground" self-image as the general staff of an obedient army of trade-unionists and socialist voters. Contrasting "the unorganized energy of the Russian Revolution" with the "organized caution of the German Party and trade unions," she launched "the first major assault from the left on the premises on which the German party, including its radicals, had operated."[151] (Ironically it was Lenin, not Luxemburg, who asserted in light of the 1905 insurrections that the workers were "instinctively, spontaneously Social Democratic.")[152]

As these mass strikes revealed, the deep structure of the workers' movement, beyond its visible official institutions and affiliates, was the unofficial, often non-party organization of struggle within factories, mines, and merchant marines. These internal networks allowed shopfloor workers to mount informal actions and, in periods of defeat and repression, to preserve their culture of militancy.

The opposition, at times even violent, of conservative trade-union bosses and moderate socialists to radical tactics like factory occupations and general strikes precipitated new leaderships from the anonymous shop floor. In some cases their networks grew into parallel or alternative unions, without the economic resources of the institutionalized unions with their dues check-off and full-time leaderships, but with a greater freedom of maneuver across the entire terrain of working-class grievances both inside and outside the factory. This is how the IWW operated in the United States during the great rebellion of immigrant workers—spurned by nativist craft unions—in the steel, rubber, textile, and garment industries from 1909 to 1913.

The national revolt began at the Pressed Steel (railroad) Car Company, a subsidiary of U.S. Steel in McKees Rocks, outside of Pittsburgh, where 5,000 workers from sixteen different national groups endured working conditions that would have appalled Czarist officials. According to the former coroner of Pittsburgh, "the Pressed Steel Car Company killed an average of one man a day at its works because of the speed-up system and the failure to protect machinery." When the workers walked out in July 1909, the company's president declared: "They're dead to us. There are more than enough idle men in Pittsburgh to fill every vacancy." The company immediately brought in armed strike-breakers, mounted state police, and the militia, panicking the small group of skilled American unionists involved in the strike. But, as Philip Foner explains in his history of the IWW, "a group of the foreign-born strikers ... had experience in revolutionary and labor struggles in Europe. They realized early in the strike that only a vigorous, militant strategy would achieve victory." They elected an "Unknown Committee" that synthesized the combined experience of the European veterans and kept the strike going despite mass arrests, a "Bloody Sunday" massacre, and evictions of strikers' families. The company, which had dismissed the strikers as little more than ignorant "Hunkie" peasants, was actually fighting a sophisticated leadership of former Hungarian socialists, Italian anarchists, Swiss social democrats, blacklisted German metalworkers, and Russian revolutionaries. The Unknowns eventually affiliated the struggle with the IWW, which mounted a brilliant national solidarity campaign on the workers' behalf, and in September the company capitulated.[153]

Another example of underground unionism was the anti-war resistance inside Berlin's huge armament factories (Siemens, AEG, Borsig, and so on) that emerged publicly in June 1916, when 55,000 workers went out on strike in protest against the imprisonment of Karl Liebknecht. The leadership, which "never numbered more than fifty members," were skilled turners (lathe operators), supporters of the far left, who, according to Pierre Broué, built "a unique kind of organization, neither a trade union nor a party, but a clandestine group in the trade unions and the Party [SPD] alike." By 1918 they effectively controlled the entire armaments industry in the German capital.

> They could set in motion, with the help of some hundreds of men whom they directly influenced, tens and later hundreds of thousands of workers, by enabling them to make their own decisions about active initiatives … Unknown in 1914, by the end of the War they were to be the accepted leaders of the workers of Berlin and, despite their relative youth, the cadres of the revolutionary socialist movement.

Indeed, Broué considered them "the finest people in Social Democracy."[154]

A half-century later, theorists of the emergent Italian far left discovered behind facile abstractions of "the masses" and "spontaneity" a similar underground of radical rank-and-file workers. Sergio Bologna recalled the secret ingredient in the ferment of the early 1960s in northern Italy's industrial triangle.

> The first autonomous, independent, self-organized wildcat strikes ... at Fiat, Pirelli, Innocenti, and in all the big factories ... were not of the masses. Rather, they were the result of a highly sophisticated political history of worker cadres and militants who had passed on the inheritance of a certain political culture to workers' groups ... they had succeeded in creating systems of struggle, maybe very partial, very local, but which were already politically mature organisms ... this completely changes the vision which makes the political elite an active subject and the mass movement a passive subject: the political elite, a kind of stratum endowed with knowledge and, instead, the mass movement, a stratum endowed only with wishes, with desires, with tensions and so on ... What we could call "spontaneity" is, in reality, the formation of microsystems of struggle which are already very mature politically, because they have been determined by a generation who came from the Resistance.

These older workers, in turn, were the "real leaven," who helped set in motion the uprising of younger workers, mostly migrants from the *Mezzogiorno*, during Italy's "Hot Autumn" of 1969.[155]

Workers can run the factories and develop the forces of production. Until the First World War, much of the applied science of production remained the quasi-property of metalworkers and other craftsmen.

Given the trends toward systematic deskilling and the "suppression of all intellectual development" in the Victorian factory, would the proletariat actually be competent to manage production? In *The Principles of Communism*, Engels was blunt:

> The common management of production *cannot* be effected by people as they are today, each one being assigned to a single branch of production, shackled to it, exploited by it, each having developed only *one* of his abilities at the cost of all the others and knowing only one branch, or only a branch of a branch of the total production."[156]

Later in "The Results of the Immediate Process of Production" (1863/64) Marx asserted that the continuing application of science to material production, the unique achievement of industrial capital, "rests entirely on the separation of the intellectual potentialities of the process from the knowledge, understanding and skill of the individual worker. ...Admittedly, a small class of higher workers does take shape, but this does not stand in any proportion to the masses of 'deskilled' workers."[157]

Yet, in his September 1864 "Inaugural Address of the Working Men's International Association," Marx celebrated the victories "of the political economy of labour over the political economy of property" with the passage of the Ten Hours Bill, but even more in the form of "the co-operative factories raised by the unassisted efforts of a few bold 'hands." "The value of these great social experiments cannot be over-rated. By deed, instead of by argument, they have shown that production on a large scale, and in accord with the behests of modern science, may be carried on without the existence of a class of masters."[158] If Marx seems to contradict himself, it is not surprising. The model of technological development in his economic writings is prescient but highly futuristic: the incipient "automatic factory" of *Capital Volume I* (Chapter 15: 4) extrapolates trends that in the 1860s were only visible in Britain's cotton textile mills and perhaps a few other industries. Overestimating the velocity of automation (the "production of machines by machines") and the reconstitution of craft labor as simple machine-tending, he simultaneously underestimated the economic persistence and social weight of the "class of higher workers": the new elite of millwrights, patternmakers, boilermakers, fitters, turners, and other precision metal workers who built, installed, and maintained the machine system.[159] (To the list of the mid-nineteenth century's new and "reskilled" occupations, we should add railroad and steamship engineers and mechanics of various grades.)

Until the rise of industrial unionism in the twentieth century, no union on earth was more powerful or widely emulated than the (English) Amalgamated Society of Engineers, with more than 90,000 members by 1897.[160] Indeed, the British term "engineer" deliberately conflated the designers and the makers of metal structures and machines, and thus testified to the stubborn resistance of skilled workers against any separation of the conceptual and practical contents of their skills. In some industries and mines, as we saw earlier, it was even common for bosses to subcontract parts of the labor process to skilled workers— the mid-Victorian aristocracy of labor—who would hire their own unskilled assistants.[161] In defending their functional autonomy (and its opacity to management) within production, the metal crafts usually played a conservative, sometimes reactionary role within labor movements, advancing their own tribal interests at the expense of less-skilled machine operators. These "mid-Victorian labour aristocrats," writes James Hinton, "often found it convenient 'to pose as the authentic spokesmen of the working class as a whole': but it *was* a pose. So long as they held to the exclusive character of their trade unionism the aristocrats could never genuinely embrace the working class as a whole, and, therefore, could never develop a politics of working-class hegemony."[162]

But they did conserve and stubbornly defend a vision of workers' control that potentially could transcend the horizons of craft property and exclusionary unionism. Until college-trained industrial engineers, as well as chemists and technicians, became a crucial part of the industrial hierarchy in the early twentieth century, and scientific management had substantially captured and analytically decomposed craft knowledge, complete capitalist control of the factory labor process ("real appropriation") was impossible.[163] As David Montgomery put it, the elite of the metal crafts kept the "manager's brain under the workman's cap."[164] At best, individual capitalists could hope to turn craft knowledge against itself by promoting machinists, electricians, and die-makers to foremen and plant managers.[165]

In the European Revolution of 1917–21, metalworkers based in the giant wartime munitions plants and shipyards led the rank-and-file labor revolt against war and immiseration. Faced with the rapid decline of craft regulation of production, an important cohort of the "aristocracy of labor," organized across Europe in ad hoc shop stewards' movements, embraced a radical program of workers' control of the factories.

The subjective position of skilled metalworkers in the class struggle, as already noted, was deeply ambiguous. They were, according to Hobsbawm, "the most active cadres of the workers' collective self-defence," yet (in the English-speaking countries at least) also "the main prop of middle-class social control and industrial discipline."[166] In Russian factories before the 1905 Revolution, these future Bolsheviks were called "barons" because of their high wages, smart clothing, and haughty attitudes toward the former peasants in the "hot shops" and labor gangs.[167] In Western Europe and North America, they often refused to support the struggles of mass-production workers, especially new immigrant groups. But their status as the "aristocracy of labor" began to quickly erode from the 1890s, with the crushing of the American Homestead steelworkers in 1892, followed by the defeat of the mighty Amalgamated in 1898.[168] Both strikes were fought over the issues of management prerogative and control of the labor process, especially the introduction of new machines (grinders, borers, punch presses, and so on) run by semi-skilled operatives, and the defeats radicalized a potent minority of younger craftsmen who came to embrace a syndicalist vision of industrial unionism and workers' control of industry.[169] The DMV, the huge German metalworkers' union, experienced a similar crisis a decade later, as its moderate "scientific" policies unraveled amidst lockouts and strike defeats, leading to a rank-and-file revolt in 1909 that prefigured the wartime shop-stewards' movement.[170] In Russia, according to Leopold Haimson, "a new generation of young workers of urban origin … impatient, romantic, singularly responsive to maximalism," repudiated the Menshevik old guard "in an atmosphere of patricidal conflict" and elected Bolsheviks to the leadership of the Union of Metalworkers in 1913, preparing the way for a riotous general strike in Petrograd the following July, on the eve of the First World War.[171]

The world war—almost as if scripted by *Capital*—produced a vast expansion in the metal-working industries and their workforces. Fiat in Turin, for example, increased its rolls by 1,200 percent in two years, while in Petrograd metalworkers came to constitute more than 60 percent of the city's workforce—an astonishing figure.[172] In Germany, 90,000 skilled metalworkers had to be demobilized to maintain production in Berlin's great outer ring of factories. As a result, DMV membership soared to almost 800,000 in 1918 and 1.6 million a year later.[173] In Paris it was the same story, except that the skilled workers (*professionnels*), some 150,000 by 1918, were technically kept in uniform, with the threat of being sent to the front if they agitated or struck.[174] In all the warring countries, and

72

usually with the complicity of right-wing or centrist union leaders, exploitation was increased to its physiological limits with seventy- to seventy-five-hour work weeks, implacable speedup, and soaring industrial accidents.

Meanwhile, the workfloor status quo was upset by the huge numbers of women and youth who were recruited for war work, often into jobs that had been "diluted"—that is to say, broken down into simpler tasks that could be performed with little formal training and paid by the "piece." By 1917 there were more than 1 million of these "dilutees" or "munitionettes," as the English called them, in the factories of the major warring powers, and in Berlin they constituted more than half of the workforce in chemicals, metal fabrication, and machine tools.[175]

To their grueling and dangerous jobs they also brought an acute concern about the deteriorating conditions on the home front, especially the food and fuel shortages. Unlike their male work-mates, dilutees could not be drafted in punishment for industrial militancy. To quote Barrington Moore, writing about the analogous case of immigrants in the Ruhr mines, these "'irresponsible' social elements freed from the inhibitions of traditions" lit a fire under the craftsmen, and it "was this fusion of limited preservation *and* destruction of their collective past that both helped and forced the miners [turners] to create a new collective identity."[176] Chris Fuller aptly portrays this "fusion of the economic with the political, the mingling of the organized with newly industrialized" as a "remak-ing" of the European working class that increasingly aligned the immediate interests of most workers with the syndicalist or revolu-tionary wing of the labor movement.[177] Radical metalworkers such as Alphonse Merrheim in France, Richard Müller in Germany, Alexander Shlyapnikov in Russia, and Willie Gallagher in Scotland helped to transform this widespread hatred of the war into active opposition with mass strikes, and eventually the occupation of the factories and shipyards.

The factory council movement synthesized two previously divergent strands of labor struggle: the semi-skilled workers' quest for inclusive industrial representation, and the metal crafts' defense of their prerogatives within the labor process. The small Owenite experiments in industrial self-management that Marx had praised fifty years earlier had now grown into a sweeping concept of workers' control of the entire industrial economy.

Wartime syndicalism in most cases eventually became Communism, and support for the creation of a new International. "Engineering shop stewards and revolutionary radicalism in the First World War," says Hobsbawm, "went together like cheese and pickles, and metalworkers—generally highly skilled men— later came proverbially to dominate the proletarian component of the Communist Party."[178] In order to incorporate dilutees and semi-skilled workers in general, a novel form of class organization emerged in a dozen European countries in 1918: the elected works council (*Betriebsrat*). Political revolution, which typically took the form of naval mutinies and army rebellions that quickly allied with local unions and workers' organizations, generated a parallel system of "workers and soldiers' councils" (*Arbeiter-und Soldatenräte* and *soviets*) that copied to some degree the model of the Paris Commune. Although varying in scale and articulation with other institutions (unions, parties, and non-industrial groups), the essence of the council movement in both of its chief manifestations was direct democracy and a commitment to workers' control of production and popular control of local government.[179]

The workers' councils arose from the radicalization of existing systems of workshop delegation such as the *sovety starost* (councils of elders) in big Petrograd factories, the shop-steward system in

British, French and German engineering works, and the "internal commissions" in northern Italian factories. Although formally responsible for representing union policy on the shop floor, stewards tended instead to become the independent tribunes of the rank and file, whose grievances often put them at odds with the compromises made by national unions during the war. In the engineering sector especially, where stewards were daily confronted with work mates' equally existential crises of loss of craft control and rapidly deteriorating family subsistence, they embraced the ideas of self-management long advocated by revolutionary syndicalists in France and industrial unionists (the IWW especially) in America. With national unions and labor/socialist parties largely coopted by *unions sacrees* and with free speech drastically curtailed, the shop floor became the major center of resistance to wartime state capitalism.

There was of course no single template for this revolution from below, but Petrograd in spring–summer 1917, with its 400,000 industrial workers concentrated in giant metal works, munitions plants, and shipyards, deserved its reputation as the most advanced laboratory of workers' control. When the newly elected factory committee for the Putilov works, which employed more than 60,000 machinists and laborers, issued instructions in April for the formation of rank-and-file committees within each of the leviathan's forty-one component shops and departments, it was explicit about ultimate goals:

> In view of the fact that the practical business of organizing shop committees is a new affair, it is necessary that these committees, which look after life at the grassroots, should display as much independence and initiative as possible. The success of the labour organisations in the factories fully depends on this. By becoming

accustomed to self-management, the workers are preparing for that time when private ownership of factories and works will be abolished, and the means of production, together with the buildings erected by the workers' hands, will pass into the hands of the working class as a whole.[180]

In his review of the Putilov experience, historian Steve Smith emphasizes that the committees were conceived as instruments of a *direct democracy always in session*:

The constitutions of factory committees [were] at pains to stress that sovereignty lies with the general meeting rather than with the committee itself. This accorded with the mood of thousands of workers who believed that power now rested with them. The significance of the February Revolution for the popular masses lay precisely in the fact that it was seen as opening the way for freedom and power to be transferred to the people. This meant not merely a "democratic republic," but also the "constitutional factory."[181]

In addition to the famous examples of Petrograd, Moscow, Berlin, and Turin, revolutionary metalworkers also gave leadership to council movements in Bremen, Chemnitz, Budapest, Wiener Neustadt, Vienna, Warsaw, and Lublin, as well as to the proto-communist parties that quickly emerged from the corresponding general strikes and insurrections. In the countries where there was no power vacuum or interruption in capitalist control of production, militant machinists, miners, and steelworkers, defending wartime gains in labor markets now being flooded with demobilized soldiers, turned toward the mass strike. Simultaneous general strikes in Seattle, Buenos Aires (the Semana Trágica, which saw 700 dead) and Glasgow in January 1919 were followed by a general walkout in Winnipeg in May, the "quasi-insurrectionary" wildcat strike of 170,000 Parisian metalworkers in June, and the U.S. Great Steel Strike in September led by syndicalist and future Communist leader William Z. Foster.

How should "workers' control" be understood? In Vienna, Max Adler, "the only Austro-Marxist theorist who granted the workers' councils any major significance for the transition to socialism," proposed a social-democratic constitution that would subordinate the councils as a second chamber of parliament to a more powerful and traditional national assembly.[182] In Berlin the shop stewards' leaders Richard Müller and Ernst Daumig saw the *Bestreibsrate* as both fighting organizations and the nuclei of a socialist economy. "The council structures' struggle from the bottom up would take from the capitalists the knowledge that had enabled them to dominate workers and employ it for the autonomous self-organization through which they would advance step by step to managing the entire economy according to plan in the future."[183] In Turin, suddenly the "Petrograd of Italy," Gramsci, writing in *L'Ordine Nuovo*, advocated a more syndicalist and utopian vision of the plant councils as nuclei of a new world government "organized on the model of a large engineering works, an International in which every people, every part of humanity acquires a characteristic personality by its performance of a particular form of production and not by its organization as a state with particular frontiers."[184] The *consigli di fabbrica* were not the future organs of the socialist state; they were that new state.[185]

IV. The Industrial City
Union militancy often attained its highest development in pit villages and textile towns, but socialism is ultimately the child of the cities: those graveyards of paternalism and religious belief. In the cities, a broad proletarian public sphere could flourish.

In Chapter 3, 'The Great Towns,' of his *The Condition of the*

Working-Class in England, the young Engels portrays a proletariat whose "making" is as much the result of urbanization as industrialization:[186]

> If the centralization of population stimulates and develops the property-holding class, it forces the development of the workers yet more rapidly ... The great cities are the birthplaces of labour movements; in them the workers first began to reflect upon their own condition, and to struggle against it; in them the opposition between proletariat and bourgeoisie first made itself manifest ... [Moreover,] without the great cities and their forcing influence upon the popular intelligence, the working class would be far less advanced than it is ... [The cities] have destroyed the last remnant of the patriarchal relation between working men and employers.[187]

Engels, who often complained about the suffocating piety of his own bourgeois background, was astonished by the casual and almost universal indifference of London laborers to organized religion and spiritual dogma. "All the writers of the bourgeoisie are unanimous on this point, that the workers are not religious, and do not attend church."[188] In Paris, meanwhile, where the Goddess of Reason had been briefly enthroned in Notre Dame in 1792, militant anticlericalism was deeply rooted in the republican petty bourgeoisie as well as the socialist artisanate. But the most dramatic and perhaps surprising example was Berlin, Europe's Chicago, where by 1912 the Socialists were winning 75 percent of the vote and the poorest districts were considered completely "dechristianized." Working-class Berlin, like Africa, was a missionary frontier.[189]

Big cities, Hobsbawm emphasizes, "tended to be disproportionately proletarian and, other things being equal, disproportionately red. In pre-1914 Germany cities over 100,000 were 60 percent proletarian as against a national urban average of 41 percent, and the situation of Stockholm in Sweden was similar."[190] Berlin, New York/Brooklyn and Chicago were the world's biggest industrial cities; London's huge proletariat was largely dispersed in small workshops or casualized as dock and construction labor. San Francisco became the first unionized city shortly after the turn of the century (a status it maintained until the end of the First World War), while Milwaukee elected the first socialist big-city mayor in 1910. (The brief golden age of municipal socialism, however, would only come after 1919, when Vienna, Berlin, and Amsterdam turned red.) Within the city or its metropolitan footprint, moreover, were the great dynamos of working-class power: the red districts, where tenements or dense row housing clustered around big industrial works and docks. Legendary examples included Packingtown (Chicago), Homestead (Pittsburgh), Govan (Glasgow), Malakoff (Paris), Sesto (Milan), Raval (Barcelona), and Viborg (Petrograd), but Hobsbawm shrewdly singles out Neukölln in Berlin as the paradigm: "In 1912–13 [it] had a population of about a quarter of a million, an electorate of about 65,000 adult males of whom 83 percent voted for the SPD; a party membership of 15,000 or one in four of the electoral roll, who were in turn shepherded by almost a thousand functionaries, each responsible for about four tenement blocs."[191] During the war it became a cauldron of left–socialist dissent, then the heart of popular support for the Spartacus League and the January uprising; by late Weimar, Neukölln, along with the neighboring district of Wedding, was the single-largest concentration of communist activism and voting strength in Europe.

The propinquity of work and residence, which ensured that industrial struggles spilled over into neighborhoods and vice versa, was a powerful

*support to class consciousness. This nexus was perpetuated, even strength-
ened, in early industrial suburbs of which Paris provided the most vivid
examples.*

After 1900, the second Industrial Revolution spurred demand
for larger sites, preferably on the periphery of big cities where
land was cheap, and for modern (meaning electrified) automobile,
chemical, and steel plants. As a rough rule of thumb, casual labor
and workers in luxury industries stayed in the center, while industrial workers followed the factories to these new suburbs. The most
famous example was the "Red Belt of Paris," already in embryo by
the outbreak of the First World War. As Michelle Perot explains,

> In this case, residence did not contribute to the assimilation of
> workers into consumer society, because these suburbs were not
> exclusively residential and domestic as in America. Work and
> residence remained inextricably linked: the factory colonized the
> neighborhood, or rather created it altogether. The French working-
> class suburb was not a void, but a place of fairly dense sociability.[192]

Unlike the scattered mining towns and small industrial cities, the
Red Belt suburbs were eventually linked to the central city by fast
street car or electric rail lines, and thus constituted a mobile reserve
for demonstrations and protests in the center. What was lost in terms
of potential voting strength in Paris was gained in the consolidation of red administrations in the suburbs. The war, moreover,
accelerated the movement of workers and production to the inner
suburbs—also a major trend in wartime Berlin and London. These
wartime establishments, writes Thierry Bonzon,

> profoundly and permanently modified the pattern of industry in
> Paris … They brought together substantial numbers of workers:

22,000 at Renault in Boulogne-Billancourt, 6,000 in the Puteaux arsenal, 5,200 in the cartridge factory at Vincennes, 11,000 with Delaunay-Belleville at Saint-Denis ... The center of gravity of economic activity thus tended to shift from the old industrial quartiers of Paris (Faubourg Saint-Antoine in the 11th and Belleville in the 20th arrondissements) towards the new industrial belt surrounding the city.[193]

The shift was dramatized by the metalworkers' general strike in June 1919:

The strike represented not just proletarian discontent but also the menace of *la banlieue* ... This was all the more true because the most radical factions of the strike, those who most consistently called for insurrection and citied the Russian Revolution as a model to emulate, arose in the suburbs. In particular Saint Denis became the epicenter of the revolutionary Left during the strike. In that community, one of the largest and most industrialized suburbs of Paris, the city's inter-union council, the various strike committees, and the municipality worked together not only to support the strike but also to give it the most maximalist orientation possible, and to try to impose that orientation upon the movement as a whole ... the "Soviet of Saint-Denis" was the true heir of the Paris Commune.[194]

Hundreds of factory towns and industrial suburbs in Europe and the United States put Socialists in city hall after 1890. They led important fights against the emerging electric power and traction trusts, and in some notable cases (Los Angeles, for example) replaced private monopolies with public utilities. In other cases, Socialist majorities in local government were crucial to protecting the rights to strike and protest, as well as

limiting the strike-breaking role of the police. But "municipalism"—the
Fabian belief that important reforms could be achieved by progressive gov-
ernment at a local level—too often degenerated into "sewer socialism,"
which differed only marginally from the middle-class reform movements
with which it was frequently allied.

Revolutionary communes aside, the workers' movement began
to face up to the challenges of civic administration in the 1880s,
when the first socialist mayors donned their sashes in Commentry
(the geographical center of France) and Imola (near Bologna).
Meanwhile, Henry George, candidate of the United Labor Party,
came breathtakingly close to becoming the mayor of New York
City, and Henry Hyndman, the irksome leader of the English
Social-Democratic Federation, published *A Commune for London*
(1887), which became an inspiration for the Fabian Society and later
London Labour governments. By the turn of the century, there were
so many socialist municipal officials that the Socialist International
began to debate a model program for red city administrations. The
key strategic questions were, first: To what extent could public
ownership, at least of utilities and infrastructure, be achieved on
a local level? and, second: How much of the maximum program
could be sacrificed in order to attract middle-class urban reform-
ers—basically the professional strata—into alliances, or even, as
was the case in the United States and Britain, into the party? The
issue was controversial, even explosively so, since the revolutionary
left rightly feared that municipalism could become an endless detour
from the road to socialism. But all sides agreed (even anarchists in
some cases) that local government should be a laboratory for testing
socialist policies. Long starved of public investment, city services
ran far behind needs, and infrastructures were largely unmodern-
ized: a crisis that socialists addressed with sweeping visions of parks,
street lights, clean water, indoor privies, public baths, municipalized

power, unionized city workers—and, above all, public housing. But where would the resources come from? "Many of the communes," writes Shelton Stromquist,

> which came under the control of socialist or workers' parties at the turn of the century in France, Belgium and Italy were very small, socially and electorally homogeneous ... and lacked the means to create the required services. Furthermore, even the most inexperienced administrators soon realized that the so-called "laboratories" could only act as such if the municipal authorities enjoyed complete legal autonomy, enabling them to seek out new financial resources by modifying local taxation, abolishing the last municipal levies, intervening in the system of ground rents, creating new services and taking over those still in private hands.[195]

The political and financial conditions for real urban "structural reformism," including large-scale housing construction, would only emerge after the First World War, above all in that extraordinary experiment known as Red Vienna.

Before the 1930s and the great victories of the CIO in the United States (a template for postwar unionism in Europe), the city itself provided the principal form or shell for the economic, as well political and cultural, organization of the working class across craft boundaries. Great class battles, with the exceptions of miners and railroad workers, were conducted by urban labor federations, or alternately the union-managed, municipally funded bourses and camere del lavoro that, from the 1890s, were the nuclei of worker militancy in France, Italy, and to a lesser extent Spain.

The once dominant "Wisconsin" or "Commons" school of labor history focused on the evolution of national unions in the

English-speaking countries, with the key motifs being the transition from exclusive craft to inclusive industrial unionism and the legal institutionalization of collective bargaining. This approach, however, drastically understated the role of urban labor federations, such as the American citywide central labor councils and the Scottish trades councils, which even when craft-dominated were more congenial than national unions to radical leadership and fighting for the interests of the unorganized. Indeed, they sometimes acted as functional equivalents of industrial unions. Unlike the German case, where the SPD and the Free Unions had formally demarcated their separate spheres of activity, the U.S., Scottish, and Australian city federations creatively blurred the boundaries between the economic and political, in some cases organizing their own municipal labor parties such as the United Labor Party, which ran Henry George for mayor of New York in 1886 (he beat Theodore Roosevelt for second place) and the Union Labor Party, which dominated San Francisco politics in the first decade of the twentieth century.[196]

The flagship of labor radicalism in North America was the Chicago Federation of Labor, which in 1903 had a membership of 245,000 and, in contrast to the national AFL, aggressively "promoted sympathy strikes and encouraged the organization of women and unskilled workers."[197] Formed after the Pullman Strike, the Chicago Fed was gangster-dominated in its early years, but after the election of the socialist John Fitzpatrick to its presidency in 1906 became the most consistently militant and progressive of the big-city centrals, flexing its muscles to support the organizing campaigns of packinghouse workers, steelworkers, and teachers. Fitzpatrick, meanwhile, was the most prominent advocate of an American Labor Party. Similarly, the Glasgow Trades Council took a lead role in the organization of dockers, carters, and gas workers usually ignored by its English counterparts. The "Red Clyde" emerged, writes William

Kenefick, "within a fiercely independent, localized and federal trade union structure with the Trades Councils at its very core. The structure promoted a greater degree of interaction between skilled and lesser skilled workers"—a strength, Kenefick argues, when compared to the more centralized British national unions.[198]

In France, where, as we have seen, industrial conflict often took on a "wildcat" character without a strong union presence, working-class solidarity was organized through the urban *bourses du travail*. These "union-managed, municipally-funded, and territorial-based labor exchanges" were a distinctly French invention, first inaugurated in 1886 when a leftish majority on the Paris council, influenced by Proudhonist and socialist precedents, established the first Bourse as a municipal hiring hall to reduce competition amongst the unemployed and prevent their recruitment as strike-breakers. The experiment spread throughout the country and the Bourses, while retaining their tax-financed employment functions, became true "houses of the people" with meeting halls, union offices, libraries, and the like. "Until the 1900s," writes Steven Lewis, "the Bourses remained the most dynamic and fastest growing branch of the labor movement, outdistancing the CGT ... the vast majority of observers agreed that the prospects of the territorial strategy of labor politics exemplified by the Bourses were superior to those of the fledgling industrial federations and confederations."[199] The Achilles' heel of "bourse-syndicalism," however, was its dependence on municipal government. As the Bourses became radical stages for anti-militarist propaganda, employers and Radical Republican patriots, often coordinated by local Prefects, combined electoral forces to cut off their municipal funding. At the same time, the increasingly national scale of strikes by miners and railroad workers favored industrial unionism and the recharged CGT, after 1906 under revolutionary syndicalist leadership.

With the exception of the powerful Federterra, the socialist union of Po Valley agricultural workers, prewar Italian unions were weak. "More important for the mass mobilization of workers were the widespread and deeply popular Chambers of Labour [*camera*], which formed the backbone of the Italian tradition of the rolling general strike, not so much to be used for collective bargaining in economic disputes but rather to gather support when workers were shot in demonstrations or strikes."[200] The *camera*, moreover,

> provided a centre for all the local unions and workers' institutions
> of a particular commune or district, and as time passed, these came
> to embrace unions, local leagues, cooperatives, savings banks. The
> focus was the *casa del popolo* ... this functioned as a hiring hall
> and workers' labour exchange, club, educational centre and head-
> quarters, and was to be a prime target for the fascists in 1921–22.

Perhaps most distinctive was that "union members were always a minority among workers, union dues irregular, organization often sketchy." "The *camera*," continues Gwyn Williams, "connected the traditional, localized revolt in anarchoid style to the new labour movement. It tended to breed a populist and communal, sometimes a class, rather than a trade or craft, mentality. It embraced a much wider range of workers. Unions tended to appeal to the more skilled, prosperous and sophisticated."[201]

Urban class struggles, especially those addressing emergencies of shelter, food, and fuel, were typically led by working-class mothers, the forgotten heroes of socialist history.

The original sin of the parties of the Second International was their lukewarm support for, or even opposition to, women's suffrage and economic equality.[202] Although the SPD had endorsed equal political rights "without distinction of sex" at Erfurt in 1891, and Social Democratic women had led the successful fight for universal women's suffrage in Finland in 1906, the powerful Belgian and Austrian parties sharply rebuffed suffrage resolutions, while the French socialists, theoretically in favor of equality, did nothing in practice to support it, as a result of which women in France did not get the vote until the end of the Second World War.[203] Socialists and trade union leaders who campaigned for a male breadwinner wage that would keep women out of the labor market simultaneously argued that women's domestic roles would make them electoral pawns of priests and conservative parties—a belief that was especially strong amongst male Socialists in France and Austria.

Yet their wives, sisters, and daughters, if not already toiling in textile mills or enslaved as domestic servants (the largest single group of wage-workers in Victorian England), were just as likely to be protesting in the streets as any male worker was to be picketing for his union. As David Montgomery reminds us, "'married women caring for their children in bleak, congested neighborhoods and facing creditors, charity officials, and the ominous authority of the clergy were reminded of their class as regularly as were their husbands, daughters, and sons in the factories."[204] Mothers were the organizers of rent strikes, demonstrations against fuel shortages, and bread riots—the oldest form of plebeian protest. Outdoor markets, dairies, and laundries, where working-class women gathered daily, were crucial information exchanges and sites of mobilization. As Temma Kaplan illustrates in the case of Barcelona in the early twentieth century, women in the new suburban factory districts still commuted to the old, central markets once a week, ensuring the rapid spread of news and protest throughout the entire metropolitan area.[205] Harold Benenson adds: "Because it assembled on a community basis, and sanctioned women's public role as the defenders of the well-being of their families, the *crowd* was an important medium of lower-class women's protest. This overall tradition of popular action persisted well past the early phases of capitalist industrialization."[206] For example, during the so-called Meat Wars in Germany, France, and Austria in 1911–12, crowds of working-class women attacked butchers' stalls and food markets in protest against the protectionist policies that inflated the prices of meat and dairy products.[207]

The Russian Revolution of February 1917, in turn, began on International Women's Day as "thousands of housewives and women workers enraged by the endless queues for bread poured into the streets of Petrograd, shouting, 'Down with high prices' and 'Down with hunger.'"[208] Just weeks later, in Berlin, 300,000 neighborhood women and war workers, mobilized by the underground network of revolutionary shop stewards, confronted the government with the famous Bread Strike.[209] The following January, during an arctic winter that decimated poor slum dwellers throughout Europe, a true "Women's War" broke out in Barcelona amidst coal shortages and soaring food prices. Spanish neutrality allowed the city's textile and metal industries to profit from war production for the combatant powers, but also introduced runaway inflation and an uncontrolled *crisis de subsistencias*. Food and fuel riots first erupted in 1915, and had grown to almost insurrectionary dimensions by early 1918 when the Guardia shot nineteen women during a protest at the Governor's Palace in Ciutat Vella. "Women's networks," writes Kaplan, "had assumed leadership of a social struggle they pursued in the name of the entire female community. Their attacks on food stores throughout the city increased, as did periodic attempts by police to repress them through armed force. They adopted a committee structure, not unlike the soviets developed in Russia in 1917, to regulate attacks on grocery stores." As the movement solidified control over working-class districts, Madrid—"fearing civil war"—recalled the governor and declared a state of siege. The struggle continued as a guerrilla war between local women and the new military governor until the beginning of spring: a remarkable example of a near-revolutionary moment due entirely to the self-activity of poor women.[210]

Geoff Eley, reflecting on such struggles in his history of European socialism, accords the slum neighborhood equal weight with the factory in the formation of socialist consciousness: "No less vital were the complex ways neighborhoods spoke and fought back. If the workplace was one frontier of resistance, where collective agency could be imagined, the family—or more properly the neighborhood solidarities working-class women fashioned for its survival—was the other … The challenge for the Left was to organize on *both* fronts of social dispossession."[211] Periodically the combined power of the neighborhood and workplace were demonstrated by strike actions in support of protests against the high cost of food and housing, as well as by labor boycotts—a tactic borrowed from the land wars in Ireland and debuted in New York City in the 1880s. Likewise, the union label (another American invention, this time from San Francisco in the 1870s) allowed consumers to reinforce the bargaining power of workers, and became a cornerstone of the ethics of solidarity.[212]

In response to the high cost of living in the great urban agglomerations, workers, inspired by the success of the Rochdale Pioneers in Lancashire, organized their own cooperative stores, believing that they were taking the first steps into a socialist future.

Consumer coops, often allied with cooperative bakeries, were popular everywhere, but in Belgium, especially Ghent, one of the most proletarian cities in Europe, they became the foundation of the movement. Ghent's famous Vooruit coop, based on the ideas of the Rochdale movement, grew into a state within a state:

The sick received free bread, medical care and medicine. Those who stopped working at the age of sixty received a small pension, calculated according to their purchases. For each birth, families received free bread for one week as well as one big celebration bread. This was how the cooperative offered the Ghent workers some protection against disease and poverty, at a time when the government was not providing any form of social security. [Edward] Anseele, who had been the manager of the cooperative for a while and had become one of the first socialist members of parliament, went even further. Through the "red factories" he aimed for Vooruit to focus more on production. The cooperative weaving mill was a first step in that direction. Vooruit was proud to offer its workers better conditions than elsewhere. Other industry branches were soon to follow: a brewery, a sugar factory, a cotton- and flax-spinning mill. To top it all off, in 1913 Anseele founded a bank—the "Belgische Bank van den Arbeid." Most of the capital it managed came from the cooperative. It was, as one liberal admirer exclaimed, *un petit univers socialiste*.[213]

Although Marx wrote little or nothing on the housing crisis, and Engels pointedly dismissed proffered solutions as utopian, rent gouging amidst a universal lack of affordable shelter was a central grievance of the urban working classes everywhere. By 1915, moreover, the rent strike had become a familiar weapon in the class arsenal and played an important role in fermenting revolts against the war.

The proletarian families crammed into New York's deadly "dumbbell" tenements, Barcelona's dark "beehive" slums, or Berlin's equally miserable "rent barracks" would undoubtedly have joined lustily in the chorus of the song that poor Parisians liked to sing at the turn of the century: "If you want to be happy /

In the name of God / Hang your landlord!"[214] From midcentury, when Napoleon III unleashed Baron von Haussman and his *démolisseurs* on Paris, most of the great cities of Western and Central Europe were violently reshaped by great waves of speculative real-estate investment coordinated with publicly financed infrastructure mega-projects. These developments unhoused entire proletarian neighborhoods while generating huge profits for the landowners, banks, and builders who typically reclaimed the sites for middle-class residences, offices, and up-market shopping. These trends, warned Engels, threatened "to turn the city into a luxury city pure and simple."

But Paris was only the most famous example of Victorian redevelopment and gentrification. "The spirit of Haussmann," Engels wrote in *The Housing Question* (1872), "has also been abroad in London, Manchester and Liverpool, and seems to feel itself just as much at home in Berlin and Vienna. The result is that the workers are forced out of the centre of the towns towards the outskirts; that workers' dwellings, and small dwellings in general, become rare and expensive and often altogether unobtainable."[215] The resulting low-income housing shortage, which Engels regarded as an integral and inescapable aspect of the Industrial Revolution, necessarily gave tremendous market power to the owners of the restricted supply of tenement housing; their rack-renting, in turn, drove working-class families to take in boarders or double up in apartments. In the worst cases humans were sometimes crammed together in densities like the cargo in the holds of slave ships. In Barcelona's Raval district (*barrio chino* or "Chinatown" to locals) one quarter of the Catalan working class was crammed into 2.5 square kilometers, and the narrow streets were in perpetual shadow from the jammed-together tenements. The result, not surprisingly, was Europe's highest rate of tuberculosis —a disease that everywhere scythed down slum-dwellers, especially young adults. No wonder Raval was called a "Nursery for Revolutionaries."[216]

Engels and most of the founding leadership of the Socialist International considered the housing problem to be intractable under capitalism, with no reformist solution. It was, he wrote, with rather odd understatement, "one of the innumerable *smaller*, secondary evils which result from the present-day capitalist mode of production."[217] But the "inevitable slum" was nonetheless contested vigorously by socialists in New York and Vienna, syndicalists in Paris and Glasgow, and anarchists in Barcelona and Buenos Aires. "In Paris, for example, tenants went on strike in the 1880s. Led by Socialists, they withheld the rent and, to cries of 'Long Live the Commune,' attempted to block evictions."[218] A generation later, the "decidedly revolutionary" Union Syndicale des Locataires, whose "members saw the fight against landlords as a crucial part of the class struggle in general," became a potent force in Belleville (19th and 20th arrondissements) and other proletarian districts.[219]

In New York, the tenants' movement in the Lower East Side was galvanized by the apartment shortage and rising rents that followed the construction of the Williamsburg Bridge in 1900, which displaced 17,000 residents. The socialist *Daily Forward*, the Yiddish-language newspaper of the Lower East Side, instigated the United Hebrew Trades, the Workman's Circle, and the Socialist Party to organize a tenants' movement that, after a preliminary strike in 1904, regrouped under more strictly Socialist leadership for the "great rent war of 1907," in the midst of a short but severe national recession. Jewish tenants in the Lower East Side, Harlem, and Brownsville (a "Socialist stronghold") hung red flags in their windows, battled police to prevent evictions, and mobbed the *schleppers* (movers). In the end, Robert Fogelson concludes, "the strike fizzled out in January 1908," but New York's Socialists had learned

92

important lessons: "The strikers would have to come not from one or two neighborhoods, but from dozens. They would have to include not just Jews, but Italians, Irish, Germans, and Poles—and even native-born New Yorkers."[220]

Simultaneous with the last New York struggle, an even larger tenants' strike broke out in the tenement (*conventillo*) districts of Buenos Aires, and by October 1907 an estimated 10 percent of the city's population (about 120,000 residents) was refusing to pay rent to their landlords. The largely immigrant Argentine working class was the fastest growing in the world at the turn of the century, and Buenos Aires, which doubled its population in the decade after 1895, was an overcrowded boomtown where rack-renting was profligate. The more energetic of the country's two labor federations, the anarchist Federación Obrera Regional Argentina (FORA), had decided at its Sixth Congress in 1906 to encourage the formation of a tenant strike movement. The strikes a year later were largely unsuccessful in their immediate objectives, but, as James Baer emphasizes, were strategically important in mobilizing proletarian women and non-union workers for general strikes that were soon to follow.[221]

The major New York and Buenos Aires rent strikes, as well as smaller struggles in dozens of contemporary cities, were propelled by sudden rent hikes and their ad hoc organization did not survive the immediate struggles. But the food and fuel shortages of the First World War, affecting non-belligerent as well as combatant countries, generated a deeper, more organic subsistence crisis, lasting years, that made all cost-of-living issues explosive. When landlords in Glasgow, for example, hiked rents in 1915, they were soon faced by resistance on a scale hitherto unimaginable. "The movement was particularly strong in Govan," writes James Hinton, "where a women's housing committee led by a previously unknown housewife, Mrs Barlow, organized constant propaganda meetings (including factory gate meetings), rent strikes and physical resistance to evictions." In October a general rent strike was declared. When landlords' agents ("factors") took the female strike leaders to court, workers poured out of the shipyards and 15,000 angry protestors surrounded the Courthouse. One of the rent strikers accosted the Sheriff: "You hear the voice of the people out in the street. That is the workers of the upper reaches of the Clyde. These men will only resume work in the event of you deciding against the factors; if you do not, it means that the workers on the lower reaches will stop work tomorrow and join them." As Hinton notes in his history, "legal niceties tumbled before the blast, and the Sheriff did as he was told." When the movement spread to Birkenhead and London, the Asquith government capitulated and froze rents at the 1914 level.[222]

Two years later, a new cycle of cost-of-living and anti-landlord protests was an integral part of the great labor revolts of 1917–19. New York, with the Socialist Party in a leadership role, was again in the vanguard of these struggles, along with Petrograd, Berlin, Barcelona, and Paris. What aggravated the situation to the breaking point was the acute fuel shortage in the winter of 1917–18, the result of the near breakdown of the eastern seaboard rail system as the Wilson administration rushed arms and supplies to the ports to re-equip European allies while simultaneously building huge stockpiles for an American expeditionary force. In the face of these priorities, there was simply not enough rolling stock to supply adequate quantities of coal to the big cities. In the midst of the bitterest winter in a generation, landlords turned off heat while refusing to reduce rents or, in some cases, brazenly raising them. "Life in the tenements was 'beyond description,' said a social worker. 'Gas is frozen, homes are dark, no water in the toilets, sanitary conditions unspeakable, faces blue and pinched from the bitter cold and ever so many kiddies down with pneumonia.'"[223]

A massive rent war was fought out in a series of battles from 1917 to 1920, and spread across the East River from Harlem and the Lower East Side to Williamsburg and the south Bronx under the aegis of the Greater New York Tenants League. As news of the revolutions in Russia electrified New York's tens of thousands of Socialist Party supporters, the "Bolsheviki rent strikes," as landlords began to call them, sometimes took on the air of revolutionary rather than merely reformist struggles. "At a mass meeting of the East Side Tenants League," for example, "several Socialists spoke out in favor of taking the tenement houses from the landlords and turning them over to the tenants." Despite the continuing repression of the Socialist Party, followed by the infamous Palmer raids and the mass deportations of immigrant radicals, the stubborn movement ultimately prevailed, forcing the legislature in Albany to introduce rent controls in 1920—a major and enduring working-class victory.[224]

V. Proletarian Culture
Within this urban matrix, already richly endowed with artisan traditions, a proletarian public sphere developed. The ideas of socialism (or anarcho-communism) became embodied in well-organized counter-cultures that projected the solidarities of the workplace and neighborhood into all aspects of recreation, education, and culture.

If one of the historic achievements of the workers' movement was to create leisure time for the masses through a reduction in hours of toil, the other equally important accomplishment was to collectivize consumption and recreation in forms such as the coop store and workers' sport societies, which reinforced solidarity and class identity. The movement in some countries was almost a complete socio-cultural world unto itself.[225] The most celebrated example was the national network of cycling, hiking, and singing clubs, sports teams, adult schools, theater societies, readers' groups, youth clubs, naturalist groups, and the like that was sponsored in Wilhemine Germany by Social Democracy and the Free Unions.[226] In the period of the Bismarckian anti-socialist laws (1878–90), these labor associations had provided a crucial legal shelter for workers' gatherings and the training of activists. "The subculture was formed out of elements of journeymen's social life and liberal bourgeois associational culture, both of which were taken over, partly reinterpreted, or brought together in a new functional union and welded to new, independently developed elements." Although Lassalle, the father of the General German Workers Association (ADAV), one of the two major currents of German radicalism ultimately united in the SPD, had envisioned "a decisive, powerful organization, in which the members functioned as party soldiers who took orders from the executive level," the movement evolved more toward what Toni Offermann describes as a "festival culture" of comraderie and socialist celebration: "The ADAV developed a varied and colorful associational life, one that emerged out of the independent learning process that the varied local organizations underwent."[227]

Some historians have proposed that Germany's "proletarian world of its own" was too hermetic or "negatively integrated" to constitute a radical threat to the Wihelmine system, but in his important 1985 book *The Alternative Culture*, Vernon Lidtke offered an eloquent rebuttal: "This alternative may be called radical not because it proposed to overturn the *Kaiserreich* in one bold stroke, but because it embodied in its principles a conception of production, social relations, and political institutions that rejected existing structures, practices, and values at almost every point."[228] The real weakness of the German counter-culture, Lidtke says, was the SPD's emphasis on *Bildung*—cultural and intellectual self-cultivation—and the democratization of bourgeois high culture rather than an exploration of the "possibility that workers ... might develop a unique culture of the labor movement, one that would draw its inspiration directly from the lives of workers themselves."[229]

The alternative organization of urban daily life, however, was not limited to the contestation of bourgeois values and institutions or to the self-organization of important cultural and social services, but aspired to educate a new socialist humanity.

The New Woman and Man, as envisioned by the *fin de siècle* socialist movement, would be the children of disciplined mass struggle, punctilious industrial habits, and constant self-improvement. The SPD was not the only socialist party that placed *Bildung* on a pedestal. Although *fin de siècle* Vienna is usually celebrated for its creative decadence, its powerful socialist movement, which organized activities from stamp collecting to choral singing, was anything but avant-garde in its attitudes toward proletarian recreation and social hygiene:

> The atmosphere permeating the Movement was one of highmindedness mingled with socialist puritanism. Every activity was scrutinized for its effect on the class struggle; pleasure for pleasure's sake was frowned upon. Membership, and particularly active participation in the Party, implied acceptance of a socialist attitude in daily life (*Haltung*) in which the virtues which were assumed to be the inevitable product of the future socialist society were to be present characteristics of Socialists fighting for the realization of that society.

The Austrian social democrats, moreover, established a Central Education Office (*Bildungszentrale*) "through which general *Kultur* and particularly socialist doctrine were to be passed on to the working class."[230]

Nor was this cultivation of disciplined and rational habits solely an obsession of northern European socialists. The Spanish party under Pablo Iglesias, a printer, waged war against the disorderly customs of its largely Castilian membership: no drink, no brothels, no flamenco, no bull fights. Their opponents caricatured the party as cloistered and austere, a *cosa de los frailes*. "But perhaps monkish," writes Gerald Brenan in *The Spanish Labyrinth*,

> was not quite the word. This closed and narrow congregation, set on maintaining the purity of its doctrines, with its strict discipline, its austere enthusiasm and its unshakeable faith in its own superior destiny, could better be described as Calvinist. There was something almost Genevan in the standard of self-respect, personal morality and obedience to conscience that it demanded of its followers.

This steeled intransigence, however, enabled the Socialists alone to resist the "policy of attraction"—that is to say, rampant corruption, bribery and cooptation—that characterized Spanish political life.[231]

In Catalonia a very different kind of proletarian counter-culture, less puritanical and patriarchal but more utopian, flourished in some of the most wretched slums in Europe. Anarcho-syndicalism, differentiating itself from the anarchist underground of the 1890s, gained tremendous ground amongst the immigrants from rural Catalonia, Valencia, and Andalusia who flocked to Barcelona's docks and textile mills in the first decades of the twentieth century. Sharing almost no common ground with bourgeois morality, the local anarchist press was a fount of practical advice on "rational" approaches to hygiene, sexuality, infant care, and anti-clerical education. Central institutions of urban proletarian life included the athenaeums which taught literacy, lent books, and organized neighborhood theater and musical recreations; the hiking and naturist clubs, which allowed working-class youth to escape the suffocating *barris*; and the district headquarters of the Solidaridad Obrera (after 1910, the CNT) and its component unions, which operated as command centers for mass mobilization and strike support. Nowhere in Europe were unions and neighborhoods so completely fused together in struggle as in Barcelona, where the CNT (which by 1918 had 250,000 members in the city and its factory environs) would one day organize a strike and the next day provide "armed escorts for groups of working-class women who requisitioned food from shops."[232] The police and the Catalan militias were universally despised, and the neighborhoods relied upon the *cenetistas* as well as armed anarchist *grupos* to defend them against incessant repression. In dramatic contrast to English and German unions, moreover, the CNT operated without a bureaucracy or a stratum of professional organizers and agents. "Anarchist leaders," claims Gerard Brenan in his classic study, "were never paid—in 1936, when their union, the CNT, contained over a million members, it had only one paid secretary."[233]

A proletarian public sphere, of course, depended upon the existence of spaces for meetings, classes, agitation and recreation. Even in countries where the labor movement was legal, it sometimes required a long fight to create such spaces at the neighborhood level.

Although temperance had celebrated supporters amongst socialist workers, including Keir Hardie, James Connolly, and most of the leadership of early Swedish Social Democracy, social drinking largely defined convivial working-class leisure, and public houses acted as informal social centers, hiring halls, and information exchanges, as important to the labor movement as coffeehouses had been to mercantilism in the time of Addison and Steele.[234] The local pub's "main advantage for political mobilization," writes Pamela Swett, "was that it was a semiprivate space. Though open to the public, regular patrons knew each other well and outsiders were easy to identify." This "intimacy" was doubly important in periods of repression or when bosses' surveillance made the plant floor unsafe for political conversation.[235]

Mary Nolan, in her study of the SPD in pre-war Düsseldorf, a stronghold of political Catholicism, underlines the centrality of the local *Kneipe* ("tavern") to the party's campaign to make itself "a viable presence in every working-class neighborhood in the city." From 1903 to 1906, most innkeepers, under pressure from employers and the Church, refused to rent meeting rooms to Social Democrats and only changed their policy after the Party organized a workers' boycott. Almost immediately, participation in party life increased.[236] In Wilhelmine Germany as a whole, adds Peter Nettle, "the *Zahl-abend* ['dues night'], when members of local organizations gathered in the pub to pay contributions and talk things over, became not only the most important social institution of Social Democracy at the grassroots, but the focus of political opinion and the accepted means by which Executive and opposition could reach the members."[237] The *lokal* was equally the hub of German-language radicalism in the United States; Tom Goyans, in his delightful *Beer and Revolution*, identifies scores of German anarchist saloons and beer halls in New York's Lower East Side—*Kleindeutschland*—and, later, Yorkville neighborhoods.[238]

Street corners were another public space essential to the propagation of socialist ideas through oratory and newspaper sales. Ironically, radical labor's most protracted battle for open-air free speech wasn't fought in Russia or Hungary, but in the United States. On the West Coast, where a vast army of migrant lumber and agricultural workers annually wintered in local "skid rows" (a corruption of "Skid Road"), the IWW conducted a ten-year campaign involving thousands of arrests and hundreds of casualties for the simple right to speak on street corners and sell the *Industrial Worker* in front of employment agencies. As Melvyn Dubofsky explains in his history, the great IWW "free speech fights" were essential to their organizing strategy: "Experience had demonstrated that it was almost impossible for organizers to reach timber workers, construction hands, and harvesters out on the job where watchful employers harassed 'labor agitators' and where workers were scattered over a vast geographical area ... only in the city did the 'agitator' have a measure of freedom to recruit without interference by employers."[239] In Seattle, Spokane, Vancouver, Oakland, Los Angeles, Missoula, Kansas City, Fresno, San Diego, and elsewhere, the Wobblies (usually supported by the Socialists) braved mob violence, brutal jailers, and finally a "massacre" (Everett in 1916), but kept the struggle alive with militant reinforcements who hoboed to battle from all over the West. Although Woodrow Wilson eventually crushed the Wobblies by imprisoning their organizers and sending the army into the timber camps and mining towns, the free-speech fight was renewed by the industrial unions in the 1930s as they challenged the local despotism of the steel companies in the mill valleys of Pennsylvania and Ohio.

The ultimate symbol of proletarian public life in most cities (and later, a chief target of fascist attack) was the maison du peuple, casa del popolo, Volkshaus, *or labor temple.*

In the early 1840s, Flora Tristan had proposed the construction of Workers' Palaces "where children of the working class will be instructed, intellectually and professionally, and where working men and women who have been injured at their jobs, and those who are infirm or aged, will be cared for." In Britain (and by imitation the United States) in the same period, Mechanics' Institutes were at the height of their popularity. But in most countries the financing of special buildings for working-class meetings, education, culture, and welfare was beyond reach until the 1890s, when unions and socialist cooperatives began to amass large, stable memberships. Their pooled contributions, sometimes topped up by donations and loans from middle-class sympathisers, allowed the construction of proletarian versions of the *hôtel-de-ville*. By 1900, virtually every industrial city or town in countries where unions were legal had a central building for workers' meetings, union offices, party papers, and the like. Almost all had libraries, and many had cinemas, gyms, and recreational space. Some were expansions of already established coops or *bourses*. They were especially important in Europe and Latin America where, in contrast to the United States with its universal public schools and new culture industries, workers organized their free time, if not in taverns, through activities sponsored by unions, parties, and cooperatives.

As Margaret Kohn emphasizes, their construction was "also an important intervention in the symbolic landscape. It was part of a polemical challenge to authority and dominance of the church, the state, and private capital." She cites the example of the *casa de popolo* in Abbadia di Montepulciano, a town of 1,000 near Siena, dominated by two large agricultural companies, where socialists had fought for years to establish a presence.

> The breakthrough came in 1914 (after the electoral reform granting almost universal male suffrage) when the first socialist municipal councilor was elected. This success, however, precipitated repression by local elites, who refused to rent rooms to the socialist organizations. The local socialists responded by starting a collection that generated 25,000 lire for materials. All work was

completed voluntarily by laborers on Sundays and after the normal working day. The House of the People, completed in 1917, included a library, a consumer cooperative, meeting rooms for a youth and a women's group, and the seat of the PSI. The *Almanacco socialista italiano* of 1918 interpreted the construction ... as an important political victory[:] "The red flag that waves in one of the towers of our House of the People, pride of this proletariat, nightmare of our adversaries, is our model and stimulus to work, propaganda, and organization."[240]

In the cities, where the left had large, organized constituencies, the houses often became authentic proletarian cathedrals. The great Festival Hall of the workers' coop in Ghent, already mentioned, was the city's architectural wonder, while the ultra-modern Parisian Bourse du Travail pioneered electric lighting and central heating; likewise, La Maison du Peuple in Brussels, home of the International Socialist Bureau as well as the Belgian Labor Party, was an international art nouveaux icon whose wanton demolition in 1965 is still mourned by architectural historians. Equally renowned were the Urania in Vienna and the Volkshaus in Leipzig.[241] The Soviet Constructivists in the 1920s, in turn, made workers' clubs—rendered in modernist masterpieces such as the Zuev and the Rusakov in Moscow—the hubs of the new culture and its utopian hopes.

The generational stratification of the working class, like gender and skill divisions, was a source of both internal conflict and creative energy. After 1905 the so-called "Young Guard" movements led the revolt of a third generation of worker socialists against the reformist, evolutionist policies of second-generation political and union leaders. Attracted to syndicalist and maximalist positions, and wholeheartedly anti-militarist, the younger cohort was accused by its elders of embracing a "socialism of the

103

Dream."[242] *In fact, the youth movements incubated the future leadership of European Communism.*

Before the First World War, working-class children typically entered the labor force at age fourteen or fifteen; a twenty-four-year-old accordingly might already have ten years of full-time work experience, during which he or she had gained a bitterly matured understanding of their life's few options.[243] Young workers, moreover, were the victims of abusive apprenticeship laws, and had little standing, if any, to contest employers' efforts to squeeze out their last drop of youthful energy with longer hours, lower wages, and appalling working conditions. Male teenagers, more-over, were canon-fodder for the modern conscript armies—more or less universal in Europe apart from Great Britain—that awaited the inevitable day of mobilization for an Armageddon that Engels in 1887 had predicted with uncanny accuracy:

> No war is any longer possible for Prussia-Germany except a world war and a world war indeed of an extent and violence hitherto undreamt of. Eight to ten millions of soldiers will massacre one another and in doing so devour the whole of Europe until they have stripped it barer than any swarm of locusts has ever done. The devastations of the Thirty Years' War compressed into three or four years, and spread over the whole Continent; famine, pestilence, general demoralisation both of the armies and of the mass of the people.[244]

Although workplace and social issues never ceased to be important, it was opposition to conscription that spurred the emergence of autonomous socialist youth movements, especially in countries where the military had been regularly used to break strikes or quell public demonstrations.

Belgium was the classic case. In one of the leaflets he wrote for the General Council of the First International, Marx explained that "there exists but one country in the civilized world where every strike is eagerly and joyously turned into a pretext for the official massacre of the Working Class. That country of single Blessedness is *Belgium*, the model state of constitutionalism, the snug, well-hedged, little paradise of the landlord, the capitalist, and the priest."[245] Marx was writing about a deadly cavalry charge against striking iron puddlers at the great Cockerill works in Seraing, but Belgium's conscript army (larger than the regular armies of the United States or Great Britain) would continue to be deployed to shoot down miners, arrest textile workers, and smash suffrage demonstrations. In the face of this ruthless repression—in a country ruled by the Liberal bourgeoisie—socialists formed the "Young Guards" in 1894 to fight conscription and organize radical soldiers' unions. They also published several anti-militarist papers, including Antwerp's fierce *De Bloedwet* ("The Rule of Blood"). After 1905, the Young Guards grew spectacularly, inspiring similar movements in Italy, Germany, Switzerland, Sweden, and the Austrian Empire.[246]

One of these, the League of Young Workers of Germany, was forced underground in Prussia and Saxony by draconian laws banning women and youth from political activity; in the more tolerant atmosphere of southern Germany, however, the League— which kept up an active liaison with its Belgian youth counterparts—was able to publicly agitate against militarism, much to the discomfort of trade-union leaders and the right wing of the SPD. The "graybeards" feared that the League—founded by rebellious apprentices but soon a home as well for Marxisant university students—would set its own reckless agenda, upsetting the reformist strategy and inciting repression against the entire movement. The irony, as Carl Schorske pointed out, was that the League was only trying to reclaim the SPD's old ardour: "[With] the adult movement … already sharply divided into economic and political sectors, the youth movement thus set out somewhat quixotically to recreate a sense of unity from below with Marxian theoretical knowledge as the fluxing substance."[247] The youth, moreover, were passionately concerned with the *actuality* of socialism and its achievement in their lifetimes. This did not seem to be an urgent concern of their elders. As Peter Nettle rather acidly points out, "in all the years from 1882 to 1914 there was only one article in *Neue Zeit*, the theoretical organ of Social Democracy, on the subject of post-revolutionary society, and this treated the problem merely in a historical context—as a discussion of past millenarian societies. Even the revolution itself was little discussed, the technique of it not at all."[248]

Within the SPD, the radical and staunchly anti-militarist wing represented by Clara Zetkin and Karl Liebknecht welcomed this renewal of revolutionary spirit, but the SPD executive launched an all-out attack on independent youth organizations which coincided with the extension of the Prussian "law of association" to the rest of the Reich. Friedrich Ebert, advocate of German colonialism in Africa and the future murderer-in-chief of Liebknecht and Rosa Luxemburg, was appointed by the Executive to keep the party youth in line: "the youth 'movement' was transformed into youth 'cultivation.'" But, as Schorske emphasizes, "under the aegis of parental 'protection' the radicalism of youth smouldered on, fanned after 1911 by increasing state persecution, until it burst into flame during the war."[249]

The youth revolt, however, had already passed the incendiary threshold in Sweden and Italy. In 1908 leaders of the Swedish Young Socialist League, opposed to the reformist direction of the SAP, were expelled from the mother party and, after the defeat of the 1909 general strike, organized the anti-parliamentary Young

Socialists Party (SUP) along syndicalist principles. In Italy, a majority of socialist deputies supported Giolitti's 1911 invasion of Libya—a vicious colonial war that lurched from one Italian atrocity to another—and the PSI "looked as if … it were finally about to disappear into bourgeois democracy." But, as Gwyn Williams emphasizes, "the peasant and working classes [were] imperfectly if at all integrated into the patriotism and nationalism which were universal among the middle and lower middle classes." The ensuing revolt against the war, which grew into a general strike, marked the entry of a "new generation of proletarian and some student militants into left-wing politics." The fiery tribunes of this generational insurgency were the "rising young socialist star of the Romagna," Benito Mussolini, and, in the South, the brilliant and intransigent Amadeo Bordiga. By 1914, as a result, the socialist youth movement, the FGS, had grown dramatically—a nursery school for both future Communist and Fascist leaders.[250]

Finally, as we have already seen, younger industrial workers in Russia had already begun to align with the Bolsheviks well before the outbreak of the war: indeed, in many factories the Menshevik–Bolshevik split became a generational conflict. As in other countries, the war conscripted hundreds of thousands of women and youth to fill labor shortages in munitions factories and shipyards. In Petrograd, there were an estimated 40,000 young people under the age of twenty-one employed in the metal industries alone, with the greatest concentration in the Vyborg industrial district, the center of Bolshevik agitation.[251] Youth of both sexes had been prominent in the February uprising, and in the spring an autonomous young workers' movement, loosely affiliated with the Petrograd factory committees, emerged as a major social force. "An impressive mobilization of 100,000 young workers for the May Day demonstration highlighted the movement's remarkable capacity for self-organization."[252] A broad youth front—"Labor and Light"—coalesced with 50,000 members, and a platform of demands for wage parity, the right to vote for eighteen-year-olds, representation on factory and district committees, and a six-hour day that left time for schooling. The most militant sections, which became the Socialist League of Young Workers, quickly allied themselves with the Bolsheviks: the only party, apart from the anarchists, that supported an autonomous movement of young workers. Amidst grumblings from older workers, Lenin's wife, Nadezhda Krupskaya, a delegate on the Vyborg district committee, became one of their most passionate advocates. When the democratic revolution was threatened in August by the Kornilov putsch, "virtually the entire Vyborg district youth organization joined the [Red] Guards" and rushed to battle. This set a precedent for the "disproportionate burden" of fighting and sacrifice assumed by socialist youth in the second revolution and the long Civil War that followed.

If the Bolsheviks, meanwhile, won the elite of young workers, the latter in turn soon captured the Party. "The Bolshevik party," writes Anne Gorsuch, "was itself a party of youth ... The median age of those present at the Sixth Party Congress in 1917 was only twenty-nine, and close to 20 percent of those joining the party in Petrograd were under twenty-one." In November of the following year, the Socialist League reorganized itself as the Communist Youth League (Komsomol), whose membership soared during the Civil War to 400,000, or "about two percent of the country's eligible youth between the ages of fourteen and twenty-one."[253] Tens of thousands of the Komsomol members, including many of its foremost leaders, died at the front in their new Red Army uniforms—a hecatomb of the bravest and most idealistic that would be repeated on an even larger scale in 1940–45.

"Sport is a chain-breaker for the youth of the proletariat, a liberator from physical and spiritual slavery."[254] *By the turn of the century, arguably no cultural contestation between classes was more important than working-class sports. Here were fought key battles over militarism, mass culture, and the allegiances of working-class youth.*

The original template for a workers' sports culture was the *Turnverein* movement: gymnastic clubs organized around the self-improving and liberal nationalist ideals espoused by Friederich Ludwig Jahn in his famous 1816 manual *Die Deutsche Turnkunst* ("The Art of German Gymnastics"). The Turners, banned, persecuted and sometimes jailed in Prussia, were indissolubly associated with the revolutionary democratic movements of 1848, and continued as a radical freemasonry for German laborers and artisans throughout the rest of the nineteenth century. "Some of their political leaders," writes Michael Kruger, "like the famous 'Forty-Eighters' Friedrich Hecker and Gustav Struve looked upon the *Turnvereine* as cells of the revolution ... After the defeat of the revolution, Hecker, Struve, Carl Schurz and numerous other German Turners emigrated to the USA, fought in the American Civil War on the side of Abraham Lincoln, and founded the Socialistic Turnerbund of North America in 1850." Back in Germany, however, the democratic nationalism of the *Turnverein* was gradually corroded by Wilhelmine imperialism, and in 1893, after the end of the Anti-Socialist Laws, the SPD stepped in and set up the powerful Deutscher Arbeiter-Turnerbund (ATB), which by 1914 had 2,411 clubs and almost 200,000 members, including 13,000 women gymnasts.[255]

Meanwhile, the "football codes"—the family of field sports involving kicking, running, and/or passing a ball—had emerged in England during the 1860s and, according to Robert Wheeler, were widely adopted as working-class recreation "after the reduction of the work week, specifically the introduction of the Saturday 'half-holiday' in the 1860s and 1870s. [Thereafter] so rapid and thoroughgoing was this development that from 1883 on the working class dominated what had begun as an 'old boys' competition and is recognized to this day as the premier British sports event, the Football Association Cup Final." He adds that "rather than become contaminated by the masses, many of the British public schools eventually dropped soccer and took up more 'gentlemanly' pursuits, especially cricket."[256] In the 1890s, thanks to the spread of the "weekend" on the continent, at least amongst the skilled working class, cycling was likewise converted from a bourgeois recreation into a proletarian passion, giving young workers of both sexes their first regular access to the healthy air of the countryside.[257] In the United States there were hundreds of factory soccer teams by the 1920s, often started by British immigrants, but baseball was the universal sport, and one popular league was sponsored by the socialist *New York Call*. In late 1913, the British, German, Austrian, French, Belgian, and Swiss worker sport organizations met at Ghent to form the anti-militaristic Federation Sportive Socialiste Internationale.[258] (After the war, the movement, although now split between rival Internationals, reemerged on an even larger scale with its own Olympiads and Spartakiads.) "By 1930," James Riordan writes, "worker sport united well over four million people, making it by far the largest working-class cultural movement."[259]

The organization of sports was also a class battlefield. Industrialists became keen sponsors of company teams as part of their larger effort, in the era of the mass strike, to domesticate loyal workforces, while governments, following the original example of the British public schools, embraced sports as part of basic training for conscript armies. The socialist sports movement, in contrast, considered football, hiking, cycling, and gymnastics as integral aspects of a socialist "cultural renaissance" and a key strategy for insulating youth against "the old nationalist–capitalist culture."[260] That culture, in turn, saw worker sports and other socialist cultural activities as a subversive threat, especially to the nationalist indoctrination of youth. This was most keenly felt in Germany, where the SPD's sports affiliates, boisterously internationalist and antimilitarist, had hundreds of thousands of members. In response, the state decided to take firm control over the recreation of workers' children. At the end of 1912, the War Ministry financed the creation of the Jungdeutschland-Bund to organize war games and paramilitary adventures for youth, and on the eve of Sarajevo "the Kaiser approved a measure to establish a compulsory national organization for all boys between the ages of thirteen and seventeen" (under the command of retired officers).[261] The Kaiser's scheme, of course, was realized a generation later under Baldur von Schirach in the Hitler Youth, which exercised a total monopoly over all sports facilities and activities for children and teenagers.[262]

Reading "ignited insurrections in the minds of workers."[263] The largely successful struggle for working-class literacy in the nineteenth century, accompanied by a technological revolution in the print media, brought the world—as news, literature, science, or simply sensation—into the daily routine of the proletariat.[264] The rapid growth of the labor and socialist press in the last quarter of the century nourished an increasingly sophisticated political world view.

Chartism, Dorothy Thompson explains, "was itself organized and made into a national movement by the growth of a national working-class press: indeed it perhaps makes more sense to date Chartism from the foundation of the *Northern Star* in November 1837 than from the publication of the Charter six months later."[265] Within a decade the movement published more than one hundred papers and reviews.[266] And by the American Civil War large sections of the working class, especially in England and the United States, kept as avidly abreast of news and current events as the middle classes. Indeed newspapers, Marx wrote in the *1861–63 Manuscripts*, now "form part of the necessary means of subsistence of the English urban worker."[267] Despite stringent restrictions on the press, the German socialist satirical magazine *Wahre Jakob*, founded in 1879, had 1.5 million readers by the early twentieth century, putting it on the same level as the most popular bourgeois publications. Marx himself, of course, was a journalist (as was Trotsky)—the only job he ever held—and the emergence of mass socialist parties toward the end of the nineteenth century would have been unimaginable without the dramatic growth of the workers' press (ninety socialist dailies in Germany alone!) and the counter-narrative of contemporary history that it presented.[268] *Vorwarts, L'Humanité, Het Volk, Il Lavoratore, Nepszava, El Socialista, Arbeiter-Zeitung, Vooruit, Avanti!*, the *New York Call, La Vanguardia* … these were the great editorial flagships of international socialism.[269]

Moreover, the constant defense of the workers' press against censorship and suppression made the socialist and anarchist movements the principal tribunes of civil liberties in the authoritarian societies of southern and east-central Europe. After 1848, Engels pointed out, erstwhile liberals in Germany, like their cousins in Austria and Russia, had cravenly abandoned the energetic advocacy of an uncensored free press and the unrestricted right of peaceful assembly, leaving the labor movement to face the full brunt of Bismarck's anti-socialist laws and prosecutions for *lèse-majesté*. In struggling to create a proletarian public sphere, therefore, socialists were also defending the orphaned principles of bourgeois democracy. "The German proletariat," wrote Engels in 1884, "at the outset thus appeared on the political stage as an extreme democratic party.

When we founded a major journal in Germany, the banner thereby was automatically placed into our hands."[270]

In countries such as Russia, where censorship was absolute, the underground press played an even more important function, with papers passed from hand to hand or read aloud when no foreman or spy was around. When the February 1917 Revolution drove the censors from office, it unleashed a torrent of free expression and radical opinion. In *Ten Days That Shook the World,* John Reed marveled at the frenetic war of print between classes and factions:

> In every city, in most towns, along the Front, each political faction
> had its newspaper—sometimes several. Hundreds of thousands
> of pamphlets were distributed by thousands of organisations, and
> poured into the armies, the villages, the factories, the streets. The
> thirst for education, so long thwarted, burst with the Revolution
> into a frenzy of expression. From Smolny Institute alone, the first
> six months, went out every day tons, car-loads, train-loads of lit-
> erature, saturating the land. Russia absorbed reading matter like
> hot sand drinks water, insatiable.[271]

The proletariat, not the bourgeoisie, is the ultimate "bearer of modern culture."[272] Its enthusiasm for science, in particular, confirmed its future as a hegemonic class.

In a famous speech before the Criminal Court of Berlin, where he was on trial for "inciting hatred of the propertied classes," Ferdinand Lassalle told his judges: "The great destiny of our age is precisely this—which the dark age had been unable to conceive, much less to achieve—the dissemination of scientific knowledge among the body of the people."[273] In previous social formations, the direct producers had little access to or need for formal learning, usually a prerogative of the church or a scribe class, but the American and French Revolutions generated an insatiable popular appetite for literacy and education. Industrial workers inherited a rich auto-didactic tradition from the artisan–intellectuals in Paris and Lyon who were the pioneers of socialism, and from their English counterparts who adapted classical political economy to the agenda of Chartism. As Marx always acknowledged, the development of the Ricardian "labor theory of value" into a powerful critique of exploitation, usually attributed to him, was actually achieved by plebeian intellectuals like the American-born printer John Bray, the Scottish factory worker John Gray, and the court-martialed sailor and rogue journalist Thomas Hodgskin.

Historians of technology likewise remind us that, until Thomas Edison established the world's first industrial laboratory in New Jersey in 1876, most of the key inventions of the first machine age were the creations of tinkerers, small master craftsmen, and ordinary workers, albeit highly self-educated. For example, one of the most important inventions of the early Industrial Revolution, the spinning mule, was developed by the spinner Samuel Crompton, who was too poor to afford the fee to register the patent. Similarly, the first electric motor was built by a Vermont blacksmith, Thomas Davenport, and the first high-pressure steam engine by the wheelwright Oliver Evans. Several of the most important English scientists of the nineteenth century were also self-educated plebs, notably Michael Faraday (a bookbinder's apprentice), Alfred Russell Wallace (surveyor's assistant), and the theorist of the ice ages, James Croll (university janitor). Joseph Dietzgen, a tanner without university education, became a celebrated socialist philosopher, who gave the name "dialectical materialism" (Marx never used the term) to his monistic critique of Kantian dualism.

Victorian workers flocked to reading rooms, mechanics' institutes, cheap libraries, athenaeums, and public lecture halls. In Britain, the mechanics' institutes, inspired by Dr George Birkbeck's famous 1800–04 lectures to Glasgow artisans, fed the popular hunger to understand the science of the new machines and prime movers. The first institute was created in Glasgow in 1821; when Marx moved to Soho, there were more than 700 in the British Isles.[274] By the 1860s, moreover, the scientifically literate sections of the working classes provided huge audiences for cutting-edge controversies, especially during the culture war that followed the publication of *The Origin of Species*. The London mechanics and craftsmen who flocked to Thomas Huxley's "Lectures to Working Men" were, according to Huxley, "as attentive and as intelligent as the best audience I have ever lectured to … I have studiously avoided the impertinence of talking down to them."[275]

Wilhelm Liebknecht, the 1848 veteran and founder of the SPD, fondly recalled attending six of these lectures with Karl Marx, then staying up all night excitedly discussing Darwin. The whole Marx household, in fact, was caught up in the great debates. (Mrs) Jenny Marx boasted to a Swiss friend of extraordinary popularity of the "Sunday Nights for the People":

With respect to religion, a great movement is currently developing in stuffy old England. The top men in science, Huxley (Darwin's disciple) at the head, with Tyndall, Sir Charles Lyell, Bowring, Carpenter, etc. give very enlightened, truly freethinking and bold lectures for the people in St Martin's Hall (of glorious waltzing memory), and, what is more, on Sunday evenings, exactly at the time when the lambs are usually grazing on the Lord's pastures; the hall has been full to bursting and the people's enthusiasm so great that, on the first evening, when I went there with the girls, 2,000 could not get into the room, which was crammed full.[276]

VI. Class Struggle and Hegemony

"Classes," said Edward Thompson in a famous article, "do not exist as separate entities ... class-struggle is the prior, as well as the more universal, concept."[277] Class struggle is shaped by and, in turn, reshapes its objective conditions: a process that often resembles an extended arms race. Indeed, we need only add the past tense to Régis Debray's description of the dialectic of guerrilla and anti-guerrilla warfare: "the Revolution revolutionizes the Counter-Revolution" (and vice versa).

A classical example, cited by Hilferding in his *Finance Capital* (1910), was the international proliferation of peak employers' organizations in response to the new industrial unions of the early twentieth century. In the German case, the Free Trade Unions had "developed a technique of labor struggle known as *'Einzelabschlachtung'*—literally, 'knocking them off singly.' The organized workers did not tackle an industry on a broad front but plant by plant. While the workers of one plant were on strike, their fellow-workers in other plants of the same industry would continue work and provide funds for the strikers." Initially this was a great success, and "it soon became apparent that organized labor could be fought only by an organization of employers which corresponded in scale and financial resources to the unions." The result was the formation of two national employers' organizations, one for heavy industry and textiles, and the other for light industries, which emulated the research and coordinating functions of the central union leagues, and, like the unions, provided mutual aid and financial support during strikes and lockouts. As Carl Schorske observed, "unionization [by 1914] had produced its counterpart—a powerful enemy, armed with equal or superior weapons."[278]

Likewise, during the Revolution of 1905, the banks and foreign investors in heavy industry organized a concerted resistance to worker demands by forming the St Petersburg Society of

Manufacturers and Mill Owners, which implemented blacklists and punitive lockouts.[279] In the same period, the notorious Merchants and Manufacturers Association imposed the open shop on Los Angeles: membership was not voluntary, and businesses that tried to get along with the unions soon found themselves denounced on the front page of the *Los Angeles Times*. In such circumstances unions were often forced underground or restricted to industries with smaller, less organized employers.

The best hope of countering this supercharged power of capital, at least on a local or regional scale, was to concentrate strike action against the most vulnerable nodes of commerce, above all the ports. "Any strike in the docks," writes Hobsbawm,

> tended to turn into a general transport strike which might grow into a general strike. The economic general strikes which multiplied in the first years of the new century—and were to lead to impassioned ideological debates within the socialist movement—were thus mainly strikes in port cities: Trieste, Genoa, Marseille, Barcelona, Amsterdam. These were giant battles, but unlikely to lead as yet to permanent mass union organization, given the heterogeneity of an often unskilled labor force.[280]

Thus, in the case of Los Angeles—and in fact all the cities of the Pacific littoral from Seattle to Valparaiso to Yokohama—the ultimate battleground against the open shop was the harbor; in this case at San Pedro, where IWW membership became the red badge of courage amongst maritime workers.

The centralizing tendency of the class struggle, however, did not always override the competing interests of employers, and some capitalists scouted the terrain of functional accommodations, even limited alliances with unions, laying the foundation for the future politics of corporatism. This was especially the case in labor-intensive industries such as coal-mining and men's apparel, where the most modern employers tolerated unions to the extent that contractural bargaining regulated competition and forced low-wage competitors out of business.[281] In any case, large-scale working-class militancy, whether successful or not, tended to "rationalize" capitalism by accelerating the introduction of new labor-saving technologies and promoting the centralization of ownership and control. This is exactly the point of the tenth chapter of *Capital Volume I*, where Marx recounts how the victory of the English workers in forcing the legislation of a ten-hour workday was quickly countered by their employers' investment in a new generation of machines. (Similarly, in 1917, during the general strike of metalworkers in the Department of the Seine, employers used the walkout as an opportunity to retool their factories, introducing new machines that required fewer skilled workers.)[282] Just as the competition between firms drives them to seek technological rents or super-profits by being the first to bring on line more modern machines, so too does the class struggle drive the development of new technologies to raise productivity and dismantle the power of strategically emplaced workers.

Contemporary Marxism has made several notable attempts to theorize the creative adaptation of capitalism to the challenges of working-class power. Probably the most influential (although still awaiting its English translation) has been Mario Tronti's 1966 book *Operai e Capitale*, which used the ten-hour-day example as a starting point for an ambitious and original theory of "class composition" and the role of class struggle in the development of the productive forces. "The pressure of labour-power," wrote Tronti, "is capable of forcing capital to modify its own internal composition, intervening *within* capital as an essential component of capitalist development."[283] Hobsbawm, in *The Age of Extremes*, transforms this idea into a diabolic paradox: "the most lasting result of the October Revolution was to save its adversary in war as in peace, inciting it to reform itself."[284] This is far different, to say the least, from anything imagined in the era of classical socialism.

The workers' movement can and must confront the power of capital in every aspect of social life, organizing resistance on the terrains of the economic, the political, the urban, the social-reproductive, and the associational. It is the fusion or synthesis of these struggles, rather than their simple addition, which invests the proletariat with hegemonic consciousness.

Marx and Engels, for example, clearly believed that mass social-ist consciousness would be a dialectical alloy of the economic and the political; of epic battles over rights as well as over wages and working hours; of bitter local fights and great international causes. Since the formation of the Communist League in 1847, they had argued that wage-labor constituted the only serious social force able to represent and enact a consistently democratic program of suffrage and rights, and thus provide the hegemonic glue to bind together a broad coalition of workers, poor peasants, national minorities, and radicalized strata of the middle class. While the mind of the liberal petty bourgeoisie easily amputated political rights from economic grievances, workers' lives refuted any categorical distinction between oppression and exploitation. The "growing over" of polit-ical into economic democracy, and of economic class struggle into the question of state power—the process that Marx characterized as "permanent revolution" in the contexts of 1848 and Chartism— was a recurrent motif in all the great European social crises from 1848 to 1948.

The counter-revolution of 1849–51 demonstrated not only the "persisting" strengths of classes derived from *anciens régimes*—landowning nobilities, for the most part, whose power was rooted in their great estates and domination of the upper ranks of the officer corps—but also, as Marx had experienced first-hand in Cologne, the treason of the "liberal bourgeoisie" and the panic of the commercial and professional middle classes at the first hint of social reform. Although the subject has been much debated, it is unclear whether Marx ever considered democracy the natural or default political counterpart to industrial capitalism, especially on the continent. As he often pointed out, Belgium was actually the paradigm of a bourgeois constitutional state and its bankers, textile magnates, and mine-owners were amongst the fiercest opponents of working-class suffrage on the continent. Although only two popular socialist revolutions actually succeeded in Europe—Russia in 1917 and Yugoslavia in 1945—the broad labor movement remained, in Göran Therborn's judgment, "the only consistent democratic force." Indeed, he argues that the "principal historical accomplishment … of the Second International" was "its contribution to the development of bourgeois democracy."[285]

But because economic struggles and political conflicts are only episodically synchronized—usually during depression or war—there was also a strong tendency toward their bifurcation. The inverse but symmetrical illusions of economism/syndicalism (progress by economic organization alone) and parliamentary cretinism (reform without workplace power) have always required a regular weeding of the red garden. Thus, for Rosa Luxemburg, the central lesson of the 1905 Revolution in Russia was the need to understand the economic and the political as *moments* in a single revolutionary process:

> In a word: the economic struggle is the transmitter from one political centre to another; the political struggle is the periodic

fertilization of the soil for the economic struggle. Cause and effect here continually change places; and thus the economic and the political factor in the period of the mass strike, now widely removed, completely separated or even mutually exclusive, as the theoretical plan would have them, merely form the two interlacing sides of the proletarian class struggle in Russia. And *their unity* is precisely the mass strike. If the sophisticated theory proposes to make a clever logical dissection of the mass strike for the purpose of getting at the "purely political mass strike," it will by this dissection, as with any other, not perceive the phenomenon in its living essence, but will kill it altogether.[286]

In the battle for societal leadership, the workers' movement must speak not only the language of scientific socialism but also the dialects of past popular struggles. Language does not "construct" the class struggle in any ontological sense (as devotees of the "linguistic turn" seem to believe), but it is a crucial battleground for competing claims of historical and moral legitimacy.

In nineteenth-century France and the United States, radical labor movements drew deep inspiration and moral ardor from their (constructed) revolutionary traditions. The Paineite interpretation of 1776 and 1789 as sister revolutions was, of course, embraced by Jefferson and American radicals, while Federalists disclaimed any connection whatsoever between "unique" American dispensations and the Jacobin orgy of violence in Paris. Until the 1840s, when a majority of workingmens' groups took a nativist turn, the artisan radicalism of the 1790s, even if only dimly remembered, remained a vital fluid in the body of democratic republicanism. In France, of course, the Great Revolution, like the Civil War in the United States, has continued to fissure society until today. The Bourbon restoration and its suppression of republican speech only anchored the memory of the culture of 1789 more deeply in the urban middle classes, the artisanate and proletariat, and, via the legend of Napoleon, amongst the peasantry. Different social groups within this broad array, of course, identified with different factions of the revolution, with Liberals celebrating Benjamin Constant and Condorcet, while revolutionary democrats defiantly defended the memory of Robespierre and Marat. Babouf, quite appropriately, became the hero of the Blanquists and communists. Until the "Debacle of 1871," no single group or party was able to secure complete rule of the discursive space of republicanism.

The Third Republic of Jules Ferry, however, set about institutionalizing the revolutionary tradition as a nationalist ideology that was disseminated by *instituteurs* in the new public school. The Republic's rhetoric often struck Jacobin notes, but, as Hobsbawm points out, "those who controlled the imagery, the symbolism, the traditions of the Republic were men of the centre masquerading as men of the extreme left: the Radical Socialist, proverbially 'like the radish, red outside, white inside, and always on the side the bread is buttered.'"[287] French socialism consequently found itself in a semiotic briar patch where revolutionary slogans and ideas were vulnerable to appropriation and transformation of meaning by bourgeois republicans. Likewise, shared anti-clericalism in a period of repeated monarchist threats and ominous Catholic mobilizations made it more difficult to draw clear class lines between richer and poorer sons of the Republic. Clarification eventually came in the 1900s, when Radical Party leader Georges Clémenceau renewed the tradition of June 1848 and began shooting workers and conscripting strikers in the name of the Republic.

A very different kind of interaction between socialism and what Hobsbawm has called an "invented tradition" was illustrated by the

Minjung movement at the height of Korean industrialization in the 1970s and 1980s, when collective action was still largely illegal. In his remarkable book on the making of the Korean working class, the most militant in Asia, Hagen Koo stresses the continuous dialogue between shopfloor struggles and populist resistance to the state. With no inherited working-class tradition, and faced with a repressive, pro-employer regime with a huge security apparatus, Korea's workers, especially the young women in light manufacturing industries, drew unexpected strength from their alliance with the movement of the *minjung*, or "masses," that independently arose in the mid-1970s:

> This broad populist movement was led by dissident intellectuals and students and aimed to forge a broad class alliance among workers, peasants, poor urban dwellers and progressive intellectuals against the authoritarian regime ... It introduced new political language and cultural activities by reinterpreting Korean history and reappropriated Korea's indigenous culture from the *minjung* perspective ... Thus, culture and politics have critical roles in the formation of the South Korean working class, not in the usual roles ascribed to them in the literature on East Asian development—as factors of labor docility and quiescence—but as sources of labor resistance and growing consciousness.[288]

Democratization came in 1987–90, on the crest of a wildcat strike wave (the "Great Labor Struggle") involving several million workers.

Political and economic class struggles, of course, had different "gear ratios" and velocities in diverse sectors, regions, and nations. What synchronized them as a single movement was the universal demand for an eight-hour working day. May Day was truly the foundation of the Socialist International.

The eight-hour day was first won, as early as the 1840s, by the infant labor movements of New Zealand and Australia. Some American state and federal workers (employees of arsenals and navy yards) gained it in the dramatic labor upsurge at the end of the U.S. Civil War, which also led to the formation of the short-lived National Labor Union. Although this legislation was soon effectively voided, it established goalposts for the American labor movement that were quickly adopted as a universal standard by the Geneva Congress of the First International. "The legal limitation of the working day is a preliminary condition without which all further attempts at improvements and emancipation of the working class must prove abortive."[289] In 1884 a new federation of American unions, led by Samuel Gompers of the Cigar Makers, relaunched the eight-hour movement with a call for a general walkout on May 1, 1886. The events that followed that first May Day in Chicago—the shooting of McCormick Harvester workers, the bomb in Haymarket Square, the subsequent trial of Albert Parsons and his comrades, and the unsuccessful international campaign to save their lives—electrified workers across the Atlantic. When Gompers again committed American unions to national demonstrations on May Day 1890 (only the Carpenters, deemed the strongest union, were actually designated to strike), the founding congress of the Socialist International, meeting in Paris on the centenary of the Great Revolution, endorsed the proposal.

In the earlier American campaigns, the shorter working day was argued as the precondition for workers' full development as educated and cultured citizens. Now it was also advocated as the cure for mass unemployment. "Among the numerous arguments," wrote Sidney Fine, employed during the campaign of 1888–1891 to buttress the eight-hour clause, the one most frequently voiced and the argument that found greatest favor among the workingmen was that shorter hours were necessary to solve the problem of unemployment created by technological progress. According to the popular estimate approximately one fifth of the existing labor force was unemployed, and it was maintained that not only did the jobless workers constitute a problem in themselves but that the excess supply of labor that they represented served to depress the labor standards of those who were employed and posed a threat to successful strike action.[290]

In the event, 50,000 American Carpenters won the eight-hour day with surprising ease; but the real drama was in Europe, where in apocalyptic anticipation tens of thousands of troops were moved into the capital cities and, in the case of Paris at least, the rich fled to their country homes. For the first time, workers in Christiana and Oporto, London and Milan, flexed their muscles in unison. But May Day 1890 was not without cost: hundreds were injured by calvary charges in the Place de la Concorde, beaten by police in the Prater, and bayoneted by attacking infantry outside a steel mill in Pest.[291] Future May Days (1906, for example) would be even bloodier.

The original decision to endorse Gompers's project at the Paris Congress had been a last-minute decision, almost an afterthought, but the magnitude of the 1890 turnout removed any doubts about the popularity of the demand or workers' willingness to take to the streets. But would they strike and potentially turn May Day into a catalyst for revolution? Left socialists and anarcho-syndicalists, particularly the French, insisted on general strikes and class confrontation, while reformists wanted to reserve strikes as a threat but ritualize May Day as a celebration of unity. In both cases, however, the eight-hour day and the social right to leisure remained central goals. Although one country or sector might be first to win the shorter working day, socialists broadly agreed that only a common standard of hours implemented in all the major industrial nations could ensure that such gains would be permanent. Unlike any other reformist demand, whether wages, prices, or suffrage, the campaign for the reduction of the working day required cross-national coordination and solidarity. It was internationalism embodied, and many hoped that the great annual demonstrations of solidarity, far more than mere resolutions at socialist congresses, would be a powerful deterrent to the warmongers in the palaces and parliaments.

In the end, working-class leisure in Europe was the gift of the October Revolution and the cascade of working-class struggles it helped to set into motion. "Eight-hour proclamations," writes Gary Cross in his important history of work reduction in Britain and France,

> began in the Bolshevik Revolution of 1917 and then spread in 1918 to Finland and Norway, and to Germany in the wake of the November Revolution. By mid-December, the movement then passed to the new states of Poland, Czechoslovakia, and Austria. From the revolutionary regimes of eastern and central Europe, it spread to Switzerland, where up to four hundred thousand struck for the eight-hour day in December 1918. In February the movement reached to Italy in a wave of shutdowns that first affected the metals industry and spread to textiles, chemicals, and even agriculture. This insurgency produced eight-hour laws in Spain, Portugal, and Switzerland by June and in the Netherlands and Sweden by November 1919.

In France, the CGT had pushed the demand to the top of its agenda at its December 1918 congress. Clémenceau, who had crushed the CGT's eight-hour offensive a decade earlier, now proposed its legislation as the price of social peace.[292] In Britain the "Triple Alliance" of miners, railway workers, and dockers threatened the Lloyd George government with economic Armageddon, and won major work-hour reductions in their industries, including a seven-hour day in the pits. (Attempts to rescind the miners' victory in 1926 produced the great General Strike of that year.)

To truly embody a general interest, the workers' movement had to assemble a "historic bloc" of allied oppressed groups, including the rural poor. Indeed the "agrarian question"—different in every country—was the Rubicon that socialism had to cross in order to attain a political and social majority everywhere except in England. The fate of the European Revolution of 1917–21 was ultimately determined in the countryside.

In his well-known essay, "The Antinomies of Antonio Gramsci," Perry Anderson dispelled the myth that Gramsci had originated "hegemony" as a critical concept in Marxist discourse. In fact, "the term *gegemoniya* (hegemony) was one of the most central political slogans in the Russian Social-Democratic movement, from the late 1890s to 1917."[293] It was first explicated in a systematic fashion by Peter Axelrod, the "orthodox" Russian Social-Democrat and later Menshevik leader, who, Leopold Haimson notes, "insisted most unequivocally that Russia's workers would come to perceive the differences of interests that separated them from other social groups and develop genuine class consciousness only by becoming conscious of the interests of the polity as a whole." "It was also Axelrod," continues Haimson, who drew the conclusion (which Lenin long accepted) "that Russia's proletariat should assume the leadership of the all-nation struggle for political freedom and indeed the role of *gegemon* [hegemon] in the 'bourgeois' revolution that Russia was still historically destined to undergo."[294] With the sole exception of England, whose peasantry was long extinct, hegemonic proletarian leadership above all pivoted on the positions adopted toward class struggles in the countryside in an era of agricultural globalization and overproduction. The countryside, moreover, was the permanent hearth of counter-revolution, and thus a major strategic variable in any theory of revolution. As Arno Mayer pointed out in *The Persistence of the Old Regime,* the great landowners of East Prussia, Ulster, the Mezzogiorno, the Carpathian Basin, and Russia, who had been "the chief economic and social supports of the *anciens régimes,*" survived the Age of Revolutions to become the bedrock of reaction and militarism in the early twentieth century.[295] Could the workers' movement mobilize or assist social forces in the countryside itself to blow up this reactionary monolith?

The conversion of the virgin steppes of the Americas and western Siberia to wheat cultivation in the 1880s unleashed a flood of cheap grain that was followed a decade later, after the advent of refrigerator ships, by beef and lamb imports from Argentina and the Antipodes. The resulting price depression was a staggering blow to European agriculture, forcing millions of laborers, small peasants, and rural artisans to move to industrial boomtowns such as Berlin, Lodz ("the Polish Manchester"), newly unified Buda-Pest, Barcelona, and Turin—or, if they had the resources, to emigrate to the Americas. Europe's large and medium-sized farmers meanwhile had three general options: to switch from grain production to higher-value livestock and dairy (Denmark, England, parts of northern Germany); to compensate for falling prices by expanding the scale of wheat growing for export (the large estates of the Danubian countries); and/or to impose agricultural tariffs to protect producers at the expense of urban consumers (France and Germany in the 1890s). In the special case of the Mediterranean littoral of France and Spain, the response to the "general crisis of agriculture" was a turn toward olive and grape monocultures that proved catastrophic with the arrival of phylloxera and various tree blights.

The heterogeneous social strata subsumed within the category "peasantry" were confronted with an array of choices in defining their interests and making alliances. Their dilemma illustrates the important point made by Ronald Aminzade in a sophisticated analysis of class positions and their variable political expressions:

> The complex and often contradictory interests defined by class positions are typically contested in a political arena with multiple possible enemies and allies. This means that it is rarely predetermined just how such interests will be defined in political programs and coalitions or how politically salient class-based interests (rather than nonclass interests rooted in racial, ethnic, or gender stratification) will become.[296]

The rural poor and independent small producers, in other words, were to some extent "up for grabs" according to the positions taken by major class-based parties. Large landowners, of course, were militantly organized to defend their interests, increasingly in alliance with heavy industries; but the political alignment of the rest of the countryside was the great open question of *fin de siècle* European politics.

As intensely debated inside the parties of the Second International, the "agrarian question" was actually twofold: What stance should the workers' movement take on these upheavals in agriculture and the desperate rural demands for protection, cheap money, and the division of large estates? With what strata of the countryside should it ally? An array of contending positions, responding in part to national and regional differences in agrarian class structures, were adopted by the major socialist parties and anarcho-syndicalist movements. The majority of the SPD and its Austro-Hungarian sister parties shared Engels's belief that "small production is irretrievably going to rack and ruin," and that, while socialists should do nothing to accelerate its extinction, they could not prevent it:

> It is the duty of our Party to make clear to the peasants again and again that their position is absolutely hopeless as long as capitalism holds sway, that it is absolutely impossible to preserve their small holdings for them as such, that capitalist large-scale production is absolutely sure to run over their impotent antiquated system of small production as a train runs over a wheelbarrow. If we do this we shall act in conformity with the inevitable trend of economic development.[297]

Unlike Marx himself, who harbored grave doubts about the long-term sustainability of capitalist agriculture and kept an open mind in discussions with the Russian Narodniki about the potential role of the traditional village commune (*mir*) in the transition to socialism, or some Revisionists like Bernstein who challenged the idea that the "law" of concentration of capital applied to agriculture in the same way as industry and in every country, the SPD majority enshrined Engels's views as party dogma. Thus Wilhelm Liebknecht, in a speech to the Brussels Congress of the Socialist International (1891), "prophesized that American corn would ruin the small farmers of Germany and thus drive them to the ranks of the proletariat. It was in American competition that he saw the best possible guarantee for the triumph of socialism."[298] No political solution, in other words, was needed, just patience while the world market ruined and proletarianized farmers. The SPD's principal task was to avoid at all costs the kind of populism that might dilute the class character of the party.[299] Despite prescient warnings from Bavarian Social Democrats that "we must prevent the hobnailed boots of the peasants and their sons from turning against us," the SPD did little to prevent the consolidation of a powerful right-wing agrarian bloc, allying peasants and *Junkers* after the passage of the 1902 von Bulow tariff.[300]

This "doomed peasant" dogma, which often went hand in hand with the belief that peasants were unalterably reactionary, isolated social democracy in Central Europe in several cases from elemental social struggles and potential allies in the countryside. Two vivid examples were Hungary and Bulgaria. In the former case, the Great Plain churned with such unrest in the 1890s—inspired by a fusion of chiliastic popular religiosity with vague socialist ideology—that the army eventually had to be sent into the fields; yet Hungarian Social Democrats at their 1894 unity conference refused to consider demands for the breakup of the great estates. Likewise in Bulgaria, an overwhelmingly agricultural country, the "Narrow Socialists," led by Dimitar Blagoev (an epigone of Plekhanov) considered any alliance with the militant and *sui generis* Peasant Party of Aleksandar Stamboliyski as a betrayal of Marxism. In 1918–19, as war turned into revolution in Central Europe, these anti-agrarian biases proved fatal. In Bulgaria any hope of a progressive republic was quashed after Blagoev's party refused to come to the aid of the Radomir peasant–soldier uprising, while in Hungary the Soviet government under Béla Kun doomed itself by refusing to confiscate the great estates and distribute land to the peasantry.[301] After the reds were toppled, moreover, Hungary's inchoate agrarian socialism morphed into the *nepies* (populist) movement of Dezső Szabó, which "sought land reform and proper education, but ... incorporated these reform programs into a program of nationalist hatred against the spirit of capitalism, Marxist socialism, and 'aliens'—primarily Jews—who, in the populist view, embodied all these anti-Hungarian elements."[302]

In the Mediterranean countries, in contrast, socialism and anarchism sunk deep roots in the countryside.[303] In Provence, above all in the "Red Var," small wine-growers defected en masse from the Radicals to elect a series of Socialists, beginning with former Union general and delegate for war in the Paris Commune Gustave Cluseret; in neighboring Languedoc, Jean Jaurès was deputy for the Tarn, a department famous for its vineyards and orchards. That the petty *vignerons* of the Midi became vigorous socialists, of course, is seemingly in contradiction with Marx's famous portrait of a backward Bonapartist countryside; but Tony Judt, in his *Socialism in Provence: 1871–1914*, points to the fact that the southern peasants lived in "urban villages," sharing a communal culture with artisans and radical school teachers, with whom they organized together in local *bourses du travail*.[304]

The same pattern of "agglomerated villages" (actually large towns in many cases) characterized the latifundian societies of Andalusia and Apulia, both bastions of anarcho-syndicalism. Anarchism in Andalusia, especially in the province of Cadiz, was an insurrectionary culture of exceptional militancy and tenacity, uniting day laborers on the estates, peasants from sierra villages, and artisans in the larger towns—although, as Temma Kaplan has emphasized, not without significant internal tensions between the purely proletarian (anarcho-communist) and petty producer (collectivist) wings.[305] In Italy, the crucible of rural syndicalism was Apulia, where the class structure had been violently simplified "into two radical and unequal extremes—the narrow class of capitalists and the mass of dispossessed proletarians … [The] *braccianti* worked exclusively as agricultural proletarians who sold their labour power. The workers cultivated no plot, owned no house, possessed no work animals, and cultivated the land as individuals rather than as members of a family unit."[306] Ultimately the estate owners turned to the *carabinieri* and the fascist *squadristi* to terrorize the day laborers into submission.

Meanwhile, in the fertile Po Valley, where landowners and lease-holders had responded to the world agricultural depression by intensified production of rice and fodder crops using wage-labor, socialists organized the largest and most powerful farmworkers' union in Europe. Italy indeed was the only country where great agricultural strikes (1893, 1896–97, 1901–02, 1907–08, and 1919) were frequently center stage in the class struggle.[307] The capitalist restructuring of agriculture in the region during the first decade of the twentieth century brought dramatic, even catastrophic changes in land tenure and class structure. In the province of Parma, one-third of peasant proprietors lost their land, sharecropping decreased by a quarter, and the number of agricultural laborers with annual contracts and housing fell by half. Most were forced to become day laborers, a group whose impoverished ranks grew from 22,000 to 41,000 in a single decade. These workers, writes Thomas Sykes, "had broken with the traditions of the peasant cosmos" to become "the homogeneous, combative vanguard of the working class in the countryside of the Po Valley. Desperate men, with little to lose, they were usually in the forefront of most agitations and strikes in agriculture." Spurning the moderate Socialists, they embraced revolutionary syndicalism, and in 1908 launched a regional general strike. By the end of the war, their union, the formidable Federterra, had 70,000 members, steeled in innumerable struggles—the most powerful agricultural union on earth.[308]

The sweeping electoral victory of the Socialists in November 1919 quickly led to simultaneous land occupations by sharecroppers organized into "Red Leagues" and insurrectionary strikes by day laborers—all viewed with accurate horror by landowners as the beginning of an agrarian revolution like Mexico's or Russia's. As in Apulia, they called on Mussolini and his urban thugs as saviors:

> Selective terror and violence became skillfully coordinated with a campaign by the fascists and their agrarian allies to regiment the day laborers and sharecroppers into "independent" unions. Before the March on Rome in late October 1922, the offensive had largely achieved its objectives: the destruction of a strong and effective labor movement, the re-establishment of landlord supremacy in the countryside and the installation of the fascists as the new *de facto* rulers in the province.[309]

In Scandinavia, the rise of the working class was parallel with the growth of the independent peasantry, and the two groups considerably overlapped, as poorer farmers were seasonally timber workers, miners, or, in Norway, fishermen. As "the family farm with no hired labor," Alestalo and Kuhnle argue, "became an increasingly common basic unit in farming in Scandinavia," farmers formed their own unions and demonstrated a strong consciousness of "a class *fur sich*," independent of the big landlords and power-holding aristocracies. In Denmark, moreover, a dense network of cooperative institutions powered the transition to dairy exports, mainly to Britain—and, if this cooperative culture did not exactly turn peasants into socialists, it facilitated strong farmer-labor alliances as the franchise was expanded. Extraordinary rates of emigration in the other Scandinavian countries (which carried cooperative and social-democratic ideas to North American areas like Minnesota, North Dakota, Manitoba, and Saskatchewan) relieved pressure on labor markets, and by 1907 union density in Sweden was probably half of the waged workforce. The Scandinavian countrysides, if not revolutionary, were populist, progressive, and never an insuperable obstacle to the exercise of political power by the region's highly successful Social Democracy.[310]

"The alliances between urban workers and peasants," explains Stefano Bartolini,

> that gave hegemony to Scandinavian socialism were finalized in the 1930s: Denmark and Sweden in 1933 and Norway in 1935. This compromise between urban and rural interests took the same basic form, involving policy programs organized around (1) the expansion of public employment, support for public works, social welfare programs, unemployment relief, and prohibition or regulation of strikes and lockouts in exchange for (2) reduction of agricultural property taxes, reduction of agricultural interest rates, state help for more-costly loans, debt relief in general for agriculture, and various forms of state subsidies to farmers. In sum, the alliance was based in a common farmer/worker interest in policies to stimulate the economy, and it resulted in urban workers accepting higher food prices in exchange for peasant support for public intervention and public works.[311]

Should the SPD not have adopted similar policies in southern Germany as the Bavarian socialists repeatedly urged in the early 1900s?

Finally, in Russia, the Bolsheviks successfully followed Marx's prescription for successful revolution in 1848: allying socialist uprisings in the cities to peasant war in the countryside. Amongst orthodox Social Democrats, Lenin was unusual in rejecting a single fixed trajectory for the future of the peasantry. Instead, he contrasted alternative "Prussian" and "American" paths for the development of the countryside, and, in advocating the latter, endorsed the formation of market-oriented family farms: "He considered peasant demands for land progressive in Russia because the rural economy was so backward that a choice still existed between more or less efficient paths of capitalist development."[312] Although the Bolshevik advocacy of "Black redistribution" (land to the tiller, pure and simple) was an accommodation to the reality of the revolutionary situation in summer 1917, Lenin was consistent in his strategic belief that only a peasant revolution, not a reformist "democratic bourgeoisie" as the Mensheviks argued, could help the proletariat destroy absolutism in Russia.[313] Whether any stratum of the peasantry, however, would support the construction of socialism was a different question.

For revolution to become a possibility, the workers' movement had to break the military monopoly of the bourgeois state from the inside. Socialist youth organizations, as we have seen, were the principal force contesting conscription and, on occasion, propagandizing anti-militarist ideas within the barracks. But the weakest link in wartime was the navy, where the great dreadnaughts and battle cruisers were little more than "floating factories" manned by slave labor.

The technologically advanced steel warships of the early twentieth century were crewed by large numbers of mechanical workers, as well as stokers and those performing more traditional naval occupations. Unlike conscript land armies, whose ranks were filled by the peasantry, modern navies relied on young workers, preferably with factory training or apprenticeships. The newly modernized Russian and German fleets, officered by aristocrats and junkers, were infamous for their brutal treatment of these proletarian seamen, especially on the big ships of the line. Any viewer of Eisenstein's *Battleship Potemkin* will recall the iconic images from 1905: the rotten, worm-infested meat; the executive officer's murder of the sailors' spokesman Vakulenchuk; quick revenge by his comrade, Matyuschenko; the daring voyage to Odessa during the general strike; the Cossacks' massacre of protestors on the city's Richelieu Steps; and the ultimate escape of the crew to Romania. The *Potemkin*, one of the newest ships in the navy, was unusual in having a large core of seamen who identified with revolutionary parties, but its heroic example became deeply imprinted on the entire Black Sea Fleet. Later that year, in Sebastopol, troops fired on a meeting of workers and sailors, and several of the largest ships in the fleet followed the spirit of the *Potemkin* and mutinied. A popular young torpedo boat commander, P. Schmidt, whose revolutionary oratory had delighted workers as well as sailors, was asked to lead the rebellion, with the goal of forcing the Czar to convoke a constituent assembly. But the mutiny was savagely crushed by Admiral Chukhnin, who executed Schmidt and his comrades.

Their revenge came later, in 1917, when the Baltic Fleet helped install the February republic. The Fleet's main bases at Kronstadt, just outside Petrograd, and Sveaborg, next to Helsinki, became stages for some of the most important events in the run-up to the climax in October. The Kronstadt Soviet, which represented the town's workers as well as its sailors, was the more advanced and quickly fell under the influence of "maximalists" (Bolsheviks, Left SRs, and anarchists), who were ready to overthrow the Provisional Government by the early summer. (With great difficulty, Lenin managed to persuade them to wait.) Although the main battle fleet at Sveaborg was less politicized, it was seething with hatred against its officers and at the first opportunity sailors began to drown them under the ice.[314] While Sveaborg guarded Petrograd's flank against counter-revolution, the Kronstadt sailors became the shock troops of Petrograd Soviet and ensured the semi-peaceful transfer of power in October. Indeed, the Revolution's enduring symbol became the battle cruiser *Aurora*, whose presence on the Neva, its spotlights illuminating the sky over the Winter Palace and its powerful guns shaking the city with occasional blasts (no less impressive for the fact that they were actually blanks), demoralized the motley contingents defending Kerensky.

A year later the mutiny of the German High Seas Fleet demonstrated a similar proletarian outlook and revolutionary temper in the engine rooms, gun turrets, and machine shops of the great warships. As Pierre Broué explains in his history of the German Revolution,

> The crews included a majority of skilled workers, most often metalworkers, who were class-conscious and had experience of class struggle. The circumstances of the War, which kept the ships in port, enabled the sailors to maintain close contacts with the workers in the docks and shipyards, to circulate books, leaflets and newspapers, to exchange ideas, and to organize discussions. The conditions of life, the concentration of proletarians in confined spaces, and the qualities of daring and the collective spirit which they promoted rendered the harsh conditions endured by the sailors and stokers increasingly intolerable. All this occurred with the combination of inactivity and the absurd disciplinary drills imposed by a particularly reactionary officer corps.[315]

The fuse had been lit in 1917 with the organization of an underground League of Soldiers and Sailors led by the seaman Max Reichpietsch. Inspired by the uprisings at Kronstadt and Sveaborg, he hoped to organize sailors' councils on the Russian model. When he contacted several Reichstag deputies from the USPD (the pro-peace split-off from the SPD) about organizing party branches in the Navy, he received little more than vague encouragement. Undeterred, he began recruiting members and organizing shipboard hunger strikes and walkouts in advance of a proposed meeting of the Second International in Stockholm. He had a clear vision of what must be done:

> To his comrades, Reichpietsch summed up the perspective: a movement had to be organized in the fleet to provide arguments for the Independent delegates at Stockholm, and, if nothing came out of the conference, the revolutionary sailors "will put to the soldiers the slogan: 'Arise! Let us break our chains as the Russians have done!'" He added: "Each of us knows what he will have to do."[316]

The high command, well informed of the agitation, quickly court-martialed and executed Reichpietsch along with four of his comrades. But his plan for an uprising lived on inside the Fleet.

In October, Admiral von Hipper ordered a last, desperate sortie of the High Seas Fleet against the Belgian coast, with the aim of provoking battle with the much larger British Grand Fleet. At sea off Wilhelmshaven, crews, who had little desire to be sacrificed for the "honor" of their commanders, began to mutiny, and von Hipper was forced to abandon the plan. But hundreds were arrested and sent to Kiel for court-martial. Upon their arrival, a large solidarity demonstration of fellow sailors was dispersed, with nine deaths. By the next morning, the red flag was flying over the fleet, the commanders had capitulated, and a sailors' council was in charge of the installation. The German Revolution had begun. And revolutionary sailors over the next eighteen years continued to sabotage counter-revolutionary and colonial designs: notably, in the mutiny of the French Black Sea Fleet in April 1919, led by the pro-Bolshevik boilermaker André Marty; in the extraordinary Communist-inspired mutiny by the Indonesian crew of the *De Zeven Provincien* (the largest ship in the Dutch Navy) in 1933 and their bold attempt to liberate imprisoned comrades at Surabaya; and finally, in 1936, in the hard-won victory of the Sailors Councils over their Francoist officers in the Spanish fleet.

VII. Class Consciousness and Socialism
Because of its position in social production and the universality of its objective interests, the proletariat possesses a superior "epistemological capacity" to see the economy as a whole, and unravel the mystery of capital's apparent self-movement (Lukács's theses).

The bourgeoisie and the proletariat are the only "pure classes" in modern society, but they are not symmetrical in their internal formation or capacity for consciousness. Competition between firms and sectors is the iron law of capitalism, but competition between workers can be ameliorated by organization. Marx was explicit: "if all the members of the modern bourgeoisie have the same interests inasmuch as they form a class as against another class, they have opposite, antagonistic interests inasmuch as they stand face to face with one another."[317] Rational self-interest, argued Lukács, following Marx, means that individual owners of capital "cannot see and are necessarily indifferent to all the social implications of their activities." The "veil drawn over the nature of bourgeois society," that is to say, the denial of its own historicity, "is indispensable to the bourgeoisie itself ... from a very early stage the ideological history of the bourgeoisie was *nothing but a desperate resistance to every insight into the true nature of the society it had created and thus to a real understanding of its class situation.*"[318] As soon as Capital confronted a rising proletariat, moreover, it took off its republican toga and, at least on the continent, ran into the arms of absolutism or embraced dictators like Napoleon III, and later Mussolini, Hitler, and Franco.

The proletarian, however poor and shirtless, has better vision. "As the bourgeoisie," says Lukács, "has the intellectual, organizational and every other advantage, *the superiority of the proletariat must lie exclusively in its ability to see society from the centre, as a coherent whole.*" In a famous but variously interpreted passage in *History and Class Consciousness*, Lukács introduced the idea of "imputed class consciousness"—the objective and ripened possibilities that the proletariat must recognize and act upon in order to bring about the revolution. In pre-crisis periods, however, the working class tends to be dominated by the "petty bourgeois attitudes of most trade unionists" and mystified by the conceptual and real "separation of the various theaters of war." "The proletariat finds the economic inhumanity to which it is subjected easier to understand than the political, and the political easier than the cultural."[319] The primary obstacle to class consciousness, moreover, is less bourgeois ideology, or the ponderous operation of Althusser's "state ideological apparatuses," than "the actual day-to-day workings of the economy and society. These have the effect of causing the internalization of commodity relations and the reification of human relations."[320] In depression and war, however, contradictions fissure this crystal palace of reified economic and political realities, and the deep meaning of the historical moment "becomes *comprehensible in practice*." It is finally "possible to read off from history the correct course of action to be followed." The reader? "The workers' council spells the political and economic defeat of reification."[321]

A revolutionary collective will is crystallized (and "correct courses of action" decided upon) primarily through rude, direct democracy in periods of extreme mass activity. Class consciousness is not the party program, but rather the synthesis of lessons learned in protracted class war.

If unions and left parties constituted the quasi-permanent institutions of the proletarian public sphere, the class struggle episodically generated ad hoc forms such as general strike committees, workers'

141

councils, factory assemblies, and soviets that dramatically expanded popular participation in debate and decision-making to include the non-party proletariat and unorganized workers, as well as in certain instances the unemployed, students, working-class mothers, soldiers, and sailors. Whether in Petrograd, Bremen, Glasgow, or Winnipeg, "movement democracy" reproduced many of the classic features of 1792 and 1871: great contests of oratory, unruly audiences and strong voices from the floor, delegates reporting back to their factories or neighborhood branches, all-night meetings, a blizzard of pamphlets and manifestoes, the unceasing work of committees, the organization of flying pickets and worker guards, rumors and battles against rumor, and, of course, the competition between parties and factions.

Despite the legend of their being an ultra-centralized party operating with perfect conspiratorial discipline, the Bolsheviks, with majority support in the big factories and the Baltic fleet, were the most consistent promoters of direct democracy in the larger revolutionary movement of 1917. For example, when liberals and moderate socialists proposed a Democratic State Conference to design a new parliamentary regime, Lenin (fresh from writing *State and Revolution*) urged an all-out mobilization to expand popular participation:

> Let us take it more to those down below, to the masses, to the office employees, to the workers, to the peasants, not only to our supporters, but particularly to those who follow the Socialist-Revolutionaries, to the non-party elements, to the ignorant. Let us lift them up so that they can pass an independent judgment, make their own decisions, send *their own* delegations to the Conference, to the Soviets, to the government and our work will not have been in vain, *no matter what* the outcome of the Conference.[322]

In his celebrated study of the revolutionary process in Petrograd, Alexander Rabinowitch stood the Bolshevik stereotype on its head. Explaining the party's attractiveness to a majority of the city's working class, he pointed to its "internally relatively democratic, tolerant, and decentralized structure and method of operation, as well as its essentially open and mass character ... within the Bolshevik Petrograd organization at all levels in 1917 there was continuing free and lively discussion and debate over the most basic theoretical and tactical issues."[323] Indeed, this was exactly how Preobrazhensky looked back on October when attempting in 1920 to explain the relationship between the recent erosion of party democracy and the "decline of spontaneity" in the proletariat:

> Comparing the party life of late 1917 and 1918 with party-life in 1920, one is struck by the way it has died out precisely among the party-masses ... Previously, rank-and-file Communists felt they were not just implementing party-decisions, but were also originating them, that they themselves were forming the Party's collective will. Now they implement party-decisions taken by committees that often do not bother to submit decisions to general meetings.[324]

Thanks to the world market and mass emigration, the industrial proletariat is objectively constituted as an international class with common interests that cross national and ethnic boundaries.[325] *Great international campaigns, moreover, crystallize the proletariat's understanding of its world-historical vocation.*

Concluding his speech to the inaugural supper of the Fraternal Democrats in London in September 1845, the Chartist George Julian Harney declared: "We repudiate the word 'foreigner'—it shall exist not in our democratic vocabulary!" Engels, who reported on the meeting (he called it "a communist festival") in the *Rheinische Jahrbücher*, noted that Harney's remark was greeted with "great cheers" by the delegates from nine nations. There were also repeated toasts to Tom Paine, Robespierre, and the recently deported Chartists. "The great mass of proletarians," Engels bragged, "are, by their very nature, free from national prejudices and their whole disposition and movement is essentially humanitarian, anti-nationalist."[326] This sounds incredibly naive today, but may have been a reasonably accurate observation on the eve of the "springtime of the peoples."

Indeed, the early workers' movement generally followed the well-worn tracks of revolutionary democracy, celebrating international fraternity in the confident belief that the social revolution would necessarily be a world revolution in the mold of 1789. Conspiratorial revolutionary groups like Blanqui and Barbes's Society of the Seasons were defiantly cosmopolitan in membership, and tramping artisans and migrant workers carried subversive ideas back and forth between major cities and industrial centers. German artisans—the largest pool of labor migrants in the Europe of the Holy Alliance—established radical outposts in Britain, Switzerland, and North America (especially Texas); but the true capital of the first German proletariat in the 1840s was Paris, where some 60,000 German-speaking "undocumented immigrants" toiled in garrets and sweatshops.[327]

In his writings and speeches about the American Civil War and on the founding of the First International, Marx argued that international solidarity is the crucial precipitant of class consciousness, and that the mobilization of labor on a national scale is accelerated by the international organization of its most advanced detachments. But he also warned that no labor movement could ever emancipate itself as long as it participated politically or materially in the oppression of another nation or race. In some of his most fiery articles and speeches, he argued that black freedom was the precondition for an independent American working-class politics, as was Irish freedom for a radical British working class. On the continent the independence of Poland, of course, had long been the touchstone of democratic and then socialist internationalism.

Few events crystallized deeper feelings of international solidarity than the great crusades to save doomed foreign comrades whose "crimes" were simply their revolutionary beliefs. Although there was normally little love lost between the anarchist and socialist wings of the labor movement, three of the most globally famous campaigns aimed to save the lives of anarchists: the Haymarket defendants in 1886–87, the Catalan education reformer Francisco Ferrer in 1909, and the "simple workers" Sacco and Vanzetti in 1926–27. The campaign to save Albert Parsons and his six condemned comrades found a particularly eloquent advocate in Marx's youngest daughter, Eleanor, who visited Chicago in November 1886 while they were awaiting execution. "Why only this morning," she told a huge crowd at the Aurora Turners Hall,

> in the Chicago *Tribune*, you will find the statement that "they hang anarchists in Chicago." That is they are going to hang these men, not as murderers, but as anarchists ... Not we, but our opponents, say it—that seven men are to be done to death not for what they have done, but for what they have said and believed. That cowardly and infamous sentence will *not* be carried out ... Should these men be murdered, we may say of their executioners, what my father said of those who massacred the people of Paris: "They are already nailed to the eternal pillory which all the prayers of their priests will not avail to redeem them."[328]

There is a legend about a certain species of caterpillar that can only cross the threshold of metamorphosis by seeing its future butterfly. Proletarian subjectivity does not evolve by incremental steps but requires non-linear leaps, especially moral self-recognition through solidarity with the struggle of a distant people, even when this contradicts short-term self-interest, as in the famous cases of Lancashire cotton workers' enthusiasm for Lincoln and later for Gandhi. Socialism, in other words, requires non-utilitarian actors, whose ultimate motivations and values arise from structures of feeling that others would deem spiritual. Marx rightly scourged romantic humanism in the abstract, but his personal pantheon—Prometheus and Spartacus, Homer, Cervantes, and Shakespeare—affirmed a heroic vision of human possibility that no longer seems to have any purchase in our fallen world.

The ground condition for the socialist project is the realm of freedom immanent in the advanced industrial economy itself. To achieve the principal goal of socialism—the transformation of surplus labor into equally distributed free time—radical chains must be translated into radical needs.

Revolutions of the poor in backward countries can reach for the stars, but only the proletariat in advanced countries can actually grasp the future. The integration of science into production, compelled both by inter-capitalist competition and working-class militancy, reduces the *necessity* (if not the actuality) of alienated toil. Already in *The Poverty of Philosophy* (1847), Marx had argued that "the organization of revolutionary elements as a class supposes the existence of all the productive forces which could be engendered in the bosom of the old society."[329] A decade later, in the *Grundrisse*, he predicted that, "to the degree that large industry develops, the creation of real wealth comes to depend less on labour-time and on the amount of labor employed" than upon "the general state of science and on the progress of technology, or the application of this science to production." At this point, "the *surplus labour of the mass* has ceased to be the condition for the development of general wealth, just as the *non-labour of the few* has ceased to be the condition for the development of the general powers of the human mind." Then it will be both materially possible and historically necessary for the workers themselves to appropriate their own surplus labor as free time for "the artistic, scientific etc. development of the individuals." "The measure of wealth is then not any longer, in any way, labour time, but rather disposable time."[330]

But such an appropriation can never occur if the goal is framed simply as redistributive justice, income equality, or shared prosperity.[331] These are preconditions for socialism, not its substance. The new world, rather, would define itself by the satisfaction of "radical needs" *generated by the struggle for socialism itself*, and incompatible with the alienation of capitalist society. According to Lebowitz, "They include the need for community, for human relationships, for labor as an end (life's prime want), for universality, for free time and free activity and for the development of personality. They are *qualitative* needs—in contrast to the needs for material products, which decline relatively in a society of associated producers (as the need to 'possess' disappears)."[332] It is not the development of consumption or capitalist "affluence" that creates radical needs for free time and liberated work, but rather the counter-values and dreams embodied in radical mass movements. To take root in daily life, such needs must be prefigured in socialist attitudes toward friendship, sexuality, gender roles, women's suffrage, nationalism, racial and ethnic bigotry, and the care of children. Marx and Engels's well-known aversion to utopian blueprints and futuristic speculations demonstrated their scientific discipline, but was not meant to foreclose the socialist imagination, much less to discourage the profusion of alternative institutions, ranging from labor colleges to consumer cooperatives, from hiking clubs to free psychoanalytic clinics, through which the workers' movement both addressed existing needs and envisioned new ones.[333]

Socialism is economic democracy, exercised at a plurality of levels. But the practicalities of workers' control over their factories and workshops (the goal and praxis of revolutionary syndicalism) must be distinguished from the incomparably greater challenges of national economic planning.

The proletariat clearly has a fundamental interest in the development of the forces of production to the extent that this equals less toil, more free time, and guaranteed economic security. But the great question that roiled the European labor movement in the early twentieth century was whether this could be achieved by free association and cooperation, or, given the scale and complexity of modern production and reproductive investment, it would require the existence of a *centralized economic state*, albeit a bureaucratic apparatus subject to the control of a working-class parliament. In his great defense of the Paris Commune, Marx clearly embraced a vision of direct democracy at every level of the economy: "united co-operative societies are to regulate national production upon a common plan, thus taking it under their own control and putting an end to the constant anarchy and periodical convulsions which are the fatality of Capitalist production."[334] Since workers themselves would participate in making both small- and large-scale decisions about investment, production targets, and work intensity, there would be ample motivation for continued technological innovation, making machines the slaves of men rather than the other way around.[335]

In its 1891 Erfurt Program, however, German Social Democracy tacitly abandoned the Paris Commune model as primitive. In the conception of Karl Kautsky, the chief ideologue of the new orthodoxy, socialism would require the expertise and efficiency of modern administrative structures—that is to say, the bourgeois state apparatus rebuilt to democratic specifications. "Kautsky," writes Massimo Salvadori,

> arrived at conclusions ... singularly analogous to those of Max Weber on the relationship between firm, state and parties. This emerges particularly clearly in his 1893 essay on parliamentarism and direct legislation. Kautsky maintained that any project of "direct democracy" was doomed to failure in a society dominated by large-scale modern industry—that is, by a mode of production whose very essence requires not only central planning and coordination of the economy and the state, but also a bureaucratic apparatus as a professionally selected technical apparatus for its implementation ... When [he] saw the Bolsheviks in practice abandon the model of the Commune and instead establish a super-centralized, bureaucratized state machine, he judged that force of circumstance and "rationality" had prevailed, but in the worst possible form, so to speak.[336]

Certainly, "associated labor" in Russia (1917–18) and Italy (1919–20) did prove that it could run the factories, as did the CNT even more sensationally in Barcelona in 1936–37; but these experiments in workers' control of production, however inspiring, were obviously of a different scale from the democratic planning of economic development on national or international levels. Although the abolition of factory committees and workers' control in early Soviet Russia was a result of civil war, economic devastation, and isolation—circumstances that Lenin openly acknowledged as catastrophic and hoped to reverse with a restoration of soviet (although not workplace) democracy—Kautsky seemingly had the last word on the fate of backward post-capitalist societies, where the growth of productive forces (especially heavy industry) at a rate necessary to guarantee state survival in a permanently hostile international environment required centralized planning, a tightly disciplined management cadre, a draconian code of labor discipline, and massive coercion of the peasantry.

Stalinism deified Marx and Lenin, but its secret gods were really Weber and Taylor, and its high priests after the 1937 decimation of the Party and Army, as Kendall Bailes has shown, were members of the new and rapidly expanding technical intelligentsia, especially engineers and agronomists.[337] The usual stereotype of a plodding, incompetent bureaucracy producing millions of mismatched shoes can hardly explain the miracles of production achieved during the Second World War or the success of the Soviet space program. Conversely, it is difficult in the first iteration to explain how an economy that could put Sputnik in orbit was unable to manufacture a decent toaster or put phones in homes.[338] This paradox, of course, became one of the major subjects of the famous "socialist calculation debate" between the disciples of Ludwig von Mises and advocates of state planning, such as the great Polish economist Oskar Lange. Attempts in the late 1950s and early 1960s to substantially reform the imposed Soviet planning model in Yugoslavia, Poland, and Czechoslovakia through a combination of enterprise autonomy and the "socialist market" had only moderate success.

By the outbreak of the First World War, several advanced economies had achieved the thresholds of industrial productivity and net national income that satisfied the minimal conditions for "socialist affluence" and the gradual conversion of surplus into free time. Furthermore, "state capitalism," as modeled by the American and German war economies of 1918, demonstrated new possibilities for allocating investment and resources through central state planning—a development whose significance was most keenly grasped by Lenin. But the communications and control technologies required for broad democratic participation in economic decision-making did not exist, and would not be created until the end of the twentieth century.

Socialist critics of the Gosplan paradigm, following in the footsteps of the Left Opposition of the 1920s, correctly identified the absence of democracy as the fundamental contradiction in state economic regulation, but seldom pondered the actual prerequisites for participatory planning. Like Marx, they failed to make a clear distinction between the development of the productive forces per se and the creation of counterpart social capacities for democratic coordination and planning. Nor, with few exceptions, did they recognize that the latter requires both sophisticated institutions of workers' control at multiple levels *and* technologies that process massive economic data in real time and present it in formats that allow for broad participation in final decisions about allocation. Although Soviet planners in the 1960s, led by the famed mathematician Leonid Kantorovich, the father of linear programming, pinned hopes on computerization to "overcome the informational overburden of traditional data channels," their "computopias" were undermined by bureaucratic opposition and the lack of computing power to process the 50,000 different variables representing the Soviet economy. Kantorovich and his colleagues, moreover, focused exclusively on the problems of centralized economic management, not decentralizaton and workers' control.[339]

The radical exception was Project Cybersyn, a quasi-utopian collaboration between the Allende government and British theorist Stafford Beer to create a cybernetic management system for nationalized industry that workers would help design and operate. Cybersyn, explains Eden Medina in her splendid history, aimed to solidify "workers' participation in management, not only by putting the workers in charge of the system but also by incorporating worker knowledge in its software." Beer, a wealthy business consultant who evolved into the leading proponent of "cybernetic socialism," viewed Cybersyn as "an instrument of revolution" whose ultimate goal was "dismantling the Chilean bureaucracy." But Chile had too few mainframes (Burroughs and IBM embargoed sales after Allende's election) and Popular Unity had too little time.[340]

Cybersyn, like the Soviet experiments, was probably premature, but thanks to the exponential increase in computing power over the last forty years the requisite informatics for democratic planning now exist in the form of computer information systems, business process re-engineering, managerial dashboards, smart phones, the internet of things, the collaborative commons, and peer production.[341] Global capitalism itself, driven by the requirements of managing international value chains (Walmart) and immense distribution networks (Amazon.com), has subtly transcended the invisible hand in economic calculation. The classical arguments against socialism—Mises' "demonstration" of the irreplaceable role of market pricing in rational allocation and von Hayek's argument that socialist planning models would never achieve the computational power to solve the hundreds of thousands of equations required to keep up with the markets—have lost much of their force. Meanwhile, the observational platforms and scientific paradigms for evaluating the impacts of the economy and its spatial organization upon the carbon cycle—that is to say, an informational infrastructure for sustainable *industrial ecology*—now exist, at least in prototype. There is no longer any insuperable obstacle to unifying economic and ecological parameters—say, job-creating investments and their natural impacts—in dynamic planning models that, in turn, are accessible to public participation. Thanks to Moore's Law, in fact, the forces of production and science are finally ripe for transformation into the kind of decentralized economic democracy envisioned by Marx in *The Civil War in France*.

Labor must *rule because the bourgeoisie is ultimately unable to fulfill the promises of progress. If the socialist project is defeated the result will be the retrogression of civilization as a whole.*

The "Final Crisis" as envisioned by most socialists *did* occur from the Pyrenees to the Urals in 1914–21, at immense human cost, but not in North America, and therefore the European catastrophe was not the *lutte final*. "The last imperialist war," Trotsky told the Third Congress of the Communist International in 1921, "was an event which we rightfully appraised as a colossal blow, unequaled in history, to the equilibrium of the capitalist world. Out of the war has actually risen the epoch of the greatest mass movements and revolutionary battles." Europe was ruined and ruled by hunger, but

we get an entirely different picture when we step into the Western Hemisphere. America has passed through a development of a diametrically opposite character. She has meanwhile enriched herself at a dizzy pace ... Has a new world division of labor been established? Of decisive importance in this sphere is the fact that the center of gravity of capitalist economy and bourgeois power has shifted from Europe to America.[342]

The aftermath of the Second World War, with Europe and the USSR again in ruins, re-confirmed American hegemony on a truly global scale, but almost all Marxist and left-Keynesian economists—Eugen Varga, Fritz Sternberg, Michal Kalecki, Gunnar

Myrdal, Paul Baran, and so on—expected a new depression, or at least a resumption of the prewar business cycle. None of them predicted the long postwar boom, the success of the Marshall Plan and NATO, or, for that matter, the radical uprisings of students and workers in 1968–69 amidst relatively full employment in Europe and North America. But history has come full circle in the early twenty-first century in a world economy that cannot create jobs in pace with population growth, guarantee food security, or adapt human habitats to catastrophic climate change. Barbarism is all around us.

2

Marx's Lost Theory

The Politics of Nationalism in 1848

What do we talk about when we talk about nationalism? Too much, it would seem. One sociologist complains that "the scholarship on ethnicity, race, and nationalism has become unsurveyably vast"; a leading intellectual historian deems it "intolerably protean."[1] In his recent primer, the British sociologist Anthony Smith—who is, amongst other distinctions, the chief bibliographer of nationalism studies—describes an intellectual sprawl rather like Los Angeles: "These debates are diffuse and wide-ranging. They concern not only competing ideologies of nationalism nor even just the clash of particular theories. They involve radical disagreements over definitions of key terms, widely divergent histories of the nation and rival accounts of the 'shape of things to come.'" Amongst the currently warring camps, Smith distinguishes "primordialists," "perennialists," "neo-perennialists," "instrumentalists," and "modernists." (He might have added "constructivists," "neo-Weberians," and "neo-Beardians" as well.) He describes himself meanwhile as an "ethno-symbolist," investigating nationalism as the modernization of pre-existing cultural identities.[2] In the face of so many categorical elisions, conflicting typologies, and incongruent disciplinary perspectives, nationalism studies is seemingly embalmed in what Clifford Geertz called a "stultifying aura of conceptual ambiguity."[3]

Yet until recently most of the voices in this cacophony have shared three core and rarely challenged assumptions. The first is a "methodological nationalism" that equates modern societies with nation-states and the state with the political nation. The second is the autonomy, or even primordiality, of nationalism as a historical force. (Political philosopher Erica Benner has lampooned this belief in a "unique set of national values, cherished by most of a nation's members, which easily takes precedence over other values and interests whenever nationalists say they should.")[4] The third presupposition is that liberal and reactionary nationalisms can be fundamentally distinguished. This dichotomy was given its most influential form by the Czech exile Hans Kohn in his monumental *The Idea of Nationalism* (1944), where he opposed "Western civic" (political) versus "Eastern ethnic" (cultural) nationalisms.[5]

NATIONALISM WITHOUT THE NATION

These cornerstone assumptions, along with the warring paradigms itemized by Smith, came under radical scrutiny from younger sociologists of Bourdieusian and neo-Weberian persuasions during the 1990s: a paradoxical decade defined both by the integration of formerly state-planned economies into the global market and an unexpected wave of extreme nationalism and civil war in what was once called the "Second World." Whereas the previous generation of scholarship in the 1970s and '80s (Gellner, Anderson, Smith, Hobsbawm) had been primarily interested in the conditions and transformations that created modern nation-states, taking for granted their subsequent existences as "static, bounded, homogenous entities," the new generation, confronted with the sudden emergence of catastrophic post-communist nationalisms in a supposedly "globalized" world, has had a greater interest in "the dynamics of relatively rapid changes in degrees of ethnic, racial or national groupness." The Kohnian dichotomy, in particular, began to seem irrelevant. Nationalisms, wrote Rogers Brubaker, are too "normatively and empirically unruly" to be parsed "into types with clearly contrasting empirical and moral profiles," especially when modifiers like "ethnic" are equally abstract. Elsewhere he proposed that "groupness," whether as ethnicity or nation, "is a variable, not a constant; it cannot be presupposed." Therefore it was necessary to "decouple the study of nationhood and nationness from the study of nations as substantial entities, collectivities or communities."[6]

Brubaker, at UCLA, has been one of the prime movers of this revolt against "substantialism." In his seminal 1996 book *Nationalism Reframed*, which surveyed the resurgence of nationalism in the collapsing state systems of the USSR and Yugoslavia, he asked how complex, layered identities could suddenly be nullified by "the terrible categorical simplicity of ascribed nationality." He rejected the "Sleeping Beauty" thesis that the nations federated by Communism were simply waiting for a wake-up kiss from Western democracy. He proposed instead that theorists needed to abandon the search for the Holy Grail of the essential "nation" and concentrate instead on the "processual dynamics of nationalism":

> Reduced to a formula, my argument is that we should focus on nation as a category of practice, nationhood as an institutionalized cultural and political form, and nationness as a contingent event or happening, and refrain from using the analytically dubious notion of "nations" as substantial, enduring collectivities.

Nationalism, moreover, "is not engendered by nations. [In Bourdieu's terminology] it is produced—or better, it is induced—by *political fields* of particular kinds." "Reification," he added, "is a social process, not only an intellectual practice. As such it is central to the phenomenon of nationalism."[7]

Siniša Malešević, a sociologist at University College, Dublin's Centre for War Studies, offered a more pungent judgment. "National identity," he declared, "is a conceptual chimera not worthy of serious analytical pursuit. It is a concept that is theoretically vapid while also lacking clear empirical referents."[8] Malešević's *bête noire* has been the promiscuous use of "identity" as "an umbrella term for anything and everything, a short-cut which evades the rigour of explanation."[9] "Cultural difference framed as ethnic difference is sociologically relevant only when it is active, mobilized and dynamic"—that is to say, politicized.[10] Because ethnicity is a politically edited construct ("not a group but a form of social relationship"), suggesting that the nation is politicized ethnicity is simply a tautology: "More importantly such a view does not clearly distinguish between the near universal and trans-historical processes of politicization of collective difference at work in all ethnic relations, and the historically specific series of events and practices that characterize nation-formation. Nationness is a complete historical and profoundly contingent novelty."[11]

Malešević, echoing Ernst Haas's idea of "a synthetic *Gemeinschaft*," attributes the secret power of nationalism to its ability to reconcile the "warmth" of intimate social worlds with the "coldness" of bureaucratic society: "In other words, nationalist ideology attempts to bridge the ongoing division between the 'state' part and the 'nation' part of the nation-state by depicting the nation as a community of close friends or a giant extended family."[12] He is emphatic, however, that this fusion of domestic emotion and abstract belief is *not* the "religious structure of collective action" presumed by Anthony Smith and Régis Debray.[13] "Although nationalism often does exhibit a quasi-religious appeal, builds on deified rituals, borrows from spiritual language and imagery, and is likely to portray nations as semi-divine entities, this does not explain the large part of the story of its relations between the social and the sacred." Claiming that Smith's ideas are "still chained to the Durkheimian legacy," Malešević reminds us that Durkheim trapped himself in the vicious circle of explaining the sacred by the social and the social by the sacred. "Do religion and nationalism, as a form of political religion, 'express the pre-given solidarity of the group, or bring it about?' Neo-Durkheimians cannot have it both ways." Malešević also criticizes Smith for putting too much emphasis on normative integration while downgrading the role of social conflict: in the last instance, "what is essential for any sudden and intensive display of group membership is precisely the contest of potential or actual social conflict."[14]

Although Brubaker and Malešević are committed to the renewal of classical sociology, especially the formidable legacy of constructivist Number One, Max Weber, their work also opens the door to political economy and invites a creative response from radical historians. By steering the debate away from "national substance" or "ethnic core," they direct attention to the actual wages of nationalism, the interests aggregated and served by manufactured national identities. Their disciplinary focus is on the *physics* of social interaction and conflict, starting with the intimate solidarities— families, churches, platoons, football clubs, and so on—from which imagined national communities derive their emotional charge.[15]

The political *chemistry*, however, of transmuting sectoral into national interests—or creating national interests to reconcile competing sectional interests—and the changing configuration of these

159

interests over time, must be addressed from another direction; and preferably from a theoretical viewpoint that is able to engage with the hoary problem of how the socioeconomic macrostructure (relations of production, class divisions, forms of property), as well as entrenched internal systems of racial, ethnic, or religious oppression, influence or even generate nationalist doctrines. Such a theory, historically explicated, cannot make categorical partitions but must locate nationalism in the broader political field. As useful as it might be for simplifying analysis, there is no Chinese Wall between the political history of nationalism and the economic and social histories of the nation-state.

MARX CONTRA MARX

Erica Benner, another participant in the 1990s debates, claims that the skeleton of such a theory can be found hidden in a surprising closet. She has long urged nationalism theorists to take a fresh look at the writings of Marx. Her Oxford doctoral thesis, published in 1995 as *Really Existing Nationalisms: A Post-Communist View from Marx and Engels*, was an invaluable, if sometimes overlooked, contribution to the critique of nationalism theory during the 1990s. Like others she wanted to travel beyond the endless debate between partisans of Anthony Smith and those of Ernest Gellner over "whether nations (not nationalisms) are perennial entities or the novel—and hence probably transient—creations of modernity."[16] By returning to Marx, however, she was rowing against a strong contemporary current of post-Marxist thought that had revived Franz Borkenau's old canard that "nationalism is the fact against which Marxist theory breaks itself."[17] Tom Nairn thus wrote in 1975 that "the theory of nationalism represents Marxism's great historical failure"; while

Ernesto Laclau agreed and pointed to Marx's refusal to recognize "the specificity and irreducibility of national identities."[18] Régis Debray was characteristically hyperbolic: Marxists had simply failed to understand the laws governing the "cultural organization of the human collectivity." "The nation is like the atomic nucleus in a general conflagration of Marxism as theory and socialism as practice." "Like language," he claimed, "the nation is an invariable which cuts across modes of production." He also charged that Marx had no theory of politics.[19]

But Benner, who has become a well-known authority on Machiavelli,[20] found Marx (and Engels to a significantly lesser extent) all the more interesting because they stressed "the limited autonomy of nationalism" while emphasizing "the role played by transnational processes in activating modern 'national' consciousness and nation-building efforts." Too many exegetes, she claimed, "had a tendency to reconstruct Marx and Engels's views on national issues from their most abstract statements of theory, while overlooking the concrete strategies they recommended in specific political contexts." Or, to put it more strongly, they failed to recognize the elements of "a *strategic theory of politics* centred on, but not reduced to, the analysis of class conflicts." "Marx and Engels," she explained, "continue to treat class as the basic unit of analysis and framework for collective action. But the relations between class and nationalist aims, class and national 'consciousness', appear as far more complex and variable than the standard class-reductionist account allows." As for the post-Marxists, "many of their most cutting criticisms are grounded in flawed assumptions about what constitutes an adequate account of nationalism." In part this was simply historical naiveté. After the fall of the Wall, "it seemed reasonable to think that all post-communist nationalism must be democratic and westward-looking. This easy assumption was confounded after the upheavals of 1989, just as the events of 1848 upset the Mazzinian equation between nationality and republican brotherhood."[21]

Benner may occasionally find more meaning in a passage from Marx than another reader might, but her reconstruction of his ideas is a *tour de force*. Although a considerable literature has long sparred over Marx and Engels's views on colonialism, so-called "nations without histories," and the right to self-determination, she's the first to place their ideas about nationalism squarely in the context of a materialist theory of politics.[22] Benner's interpretation, along with my interpolations, are best framed in the paradoxical context of Marx and Engels's most extended analyses of class politics and nationalism: their celebrated yet still in many respects unknown articles, commentaries, and pamphlets on the revolutions of 1848. In the *Neue Rheinische Zeitung*, the Cologne paper founded by the Communist League, Marx and Engels comprehensively chronicled the progress of the insurrections in Paris, Berlin, Vienna, and Budapest, and championed German unification from "the bottom up" by a broad coalition of democratic forces. In a striking formulation that would resurface in later polemics on Ireland and Afro-Americans,[23] Engels proposed that "the creation of a democratic Poland is the first condition for the creation of a democratic Germany." He and Marx agreed that war with Russia, in alliance with revolutionary France and with Poland's emancipation as a principal goal, was the only path that could bring democratic nationalism to power in Central Europe.[24]

In London exile from August 1849, Marx turned his attention to the fate of the February Revolution in France; indeed, he wrote its obituary. *The Class Struggles in France, 1848–50* and its sequel, *The Eighteenth Brumaire of Louis Bonaparte*, are best read as a single text: the failure to appreciate the former has often led to distorted interpretations of the latter. (In addition, one should also read the "Review: May–October 1850," published in the exiled *Neue Rheinische Zeitung Revue*, where Marx boldly sketched the global geopolitical and economic coordinates of the earthquake in Europe.) The French pieces defy simple classification as theory, journalism, or instant history, and perhaps are best understood as an original genre of political writing in which theoretical concepts are developed and applied, but not abstractly formalized, in the course of trying to think and enact socialist politics. Marx, moreover, uses a terminology—"class fractions," "coteries," "conjugation of factions," "lumpen proletariat," and so on—that can be construed as an incipient political sociology of the middle landscape between the relations of production and the collision of politically organized economic interests. Indeed, Terrell Carver argues that "Marx's colourful, extravagant, untidy and apparently atheoretical vocabulary is actually political theory at its best."[25]

Translated into theoretical propositions, Marx makes important claims in the French writings that hardly jibe with the post-Marxist stereotypes of "class *versus* nation" or the invariable causal primacy of the relations of production.

- The revolutions developed simultaneously in the triadic spaces of the nation (existing or aspirant nation-state), the world market and the European state system (the Holy Alliance). Marx was particularly interested in the interconnections of these spaces: for example, how the dramatic thrust of capitalism into East Asia and the Pacific—the opium trade, the Dutch conquest of Java, and the Australian and Californian gold rushes—affected the climate of insurrection in Europe; or how the continental revolutions might radicalize Chartism in Britain.

- In the *Manifesto*, Marx and Engels wrote that "working men have no country [*Vaterland*]," but immediately added that the proletariat is "itself national" to the extent that it "must rise to be the leading class of the nation, must constitute itself as the nation" in order to achieve "political supremacy." This opaque formulation was clarified later in Cologne and London, with Marx arguing that a defensive war against the Holy Alliance was the necessary mode through which proletarians in France and revolutionary democrats in Germany could hope to win that "supremacy" en bloc with the peasants and middle classes.

- Initially the 1848 revolutions were an archipelago of exclusively urban uprisings. Marx stressed that the next step forward must be a democratic alliance with the peasantry. The countryside would either ensure the triumph of the revolutionary-democratic insurrection or be its gravedigger. Such an alliance must be built on the terrain of revolutionary nationalism and against foreign intervention. Far from denouncing nationalism, socialists should organize national defense.

- Under certain conditions of stalemated or immature class struggle, the state apparatus can become an "executive committee of itself," capable of wielding power in its own kleptocratic interest.

- The economic content of politics/nationalism—except in periods of crisis or in the most advanced nations—usually derives from "secondary forms of exploitation" or clashes between different categories of property. Marx, in fact, would spend much of the 1850s trying to understand the autonomous politics of money and credit which played such a large role in the events in France and elsewhere.

CLASSES AND NATIONALISM

In prose suffused with razor-sharp irony and "almost Rabelaisian verve," Marx proposed a remarkable if imperfect analysis of the differential capacities of French social classes to act strategically on a national level and through a discourse of national interest.[26] The events in France in 1848 were a battle between labour and capital only in a premonitory sense: the June insurrection in the name of the Social Republic was a bolt of lightning announcing a new historical era, but no more than that. The French economy, still largely agricultural, was in transition between modes of production and forms of exploitation. If the Industrial Revolution had created islands of modern production in some cities and regions, the factory working class and its bosses were not yet social classes consciously organized on a national scale. Socialism in many flavours, to be sure, was stronger in Paris than anywhere else in the world: in 1851, for example, there were almost 200 "socialist-inspired workers' associations" in the city. The left, however, was rooted in a cosmopolitan but pre-industrial culture of artisanal labor that formed a Jacobin continuum with the democratic-republican petty bourgeoisie.[27] The largest tendency, the followers of Proudhon, were anti-authoritarian associationalists and federalists for whom *pays*—the home ground, town, or region—was the authentic *patrie*.

Nationalism, in Marx's view, was in the first place the opium of the two amorphous social worlds or "quasi-classes" that comprised a majority of the French population: the urban artisans, shopkeepers, and small merchants on one side, and rural smallholders on the other. As Zola would later chronicle in extraordinary detail in his twenty Rougon-Macquart novels, these groups had the most to lose from the modernization of French society and the resulting polarization between a factory proletariat and big capital. For small property owners and independent producers, the "nation" in 1848 represented a magical abolition of class struggle and an imaginary equilibrium of social forces. The city and countryside adhered to different if partially overlapping versions of popular nationalism and historical memory. The urban petty bourgeois, still loyal to 1792–94, embraced a largely democratic nationalism, while much of the countryside yearned for the Empire and the Napoleonic glory that mantled their fathers and grandfathers. In the Constituent National Assembly, after the June massacre of the socialists, a republican majority led by Ledru-Rollin waved the tricolor in the name of the nation, but in Marx's opinion they were not a genuine political party but rather a fractious "clique of republican-minded bourgeois, writers, lawyers, officers and officials that owed its influence to the personal antipathies of the country against Louis Philippe, to memories of the old republic, to the republican faith of a number of enthusiasts, above all, however, to *French nationalism*, whose hatred of the Vienna treaties and of the alliance with England it always kept awake."[28]

Meanwhile, in the smallholder countryside the sons and grandsons of Napoleon's "Immortals" were crushed by debt and taxes from one direction, while from the other, partible inheritance was slowly but relentlessly reducing farm size—a situation that varied by *département* but in the aggregate was progressively pauperizing the countryside and turning the peasants into "troglodytes." Marx estimated that "the mortgage debt burdening the soil of France imposes on the French peasantry payment of an amount of interest equal to the annual interest on the entire British national debt." Rapid disillusionment with the Republic, which had immediately hiked taxes on the countryside, only increased nostalgia for the Empire, which peasants equated with land and unmortgaged tenure as well as national glory. For Marx, Solomon Bloom observed, "Every class had the tendency to picture the nation, and sometimes the whole species, in its own image. It then proceeded to worship that image. For each class there was a different 'fatherland.'" In the case of the peasantry, "the uniform was their own state dress; war was their poetry; the small-holding, extended and rounded off in their imagination, was their fatherland, and patriotism was the ideal form of their sense of property."[29] The intense localism of the French countryside, so famously described by Eugen Weber, may have made national identification with big cities and distant regions difficult until the very late nineteenth century, but the memory of "empire" was the cow in the field.

But neither the debt-ridden urban petty bourgeoisie nor the tax-burdened rural smallholders necessarily acted in a purely reflexive or predetermined manner; rather, they were oriented toward the organized class or party that best addressed their economic survival. "Marx—though not always Engels," writes Benner, "denied that the members of quasi-classes were congenitally xenophobic or prone to the manipulative ruses of 'false consciousness'. Their support for specific nationalist policies was seen as conditional, not wholly irrational; and the decisive conditions involved concrete interests in security and material well-being."[30] Marx suggests that the popular logic of nationalism depends upon a calculus of sacrifice and gain: the promise not just of heaven and glory, but also of lifting the yoke of oppression or, even better, a favorable redistribution of someone else's property. Only the conservative peasantry, in other words, was necessarily a "sack of potatoes." Marx clearly views class formation as an ultimately contingent process, conditioned by the level of economic development and the capacity of class-political actors to legitimate themselves as representatives of the nation. "National ideology," Benner emphasizes, "appears in this context not as a fixed or monolithic mechanism of a single class's ascendancy, but as a key doctrinal arena in struggles for political power."[31]

Much of the *Eighteenth Brumaire*, in fact, is a hypercritical balance-sheet of the strategic decisions made by the principal actors, with Marx making clear distinctions between class positions, negotiated group interests, and the political representation of those interests.[32] In the Second Republic, parties in the modern sense were at most embryonic, and no social class possessed the unity or political technology to impose a single rhetoric of nationalism upon the others. The Paris proletariat, defeated in a premature uprising in June 1848 and unorganized nationally, was pushed off the stage early on, while the nebulous broad bourgeoisie was unable to organize as a hegemonic class once the barricades were dismantled and the socialists were summarily executed or transported to Algeria. (As Marx pointed out earlier in *The German Ideology*, "the separate individuals form a class only insofar as they have to carry on a common battle against another class; in other respects they are on hostile terms with each other as competitors.")[33]

After a complicated choreography of alliances and conspiracies, Napoleon's quondam nephew Louis Bonaparte was elected president by a rural majority, while the traditionally divided *haute bourgeoisie*—that is to say, the large landowners (Legitimists) and the speculator-financiers (Orléanists)—precariously united in the Party of Order. They proceeded to dismantle the gains of the February Revolution piece by piece, including universal suffrage, and with Bonaparte sent an expedition to overthrow Garibaldi's brave republic in Rome. The republican opposition, the "Mountain," made a tepid attempt at insurrection on June 13, 1849 that was easily dispersed. But the Party of Order's successful offensive against democracy simultaneously undermined the legitimacy of the National Assembly and strengthened Bonaparte's demagogic claims to represent the nation rather than classes. In an extraordinary denouement, the "extra-parliamentary bourgeoisie"—seeing political turbulence as the cause of the ongoing commercial depression—repudiated its own political and literary representatives and acquiesced in Bonaparte's coup d'état and plebiscite. He punctually swept the Second Republic into the gutter.[34]

What has always surprised, even scandalized his readers is the scope that Marx gave to that heirloom of absolutism, the French state, as an "independent power." When the conflicts within the Second Republic fail to bring any class or alliance of classes to power with the capacity to stabilize parliamentary rule, the crisis is resolved by a plebiscitary dictatorship. The *Eighteenth Brumaire* ends with the bizarre victory of state over society, clique over class, and nationalism (in atavistic form) over democracy.[35] If the Second Empire had quickly collapsed (Marx's original expectation), it could easily have been dismissed as an aberration; but the regime's generation-long lifespan and Napoleon III's predominance over continental politics gave the formulations in the *Eighteenth Brumaire* an importance beyond what Marx had initially intended. Thus "Bonapartism," as an authoritarian state-form to which the bourgeoisie prudentially abdicates power, would episodically re-emerge as a category of classical socialist analysis, notably in Engels's description of the Bismarckian Reich, Lenin's characterization of the Kerensky regime, Thalheimer's theory of fascism, and Trotsky's autopsy of the Hindenberg–von Papen government that preceded Hitler.[36]

Marx himself returned to this terrain one more time, in articles on the Crédit Mobilier published in Dana's *New York Tribune* in June and July 1856 and May 1857. Thanks to an enormous but highly original exegesis by Sergio Bologna in 1973, these otherwise forgotten texts became seminal to Italian autonomist Marxism's analysis of inflation and monetary policy during the crisis years of the 1970s.[37] The Crédit Mobilier was a limited-liability investment bank-cum-holding company organized by the Péreire brothers, former apostles of Saint-Simon, to "mobilize" capital for industry and public works, including Haussmann's rebuilding of Paris. By only investing in joint-stock companies, the Crédit stimulated the combination and reorganization of French industry. Marx denounced it as a vast speculative swindle, reminiscent of Law's South Sea Bubble, whose collapse would soon bring down the regime: "the ruling principle of the Crédit Mobilier, the representative of the present mania, is not to speculate in a given line, but to speculate in speculation and to universalize swindling at the same rate that it centralizes it."[38] Yet he also acknowledged that it had "revealed the productive powers of association, not suspected before, and called into life industrial creations, on a scale unattainable by the efforts of individual capitalists."[39] In the event, "Napoleonic socialism" was more robust than Marx suspected. The Crédit Mobilier–induced construction boom and capital-investment mania allowed the Second Empire to ride out the Depression of 1857 comfortably.

For whatever reason—perhaps his visceral loathing for Little Bonaparte—Marx never expanded upon his analysis of "Napoleonic socialism," nor did he write more chapters of what might have been, if not the *Capital*, then perhaps the *Grundrisse* of materialist political theory. His occasional short articles or letters on the French home scene (usually ending with hopeful observations like "Bonaparte appears to me shakier than ever") provide barely a glimpse of the Second Empire's staggering culture of speculation and spectacle: the *grands projets*, including the rebuilding of Paris and digging of the Suez Canal; the minting of a "Latin race" and an accompanying sphere of influence for the purposes of French foreign policy.[40] The cornerstone of the regime's identity, moreover, was the *fête* Saint-Napoléon established in 1852. It was the largest annual patriotic event or nationalist carnival staged during the nineteenth century, mobilizing colossal crowds in Paris to bask in "a common sentiment of national glory."[41] If Marx overestimated Bonaparte's military power, he greatly underestimated the perverse dynamism of the Empire, as well as the continuing preeminence of France (resumed in the Third Republic) in generating templates for modern nationalism.

But he did not underestimate nationalism per se. The major political lesson of the French writings is seldom recalled. Without the slightest ambiguity, Marx argued, *contra* the post-Marxist stereotype, that martial nationalism was an essential fuel for social revolution, as well as a precondition for socialist leadership of the peasantry and the lower middle classes. He and Engels had already made this argument in the case of Germany, and it was resumed in *The Class Struggles in France*, where he contrasted 1848 to 1792, regretting the absence of foreign interventions and "a national enemy to face":

> Consequently, there were no great foreign complications which could fire the energies, hasten the revolutionary process, drive the Provisional Government forward or throw it overboard. The Paris proletariat, which looked upon the republic as its own creation, naturally acclaimed each act of the Provisional Government which facilitated the firm emplacement of the latter in bourgeois society … The republic [Marx is writing about the earliest period of the Revolution] encountered no resistance abroad or at home. This disarmed it. Its task was no longer the revolutionary transformation of the world, but consisted only in adapting itself to the relations of bourgeois society.[42]

Marx, of course, was not advocating proletarian nationalism per se but rather socialist assumption of leadership in national defense, with the goal of accelerating revolutionary change both internally and in neighboring countries. This was not a one-off position. For similar reasons Marx and Engels urged German comrades in 1870 to give support to the Prussian-led alliance against Napoleon III, although only as long as it remained a war of national self-defense. Marx believed that "the French need a thrashing." A German victory, he argued to Engels, would

> transfer the centre of gravity of the workers' movement in Western Europe from France to Germany, and one has only to compare the movements in the two countries since 1866 to see that the German working class is superior to the French both in theory and in organization. Its predominance over the French on the world stage would also mean the predominance of *our* theory over Proudhon's, etc.[43]

Engels, who in 1849 had predicted that "the next world war will not only cause reactionary classes and dynasties to disappear from the face of the earth, but also entire reactionary peoples" ("Slav barbarians" in particular), returned to this theme in 1891 in an extraordinary letter to August Bebel. War with Russia seemed imminent:

> This much is, I believe, certain—if we are beaten, chauvinism and retaliatory warfare will flourish unchecked in Europe for years to come. If we are victorious, our party will take the helm. *The victory of Germany, therefore, will be the victory of the revolution and, if war comes, we must not only desire that victory but promote it with all available means.*[44]

Not surprisingly, the right wing of the SPD invoked the authority of Engels and the specter of a Russian invasion when it voted for war credits in the Reichstag on August 4, 1914.

CALCULATING INTERESTS

If the nation and nationalism therefore are not quite the aporias in Marx's work that the post-Marxists depict, what of the charge by Debray and others that Marx had a simplistic, class-determinist concept of politics?[45] Since the days when Thatcherism and Reaganism supposedly proved themselves impenetrable to conventional Marxist analysis, the claim has commonly been made that "class politics" is a figment of discursive practice and political rhetoric, rather than organized economic power. But politics-as-discourse is itself a variety of reductionism that repudiates not only the economic macrostructure but also political institutions, their embedded interests, and modes of conflict. Suffrage, constitutions, and legislatures, on the other hand, all figured prominently in Marx's analyses of the 1848 revolutions. Perhaps the best de facto formalization of Marx's inchoate conception of politics is found in Ronald Aminzade's 1993 *Ballots and Barricades*, a study of voting reform and working-class identity in three industrializing French cities during the mid-nineteenth century. It is a remarkable exploration of how artisans and workers construed "Republicanism" and socialism from the standpoint of their daily struggles. Aminzade makes no explicit references to *Class Struggles in France* or the *Eighteenth Brumaire*, but his characterization of the relationship between class position, organization, and ideology is exemplary, and congruent with Benner's interpretation of Marx:

> The translation of class interests, based on one's position as a landowner, shopkeeper, worker, or capitalist, into subjective political dispositions and collective political action depends on a political process in which institutions, such as political parties, and ideologies, like republicanism, play a key role. These institutions and

173

ideologies are not independent of material conditions and class forces, nor are they capable of simply creating interests out of discourses, unconstrained by material realities. Structural positions within production (i.e. class positions) define a constellation of interests that can serve as a potential basis for collective political action. Such action depends on the building of political organizations and creation of identities that are not simple reflections of objective positions in a political arena, with rules that constitute opportunities and constraints and with multiple possible enemies and allies. This means that class factors alone never fully determine just how such interests will be defined in political programmes and coalitions, or how politically salient class-based interests (rather than non-class interests rooted in racial, ethnic or gender stratification) will become ... Recognition of the institutional and cultural determinants of political behaviour need not lead to an assertion of the autonomy of politics [read: nationalism] or to an abandonment of class analysis. One can reject a class-reductionist understanding of politics yet still acknowledge the centrality of class relations in shaping political behaviour.[46]

This admirable formulation, however, begs a more complete definition of "class-based interests." As all careful readers of *Capital* know, class struggle or competition takes many forms. Wage-earners and capitalists, for example, battle for control over the pace and organization of the production process ("real subsumption"), over the price of labor-power, and over the social reproduction of labor. Workers as individuals or collectivities compete with one another for jobs and apprenticeships. Firms in the same product-lines likewise compete for the "super-profits" made possible by increased productivity from new technologies and divisions of labor. Home-market producers favor tariff protection, while exporters seek free trade or at least reciprocity; but manufacturers in general, whether or not they demand tariffs for their own products, support global free trade in grain so as to reduce the subsistence cost of their workers. Meanwhile, the productive economy as a whole (which includes necessary commercial and financial services) confronts those who draw income from ownership of land and other natural assets. Other rent-seekers attempt to mint monopolies and acquire privileges through manipulation of the state. Financial capital, variably constituted, leases money to both the private economy and the state, while often taking ownership positions of its own.

The earlier French writings, it might be argued, prefigured the concrete categories of analysis that were the ultimate destination of Marx's critique of political economy. He characterized contemporary France as crony capitalism dominated by two largely unproductive fractions of capital: Legitimist landowners and Orléanist financiers and speculators. These rentiers in control of the state relentlessly exploited the petty bourgeoisie and small farmers through mortgages, debt, and taxes. This recognition of the multivariate nature of class conflict is a key innovation in *The Class Struggles in France*. What drove the political conflict forward after the June massacres of the proletariat, according to Marx, was "the struggle against *capital's secondary modes of exploitation*, that of the peasant against usury and mortgages or of the petty bourgeois against the wholesale dealer, banker and manufacturer." "The July monarchy," Marx adds, "was nothing but a joint-stock company for the exploitation of France's national wealth ... It was not the French bourgeoisie that ruled under Louis Philippe, but one fraction of it: bankers, stock-exchange kings, owners of coal and iron mines and forests, a part of the landed proprietors associated with them—the so-called finance aristocracy."[47]

This vampirish cartel, which contributed little or nothing to production, controlled the nation's credit and, to a great extent, government spending and taxes; it encouraged the expansion of the national debt—often on railroad projects and the like, in which it was the principal investor—and then financed the debt (which it owned) with punitive taxes on small producers. The exploitation of peasants, Marx maintained, "differs only in *form* from the exploitation of the industrial proletariat. The exploiter is the same: *capital*. The individual capitalists exploit the individual peasants through *mortgages* and *usury*; the capitalist class exploits the peasant class through the *state taxes*." The chief task of the February Republic, he argued, should have been to abolish the national debt and the financiers with it; but instead the National Assembly became their collection agency, hiking taxes on the peasants and allowing the urban trading class to sink into bankruptcy. The Party of Order's repression of the radical petty bourgeoisie in June 1849, Marx writes, "was not a bloody tragedy between wage labour and capital, but a prison-filling and lamentable play of debtors and creditors." For its part, the taxed-to-death countryside dreamt of a second Empire:

> Napoleon was to the peasants not a person but a programme. With banners, with beat of drums and blare of trumpets, they marched to the polling booths shouting: *Ne plus d'impôts, à bas les riches, à bas la République, vive l'Empereur!* Behind the Emperor was hidden the peasant war. The republic that they voted down was the *republic of the rich*.

Likewise, "to the petty bourgeoisie, Napoleon meant the rule of the debtor over the creditor."[48]

Here an interesting comparison can be made to James Madison's ideas in his famous "Federalist Paper Number 10" (1787)—the inspiration, according to Charles Beard, for his own *Economic Interpretation of the Constitution* (1913).[49] Madison argued against Montesquieu that a large, even continental republic would better contain factional conflict than the small, participatory state demanded by classical republican theory. The very multiplication of interest groups under the proposed Constitution, Madison claimed, would reduce the likelihood of destructive conflicts, encourage coalition-building, and favor bargain-making in a national legislature. But Madison, unembarrassed about the economic facts of life, believed factional struggle was otherwise irrepressible because it arose from the very nature of wealth-accumulation in a liberal economy. There were three major axes of conflict:

> The most common and durable source of factions has been the various and unequal distribution of property. Those who hold, and those who are without property, have ever formed distinct interests in society. Those who are creditors, and those who are debtors, fall under a like discrimination. A landed interest, a manufacturing interest, a mercantile interest, a moneyed interest, with many lesser interests, grow up of necessity in civilized nations, and divide them into different classes, actuated by different sentiments and views. The regulation of these various and interfering interests forms the principal task of modern Legislation, and involves the spirit of party and faction in the necessary and ordinary operations of the Government.[50]

Marx never attempted a formal taxonomy of economic conflict, but the appropriate categories stare out at us from the pages of the *Collected Works*. If, according to Aminzade, fundamental class positions "define a constellation of interests that can serve as a potential basis for collective political action," then we must make conceptual room for those "positions"—the Madisonian or Beardian categories—that derive from Marx's "secondary modes of exploitation." As Bob Jessop pointed out in his astute reading of the *Eighteenth Brumaire*, "the social content of politics is related mainly to the economic interests of the contending classes and class fractions in specific conjunctures and/or periods, in a particular social formation, rather than to abstract interests identified at the level of a mode of production."[51] Marx's "middle level" concepts—so crucial to his analysis of the February Revolution—were largely lost in the subsequent development of his inheritance, although Gramsci arguably retrieved important ideas about proletarian national leadership en bloc with the peasants and petty bourgeoisie. Otherwise it is necessary to suggest that the principal problem with most Marxist analyses of nationalism—or, for that matter, of politics in general—has *not* been a refusal to acknowledge the autonomy of the discursive, the cultural, or the ethnic, but rather the failure to map comprehensively the entire field of property relations and their derivative conflicts. Although it is heresy to say so, we need *more* economic interpretation, not less.

3

The Coming Desert

Kropotkin, Mars, and the Pulse of Asia

Anthropogenic climate change is usually portrayed as a recent discovery, with a genealogy that extends no further backwards than Charles Keeling sampling atmospheric gases from his station near the summit of Mauna Loa in the 1960s, or, at the very most, Svante Arrhenius's legendary 1896 paper on carbon emissions and the planetary greenhouse. In fact, the deleterious climatic consequences of economic growth, especially the influence of deforestation and plantation agriculture on atmospheric moisture levels, were widely noted, and often exaggerated, from the Enlightenment until the late nineteenth century. The irony of Victorian science, however, was that while human influence on climate, whether as a result of land clearance or industrial pollution, was widely acknowledged, and sometimes envisioned as an approaching doomsday for the big cities (see John Ruskin's hallucinatory rant, "The Storm Cloud of the Nineteenth Century"), few if any major thinkers discerned a pattern of *natural* climate variability in ancient or modern history. The Lyellian world view, canonized by Darwin in *The Origin of Species*, supplanted biblical catastrophism with a vision of slow geological and environmental evolution through deep time. Despite the discovery of the Ice Age(s) by the Swiss geologist Louis Agassiz in the late 1830s, the contemporary scientific bias was against environmental perturbations, whether periodic or progressive, on historical time-scales. Climate change, like evolution, was measured in eons, not centuries.

Oddly, it required the "discovery" of a supposed dying civilization on Mars to finally ignite interest in the idea, first proposed by the anarchist geographer Kropotkin in the late 1870s, that the 14,000 years since the Glacial Maximum constituted an epoch of ongoing and catastrophic desiccation of the continental interiors. This theory—we might call it the "old climatic interpretation of history"—was highly influential in the early twentieth century, but waned quickly with the advent of dynamic meteorology in the 1940s, with its emphasis on self-adjusting physical equilibria.[1] What many fervently believed to be a key to world history was found and then lost, discrediting its discoverers almost as completely as the eminent astronomers who had seen (and in some cases, claimed to have photographed) canals on the Red Planet. Although the controversy primarily involved German- and English-speaking geographers and orientalists, the original thesis—postglacial aridification as the driver of Eurasian history—was formulated inside Tsardom's *école des hautes études*: St Petersburg's notorious Peter-and-Paul Fortress, where the young Prince Piotr Kropotkin, along with other celebrated Russian intellectuals, was held as a political prisoner.

EXPLORATION OF SIBERIA

The famed anarchist was also a first-rate natural scientist, physical geographer, and explorer. In 1862, he voluntarily exiled himself to eastern Siberia for five years in order to escape the suffocating life of a courtier in an increasingly reactionary court. Offered a commission by Alexander II in the regiment of his choice, he opted for a newly formed Cossack unit in remote Transbaikalia, where his education, pluck, and endurance quickly recommended him to lead a series of expeditions—for the purposes of both science and imperial espionage—into a huge, unexplored tangle of mountain and *taiga* wildernesses recently annexed by the Empire. Whether measured by physical challenge or scientific achievement, Kropotkin's explorations of the lower Amur valley and into the heart of Manchuria, followed by a singularly daring reconnaissance of the "vast and deserted mountain region between the Lena in northern Siberia and the higher reaches of the Amur near Chita,"were comparable to the Great Northern Expeditions of Vitus Bering in the eighteenth century or the contemporary explorations of the Colorado Plateau by John Wesley Powell and Clarence King.[2] After thousands of miles of travel, usually in extreme terrain, Kropotkin was able to show that the orography of northeast Asia was considerably different from that envisioned by Alexander von Humboldt and his followers.[3] Moreover, he was the first to demonstrate that the plateau was a "basic and independent type of the Earth's relief" with as wide "a distribution as mountain ranges."[4]

Kropotkin also encountered a riddle in Siberia that he later tried to solve in Scandinavia. While on his epic trek across the mountainous terrain between the Lena and the upper Amur, his zoologist, comrade Poliakov, discovered "palaeolithic remains in the dried beds of shrunken lakes, and other similar observations [which] gave evidence on the desiccation of Asia." This accorded with the observations of other explorers in Central Asia—especially the Caspian steppe and Tarim basin—of ruined cities in deserts and arid basins that had once been great lakes.[5] After his return from Siberia, Kropotkin took an assignment from the Russian Geographical

Society to survey the glacial moraines and lakes of Sweden and Finland. Agassiz's ice-age theories were under intense debate in Russian scientific circles, but the physics of ice was little understood. From detailed studies of striated rock surfaces, Kropotkin deduced that the sheer mass of continental ice sheets caused them to flow plastically, almost like a super-viscous fluid—his "most important scientific achievement," according to one historian of science.[6] He also became convinced that Eurasian ice sheets had extended southward into the steppe as far as the 50th parallel. If this was indeed the case, it followed that, with the recession of the ice, the northern steppe became a vast mosaic of lakes and marshes (he envisioned much of Eurasia once looking like the Pripet Marshes), then gradually dried into grasslands, and finally began to turn into desert. Desiccation was a continuing process (*causing*, not caused by, the diminishing rainfall) that Kropotkin believed was observable across the entire Northern Hemisphere.[7]

An outline of this bold theory was first presented to a meeting of the Geographical Society in March 1874. Shortly after the talk, Kropotkin was arrested by the dreaded Third Section and charged with being "Borodin," a member of an underground antitsarist group, the Circle of Tchaikovsky. Thanks to this "chance leisure bestowed on me," and special permission given by the Tsar (Kropotkin, after all, was still a prince), he was enabled to obtain books and continue his scientific writing in prison, where he completed most of a planned two-volume exposition of his glacial and climatic theories.[8]

This was the first scientific attempt to make a comprehensive case for *natural* climate change as a prime mover of the history of civilization.[9] As noted earlier, Enlightenment and early Victorian thought universally assumed that climate was historically stable, stationary in trend, with extreme events as simple outliers of a mean state. In contrast, the impact of human modification of the landscape upon the atmospheric water cycle had been debated since the Greeks. For instance, Theophrastus, Aristotle's heir at the Lyceum, reportedly believed that the drainage of a lake near Larisa in Thessaly had reduced forest growth and made the climate colder.[10] Two thousand years later, the Comtes de Buffon and de Volney, Thomas Jefferson, Alexander von Humboldt, Jean-Baptiste Boussingault, and Henri Becquerel (to give just a short list) were citing one example after another of how European colonialism was radically changing local climates through forest clearance and extensive agriculture.[11] ("Buffon," wrote Clarence Glacken, "concluded it was possible for man to regulate or to change the climate radically.")[12] Lacking any long-term climate records that might reveal major natural variations in weather patterns, the *philosophes* were instead riveted by the innumerable circumstantial reports of declining rainfall in the wake of plantation agriculture on island colonies. In the same vein, Auguste Blanqui's older brother, the political economist Jérôme-Adolphe Blanqui, later cited Malta as an example of a man-made island desert, and warned that the heavily logged foothills of the French Alps risked becoming an arid "Arabia Petraea."[13] By the 1840s, according to Michael Williams, "deforestation and consequent aridity was one of the great 'lessons of history' that every literate person knew about."[14]

Two of these literate people were Marx and Engels, both of whom were fascinated by the Bavarian botanist Karl Fraas's cautionary account of the transformation of the eastern Mediterranean climate by land clearance and grazing. Fraas had been a member of the impressive scientific retinue that accompanied the Bavarian Prince Otto when he became king of Greece in 1832.[15] Writing to Engels in March 1868, Marx enthused about Fraas's book:

He maintains that as a result of cultivation and in proportion to its degree, the "damp" so much beloved by the peasant is lost (hence too plants emigrate from south to north) and eventually the formation of steppes begins. The first effects of cultivation are useful, later devastating owing to deforestation, etc. This man is both a thoroughly learned philologist (he has written books in Greek) and a chemist, agricultural expert, etc. The whole conclusion is that cultivation when it progresses in a primitive way and is not consciously controlled (as a bourgeois of course he does not arrive at this), leaves deserts behind it, Persia, Mesopotamia, etc., Greece. Here again another unconscious socialist tendency![16]

Similarly Engels, later referring to deforestation of the Mediterranean in *The Dialectics of Nature*, warned that after every human "victory," "nature takes its revenge": "Each victory, it is true, in the first place brings about the results we expected, but in the second and third places it has quite different, unforeseen effects which only too often cancel the first."[17] But if nature has teeth with which to bite back against human conquest, Engels saw no evidence of natural forces acting as independent agents of change within the span of historical time. As he emphasized in a description of the contemporary German landscape, culture is promethean while nature is at most reactive:

There is devilishly little left of "nature" as it was in Germany at the time when the Germanic peoples immigrated into it. The earth's surface, climate, vegetation, fauna, and the human beings themselves have infinitely changed, and *all this owing to human activity*, while the changes of nature in Germany which have occurred in this period of time without human interference are incalculably small.[18]

In contrast to the seventeenth century, when earthquakes, comets, plagues, and arctic winters reinforced a cataclysmic view of nature amongst great savants like Newton, Halley, and Leibniz,[19] weather and geology in nineteenth-century Europe seemed as stable from decade to decade as the gold standard. For this reason, at least, Marx and Engels never speculated on the possibility that the natural conditions of production over the past two or three millennia might have been subject to directional evolution or epic fluctuation, or that climate therefore might have its own distinctive history, repeatedly intersecting and overdetermining a succession of different social formations. Certainly they believed that nature had a history, but it was enacted on long evolutionary or geological time-scales. Like most scientifically literate people in mid-Victorian England, they accepted Sir Charles Lyell's uniformitarian view of earth history, upon which Darwin had built his theory of natural selection, even while they satirized the reflection of English Liberal ideology in the concept of geological gradualism.

The long international controversy starting in the late 1830s over Agassiz's "discovery" of the Great Ice Age did not put this reigning anthropogenic model into question, since geologists were vexed for decades by the problem of Pleistocene chronology: unable to establish the order of succession amongst glacial drifts, or estimate the relative age of the ancient human and megafaunal remains whose discovery was a staple sensation of mid-Victorian times.[20] Although "glacial research prepared the way for insight into the reality of short-term changes in climate gauged against geological time," there was no measure of the Ice Age's temporal distance from modern climate.[21] Cleveland Abbe, the greatest American weather scientist of the late nineteenth century, expressed the consensus view of the "rational climatology" school when he wrote in 1889 that "great changes have taken place during geological ages perhaps

50,000 years distant," but "no important climatic change has yet been demonstrated since human history began."[22]

DESICCATION OF ASIA AND MARS

Kropotkin radically challenged this orthodoxy by asserting a continuity of global climatic dynamics between the end of the Ice Age and modern times; far from being stationary, as early meteorologists believed, climate had been continuously changing in a unidirectional sense and without human help throughout history. In 1904, on the thirtieth anniversary of his original presentation to Russian geographers, and amidst much public interest in recent expeditions to inner Asia by the Swedish geographer Sven Hedin and the American geologist Raphael Pumpelly, the Royal Geographical Society invited Kropotkin to outline his current views.

In his article, he argued that recent explorations like Hedin's had fully vindicated his theory of rapid desiccation in the post-glacial era, proving that "from year to year the limits of the deserts are extended." Based on this inexorable trend from ice sheet to lake land, and then from grassland to desert, he proposed a startlingly new theory of history.[23] East Turkestan and Central Mongolia, he claimed, were once well-watered and "advanced in civilization":

All of this is gone now, and it must have been the rapid desiccation of this region which compelled its inhabitants to rush down to the Jungarian Gate, down to the lowlands of the Balkhash and Obi, and thence, pushing before them the former inhabitants of the lowlands, to produce those great migrations and invasions of Europe which took place during the first centuries of our era.[24]

Nor was this just a cyclical fluctuation: *progressive desiccation*, emphasized Kropotkin, "is a geological fact," and the Lacustrine period (the Holocene) must be conceptualized as an epoch of expanding drought. As he had already written five years earlier: "And now we are fully in the period of a rapid desiccation, accompanied by the formation of dry prairies and steppes, and man has to find out the means to put a check to that desiccation to which Central Asia already has fallen a victim, and which menaces Southeastern Europe."[25] Only heroic and globally coordinated action—planting millions of trees and digging thousands of artesian wells—could arrest future desertification.[26]

Kropotkin's hypothesis of natural, progressive climate change had a differential reception: greeted with more skepticism in continental Europe than in English-speaking countries or amongst scientists working in desert environments. In Russia, where his contributions to physical geography were well known, there had been intense interest, following the great famine of 1891–92, in understanding whether drought on the black-soil steppe, the new frontier of wheat production, was a result of cultivation or an omen of creeping desertification. In the event, the two internationally recognized authorities on the question, Aleksandr Voeikov—a pioneer of modern climatology, and an old colleague of Kropotkin's from the Geographical Society in the early 1870s—and Vasily Dokuchaev—celebrated as "the father of soil science"—found little evidence of either process at work. In their view, the steppe climate had not changed in historical time, although the succession of wet and dry years might be cyclical in nature. Voeikov, like many other contemporary scientists in Europe, was intrigued if not convinced by the ideas about climate variability advanced by the brilliant German glaciologist Eduard Brückner.[27]

Brückner's 1890 landmark book *Climatic Changes since 1700* (unfortunately never translated into English) argued the case for multi-decadal climatic fluctuations in historical times.[28] In stunningly modern fashion, unequaled in rigor until the work of Emmanuel Le Roy Ladurie and Hubert Lamb, he combined documentary and proxy sources like grape-harvest dates, retreating glaciers, and accounts of extreme winters with an analysis of the previous century of instrumental data from different stations to arrive at a picture of a quasi-periodic, thirty-five-year cycling between wet/cool and dry/warm years that regulated changes in European harvests, and perhaps world climate as a whole. Brückner, who knew very little about meteorology and nothing about the general circulation of the atmosphere, was extremely disciplined in avoiding the conjectures and anecdotal claims that contaminated the next generation of debate about climate change, and wisely refused to speculate on the causality of what became known as the *Brückner cycle*. In countries whose scientific culture was largely German (most of central Europe and also Russia at the turn of the century), Brückner's cautious model of climate oscillation was preferred to Kropotkin's climatic catastrophism.[29]

In the English-speaking world, on the other hand, Kropotkin's 1904 article—seemingly buttressed by recent scientific research on the fossil great lakes and dry rivers of the American West, the Sahara, and Inner Asia—was generally received with great interest. Its most immediate and remarkable impact, however, was extra-terrestrial. Percival Lowell, a wealthy Boston Brahman, had abandoned his career as an orientalist in 1894 to build an observatory in Flagstaff, Arizona, where he could study the *canali* on Mars "discovered" by Giovanni Schiaparelli in 1877 and later "confirmed" by several leading astronomers. Until Lowell, these hallucinatory channels or fissures were believed by most to be natural features of the Red Planet, although the Belfast journalist and science-fiction writer Robert Cromie had already suggested in an 1890 novel that the canals were oases created by an advanced civilization on a dry and dying world.[30] Five years later, in his sensational book *Mars*, Lowell proposed that Cromie's fiction was observable science: because of their geometry, the canals must be an artificial irrigation system built by intelligent life. Moreover, Martian civilization had obviously put an end to "nations" and warfare in order to build on a planetary scale. But "what manner of beings they may be we lack the data even to conceive."[31]

Newspaper readers across the globe were electrified, composers wrote Mars marches, and an English journalist named Wells found the plot for a book that continues to fascinate and terrify readers. Lowell quickly acquired implacable scientific foes, such as the co-discoverer of natural selection and acquaintance of Kropotkin Alfred Russel Wallace; but with the popular press as an ally, he soon convinced public opinion that a Martian civilization was fact, not speculation. He liked to astound audiences with photographs of the "canals," always apologizing for the blurred images.[32] But what was the nature and history of this alien civilization? Lowell may have met Kropotkin when the latter gave a series of lectures on evolution at Boston's Lowell Institute in 1901, but whatever the case may be, the 1904 paper on progressive desiccation struck Lowell like a lightning bolt. Here was a master narrative to explain not only the "tragedy of Mars" but also the fate of the Earth. Lowell argued that, because of its smaller size, planetary evolution was accelerated on Mars, thus providing a preview of how the Earth would change in eons to come. "On our own world," he wrote in the 1906 book *Mars and Its Canals*, "we are able only to study our present and our past; in Mars we are able to glimpse, in some sort, our future." That future was planetary desiccation as oceans evaporated and dried into land, forest gave way to steppe, and grasslands became deserts. He agreed with Kropotkin about the velocity of aridification: "Palestine has desiccated within historic times."[33]

Two years later, in popular talks published under the title *Mars as Abode of Life*, Lowell devoted a lecture to "Mars and the Future of Earth," warning that "the cosmic circumstance about them which is most terrible is not that deserts are, but that deserts have begun to be. Not as local, evitable evils only are they to be pictured, but as the general unspeakable death-grip on our world." His prime example, not surprisingly, was Central Asia: "The Caspian is disappearing before our eyes, as the remains, some distance from its edge, of what once were ports mutely inform us." Someday, the only option left to humans in this "struggle for existence in their planet's decrepitude and decay" would be to emulate the Martians and build canals to bring polar water to their last oases.[34] Lowell, a skilled mathematician but a hapless geologist, liked to impress visitors to Arizona with the Petrified Forest as an example of desiccation at work, although the tree fossils dated from the Triassic Period, 225 million years earlier. Likewise, he took for granted the evidence for unidirectional and rapid climate change on Earth.

In fact, Kropotkin's theory, based on landscape impressions and the hypothesis of a Eurasian ice sheet, was a speculative leap far ahead of any data about past climates or their causes. Indeed, it was essentially untestable. Theoretical as contrasted to descriptive meteorology, for example, was still in its swaddling clothes. By coincidence, Kropotkin's paper was published almost simultaneously with an obscure article by a Norwegian scientist named Jacob Bjerknes that laid the first foundations for a physics of the atmosphere, in the form of a half-dozen fundamental equations derived from fluid mechanics and thermodynamics. "He [Bjerknes] conceived the atmosphere," observes a historian of geophysics, "from a purely mechanical and physical viewpoint, as an 'air-mass circulation engine,' driven by solar radiation and deflected by rotation, expressed in local differences of velocity, density, air pressure, temperature and humidity." It would take more than half a century for these conceptual seeds to grow into modern dynamic meteorology; in the meantime, it was impossible to propose a climate model for Kropotkin's theory.[35]

Quantitative evidence for understanding past climate was likewise a bare cupboard. Brückner had used instrumental records with impressive skill, but only for the period after the French Revolution. In 1901, the Swedish meteorologist Nils Ekholm, writing in the *Quarterly Journal of the Royal Meteorological Society*, had soberly surveyed the available pre-instrumental documentary evidence and found that much of it was simply worthless: "Almost the only weather phenomenon of which the old chronicles give trustworthy reports are severe winters." Comparing Tycho Brahe's pioneering instrumental weather readings in 1579–82 from an island off the Danish coast with modern measurements from the same location, Ekholm found some indications that winters were milder and that Northern European climate in general was more "maritime" than three centuries earlier. But this was the limit of disciplined inference: "The character in other respects and the cause of this variation are unknown. We cannot say if the variation is periodical, progressive or accidental, nor how far it extends in space and time." Since Ekholm reasonably assumed that insolation had been constant for at least a million years and that the Earth's orbital variability had had minimal influence over the last millennium of climate, the most likely cause of climate change (based on the famous experiments of his colleague Svante Arrhenius) was a fluctuation in atmospheric carbon dioxide, and thereby the greenhouse effect.[36]

PATHOLOGICAL SCIENCE

But there was an avid appetite amongst scientists and geographers, as well as the general public, for bolder theories, and as the Royal Society had undoubtedly hoped, Kropotkin's paper, aside from gifting Lowell's Mars mania, stimulated a far-reaching debate that lasted until the eve of the First World War. Lord Curzon, the viceroy of India, even waded into the controversy, siding with the explorers who had seen desertification first-hand, rather than with "untravelled scientists" who denied climate change.[37] One of the eminent travelers and scientists who embraced the evidence for progressive desiccation was Europe's other red prince, Leone Caetani, whose *Annali dell'Islam* (ten volumes, 1905–29) became the foundation stone for Islamic studies in the West. A skilled linguist, he had travelled widely in the Muslim world before being drawn into left-wing politics. Although a papal prince, he became a parliamentary deputy for the anti-clerical Radical Party, and in 1911 joined with the majority faction of the Socialists to oppose the invasion of Libya. After the rise of fascism, he moved to Canada and continued work on the *Annali*.[38] Caetani hypothesized that the originally fertile Arabian Peninsula was the home of all Semite cultures, but aridification and subsequent overpopulation had forced one group after another to migrate; indeed, desiccation was the environmental motor force behind the expansion of Islam. Hugo Winckler, the famed German archaeologist/philologist who had discovered Hattusa, the lost capital of the Hittites, arrived at the same idea independently, and the "Winckler–Caetani" or "Semite Wave" theory subsequently became a touchstone of pan-Arab ideology in the 1920s and '30s.[39]

The most fervent adherent to the desiccation hypothesis, however, was the Yale geographer Ellsworth Huntington, a former missionary in Turkey and a veteran of the 1903 Pumpelly Expedition to

Transcaspia and the 1905 Barrett Expedition to Chinese Turkestan. His observations from the latter mission confirmed those of earlier travelers in Xinjiang and supported Kropotkin's theory: "All the more arid part of Asia, from the Caspian Sea eastward for over 2,500 miles, appears to have been subject to a climatic change whereby it has been growing less and less habitable for the last two or three thousand years."[40] At first Huntington vigorously defended Kropotkin's ideas to the letter, but in his 1907 book, *The Pulse of Asia*, he amended the theory in one decisive regard. Considering the menu of possible climate hypotheses—"uniformity, deforestation [anthropogenic change], progressive change, and pulsatory change"—he now voted for the last. Climate change, Huntington argued, took the form of great, Sun-driven oscillations of centuries-long duration: wet periods followed by mega-droughts.[41] Although he attributed the idea to reading Brückner, his cycles were an order of magnitude longer in frequency, and had the epic effects ascribed to progressive desiccation by Kropotkin.

Like Lowell, Huntington was a superb publicist. He aggressively sought further evidence for the cyclical thesis in Palestine, Yucatan, and the American West, where he worked with tree-ring pioneer Andrew Douglas (Lowell's former assistant at the observatory) in the ancient California sequoias.[42] From each new investigation came an article or book bolstering his claim that societies and civilizations rose and fell with these climatic oscillations. "With every throw of the climatic pulse which we have felt in Central Asia, the centre of civilization has moved this way or that. Each throb has sent pain and decay to the lands whose day was done, life and vigour to those whose day was yet to be."[43] (Owen Lattimore, author of the classic 1940 work *The Inner Asian Frontiers of China*, parodied Huntington's image of "hordes of erratic nomads, ready to start for lost horizons at the joggle of a barometer, in search of suddenly vanishing pastures.")[44]

Huntington's majestic oscillations were an unexpected gift to searchers for ultimate causations in history, and *The Pulse of Asia* helped inspire Arnold Toynbee's famous theory of civilizational cycles driven by responses to environmental challenges.[45] But Huntington's sweeping claims made others nervous. Both the Royal Geographical Society and Yale University (which was considering promoting him to a professorship) discreetly canvassed the opinions of major authorities. The explorer Sven Hedin derided the whole idea of desiccation: "Men and camels, country and climate—none has undergone any change worth mention."[46] Albrecht Penck, one of the giants of modern physical geography, gently observed of Huntington that "sometimes his thoughts run ahead of his facts. He works more with a vital scientific imagination than with a critical faculty."[47]

In Vienna, Eduard Brückner, whom Huntington acknowledged as one of his masters, was also polite but devastating in his assessment:

He takes his data from historical works without examining it properly. He is not sufficiently aware to what degree he may use data as facts. In particular the archaeological results are by no means definitive enough as he himself explains in his work *The Pulse of Asia* ... He has shown several times the desire to fit the facts to his theory. During my visit to Yale Dr Huntington showed me the results of his investigations in respect to the rings of old trees in their relationship to fluctuations of climate. He has collected very interesting material, but again I had the impression that he concluded more from his curves than a cautious man ought to conclude. He claimed in several cases that he saw a parallelism in the curve where I could not see one.[48]

Huntington did not receive the promotion, and left Yale.

Brückner's critique anticipated Irving Langmuir's famous definition of "pathological science" as research "led astray by subjective effects, wishful thinking or threshold interactions."[49] In addition to the usual sins of confusing coincidence with correlation and correlation with causality, Huntington and his several prominent co-thinkers—especially the Clark University geographer Charles Brooks—were addicted to circular argumentation. "Huntington," Le Roy Ladurie wrote in his *Histoire du climat*, "explained the Mongol migrations by the fluctuations in rainfall and barometric pressure in the arid zones of Central Asia. Brooks carried on the good work by basing a graph of rainfall in Central Asia on the migration of the Mongols!"[50] In another instance, Brooks, who followed Huntington in believing that tropical climates could not support advanced civilizations, concluded that the existence of Angkor Wat proved that the climate of Cambodia in 600 AD must have been more temperate.[51]

As for spectacular ruins in the deserts, the geographer and historian Rhoads Murphey demonstrated in a 1951 article, *contra* Huntington, that in the case of North Africa there is little evidence of climate change since the Roman period. Instead, he explained the desolate landscapes where wheat fields and Roman towns once flourished as a result of the neglect or destruction of water-storage infrastructures. (Huntington seemed to have forgotten the dependence of desert societies upon groundwater rather than rain.) In a classic example of the kind of "natural experiment" that Jared Diamond would decades later urge historians to adopt, Murphey cited the example of the Aïr Massif in Niger, where the French forcibly evicted the rebellious Tuareg population in 1917: "As population decreased, wells, gardens and stock were allowed to deteriorate, and within less than a year the area looked exactly like the other areas which have been used as evidence of progressive desiccation."[52]

For all this, the Kropotkin–Huntington debate about natural climate change in history might have left a more fruitful legacy if it had stayed within the domain of physical geography. Huntington, however, fused his distinctive ideas about climate cycles with the extreme environmental determinism advocated by the German geographer Friedrich Ratzel and his American disciple Ellen Churchill Semple. They argued that cultural and ethnic characteristics were mechanically and irreversibly imprinted upon human groups by their natural habitats, especially climate. Huntington also became mesmerized by the bizarre ideas of a professor of German in Syracuse named Charles Kullmer, who believed that human mental activity, both individual and social, was governed by the electrical potential of barometric depressions. As Huntington's biographer explains, "Kullmer measured the number of nonfiction books taken from libraries and the barometric pressure at such time; 'high pressure means more serious books, and low pressure fewer.'" Huntington, "electrified" by Kullmer's findings, wrote: "I have pondered a great deal over the Italian Renaissance; and now I am wondering whether by any chance that was associated with some change in storm frequency." Huntington subsequently tested Kullmer's thesis by having a friend's children type three dictated stanzas of Spencer's *The Faerie Queene* every day for months while their father recorded the barometric pressure. Huntington then compared the pattern of errors: "There seems to be a connection between weather and mental ability far closer than we have hitherto suspected. I am at work just now trying to apply this to Japan."[53]

But Huntington soon put barometry aside, concluding that it was actually temperature, perhaps in collusion with humidity, that determined human mental acuity and industrial efficiency. This "meteorological Taylorism," as James Fleming calls it, was then subsumed by Huntington's passion for eugenics and racial engineering.[54] While an ailing Kropotkin, who had returned to Russia in 1917 to support the anarchist movement, was racing to finish his magisterial scientific testament, *Glacial and Lacustrine Periods*,[55] Huntington was publishing increasingly bizarre papers on the adaptability of white men to the Australian tropics and the impact of climate on human productivity in Korea. A few years later, he was struggling to understand the effect of overpopulation on Chinese character, decrying the immigration of Puerto Ricans to New York, and pontificating in *Harper's* about "Temperature and the Fate of Nations."[56] In effect, Huntington, like Ratzel, Semple, and many others, was aggrandizing the climatic race theories of Herodotus and Montesquieu—the first convinced that Greece was man's perfect habitat; the other, France—into an all-encompassing meteorological anthropology.

In the 1910s and 1920s, the heyday of scientific racism (of which Huntington was a fervent proponent), these ideas were easily embraced by mainstream scholarship; by the late 1930s, however, a new generation of academics began to recoil from the dark implications of environmental determinism alloyed with white supremacy and its apotheosis, fascism. As his biographer gingerly observes, "Huntington's insistence on a hierarchy of innate competence, and consistent inquiry into the eugenic cause in the 1930s, was perhaps unfortunate. When he proposed on the eve of World War II that Caucasians with blond hair and blue eyes were possessed of greater longevity than others, his utterance seemed peculiarly *non sequitur*."[57] (The Nazis, meanwhile, were integrating desiccationist ideas into their rationale for the removal and mass murder of the populations of Poland and the USSR. The Slavs were simultaneously condemned for failing to drain the post-glacial wetlands east of the Vistula and for allowing them to turn into desert—*Versteppung*. Only the master race could arrest the great drying.)[58] Huntington's wild theories and crude determinism, together with the absence of reliable historical weather data, began to taint the enterprise of climate history for most geographers and historians. In 1937, the physicist Sir Gilbert Walker, who had spent a lifetime searching for structure in weather data, wrote an obituary for climatic determinism, a theory he equated with astrology:

> I regard the widespread faith in the effective control of weather by periods as based partly on a mistaken handling of plotted data and partly on an instinct that survives in many of us, like the faith in the effect of the Moon on the weather, from the time when our forefathers believed in the control of human affairs by the heavenly bodies with their fixed cycles.[59]

In the postwar period, moreover, "a new disciplinary consensus" emerged amongst climatologists: "Namely that the global climate system contained overriding equilibrating processes providing resilience against secular climate fluctuations."[60] Meanwhile, the natural archives of deep Eurasia that hid the secrets of its climate history were off-limits: the only Westerners to visit the Tarim Basin during the Cold War were CIA agents (Lop Nor was the Chinese nuclear test site). Finally, in 2010–11, more than a century after the controversial expeditions of Stein, Heden, and Huntington, an interdisciplinary team of Chinese, American, Swiss, and Australian researchers spent a field season in the Tarim Basin, modeling relict hydrologies and sampling such potential climate archives as sediments from the now vanished Lake Lop Nor and dead trees interred in sand dunes.

Their results were published at the beginning of 2018. Desiccation, it turns out, is a modern phenomenon, not an ancient curse: "The Tarim Basin was continuously wetter than today at least as early as AD 1180 until the middle AD 1800s." This falls within the parameters, generously construed, of the Little Ice Age, and the researchers attribute the wetting to a southward shift of the boreal westerlies that produced enhanced snowfall in the mountains that feed the Tarim and its sister rivers. It was this "greening of the desert," not its relentless expansion, that was a mainspring of late medieval and early modern history:

> We propose that wetting of the interior Asian desert corridor stimulated southward migration of winter rangeland, which was essential in fuelling the horse-driven Mongol conquests across Eurasian deserts. In addition, wetter-than-present Asian deserts may have aided in the spread of pastoralism out of the Mongolian heartland, strengthening cultural and economic affinities among the Mongols and Turkic-speaking groups on the periphery of the steppe.[61]

Since the late nineteenth century, however, the progressive warming of interior Asia has produced a net drying which the researchers warn may be a prelude to the future northward expansion of the deserts. Meanwhile, other climate scientists have expressed concern that precipitation regimes in western Asia may be radically changing as well. A research group based at Columbia University's Lamont-Doherty Earth Observatory, which has been studying contemporary and historical megadroughts, recently published a paper warning that the disastrous 2007–10 drought in Syria, the most severe in the instrumental record and a principal catalyst to social unrest, was likely part of "a longterm drying trend" associated with rising greenhouse emissions.[62] This uncomfortably accords with an earlier study which predicted that the entire climatological Fertile Crescent, from the Jordan Valley to the Zagros foothills, might disappear by the end of the century: "Ancient rain-fed agriculture enabled the civilizations to thrive in the Fertile Crescent region, but this blessing is soon to disappear due to human-induced climate change."[63] The Anthropocene, it seems, may vindicate Kropotkin after all.

4

Who Will Build the Ark?

What follows is rather like the famous courtroom scene in Orson Welles's *The Lady from Shanghai* (1947).[1] In that noir allegory of proletarian virtue in the embrace of ruling-class decadence, Welles plays a left-wing sailor named Michael O'Hara who rolls in the hay with *femme fatale* Rita Hayworth, and then gets framed for murder. Her husband, Arthur Bannister, the most celebrated criminal lawyer in America, played by Everett Sloane, convinces O'Hara to appoint him as his defense, all the better to ensure his rival's conviction and execution. At the turning point in the trial, decried by the prosecution as "yet another of the great Bannister's famous tricks," Bannister the attorney calls Bannister the aggrieved husband to the witness stand and interrogates himself in rapid schizoid volleys, to the mirth of the jury. In the spirit of *Lady from Shanghai*, this chapter is organized as a debate with myself, a mental tournament between analytic despair and utopian possibility that is personally, and probably objectively, irresolvable.

In the first section, "Pessimism of the Intellect," I adduce arguments for believing that we have already lost the first, epochal stage of the battle against global warming. The Kyoto Protocol, in the smug but sadly accurate words of one of its chief opponents, has done "nothing measurable" about climate change. Global carbon dioxide emissions rose by the same amount they were supposed to fall because of it.[2] It is highly unlikely that greenhouse gas accumulation can be stabilized this side of the famous "red line" of 450 ppm by 2020. If this is the case, the most heroic efforts of our children's generation will be unable to forestall a radical reshaping of ecologies, water resources, and agricultural systems. In a warmer world, moreover, socioeconomic inequality will have a meteorological mandate, and there will be little incentive for the rich northern-hemisphere countries, whose carbon emissions have destroyed the climate equilibrium of the Holocene, to share resources for adaptation with those poor subtropical countries most vulnerable to droughts and floods.

The second part of the chapter, "Optimism of the Imagination," is my self-rebuttal. I appeal to the paradox that the single most important cause of global warming—the urbanization of humanity—is also potentially the principal solution to the problem of human survival in the later twenty-first century. Left to the dismal politics of the present, of course, cities of poverty will almost certainly become the coffins of hope; all the more reason that we must start thinking like Noah. Since most of history's giant trees have already been cut down, a new Ark will have to be constructed out of the materials that a desperate humanity finds at hand in insurgent communities, pirate technologies, bootlegged media, rebel science, and forgotten utopias.

I. PESSIMISM OF THE INTELLECT

Our old world, the one that we have inhabited for the last 12,000 years, has ended, even if no newspaper has yet printed its scientific obituary. The verdict is that of the Stratigraphy Commission of the Geological Society of London. Founded in 1807, the Society is the world's oldest association of earth scientists, and its Stratigraphy Commission acts as a college of cardinals in the adjudication of the geological time-scale. Stratigraphers slice up Earth's history as preserved in sedimentary strata into a hierarchy of eons, eras, periods, and epochs, marked by the "golden spikes" of mass extinctions, speciation events, or abrupt changes in atmospheric chemistry. In geology, as in biology and history, periodization is a complex, controversial art; the most bitter feud in nineteenth-century British science—still known as the "Great Devonian Controversy"—was fought over competing interpretations of homely Welsh greywackes and English Old Red Sandstone. As a result, Earth science sets extraordinarily rigorous standards for the beatification of any new geological division. Although the idea of an "Anthropocene" epoch—defined by the emergence of urban–industrial society as a geological force—has long circulated in the literature, stratigraphers have never acknowledged its warrant.

At least for the London Society, that position has now been revised. To the question, "Are we now living in the Anthropocene?" the twenty-one members of the Commission have unanimously answered, "Yes." In a 2008 report, they marshalled robust evidence to support the hypothesis that the Holocene epoch—the interglacial span of unusually stable climate that allowed the rapid evolution of agriculture and urban civilization—has ended, and that the Earth has now entered "a stratigraphic interval without close parallel" in the last several million years.[3] In addition to the build-up of greenhouse gases, the stratigraphers cited human landscape transformation, which "now exceeds [annual] natural sediment production by an order of magnitude," the ominous acidification of the oceans, and the relentless destruction of biota.

This new age, they explained, is defined both by the heating trend—whose closest analogue may be the catastrophe known as the Paleocene Eocene Thermal Maximum, 56 million years ago—and by the radical instability expected of future environments. In somber prose, they warned:

> The combination of extinctions, global species migrations and the widespread replacement of natural vegetation with agricultural monocultures is producing a distinctive contemporary biostrati-graphic signal. These effects are permanent, as future evolution will take place from surviving (and frequently anthropogenically relocated) stocks.[4]

Evolution itself, in other words, has been forced onto a new trajectory.

Spontaneous decarbonization?

The Commission's recognition of the Anthropocene coincided with growing scientific controversy over the Fourth Assessment Report issued by the Intergovernmental Panel on Climate Change. The IPCC, of course, is mandated to assess the possible range of climate change and establish appropriate targets for the mitiga-tion of emissions. The most critical baselines include estimates of "climate sensitivity" to increasing accumulations of greenhouse gas, as well as socioeconomic tableaux that configure different futures of energy use, and thus of emissions. But an impressive number of senior researchers, including key participants in the IPCC's own working groups, have recently expressed unease or disagreement with the methodology of the four-volume Fourth Assessment, which they charge is unwarrantedly optimistic in its geophysics and social science.[5]

The most celebrated dissenter is James Hansen, from NASA's Goddard Institute. The Paul Revere of global warming, who first warned Congress of the greenhouse peril in a famous 1988 hearing, he returned to Washington with the troubling message that the IPCC, through its failure to parameterize crucial Earth-system feedbacks, has given far too much leeway to further carbon emissions. Instead of the IPCC's proposed red line of 450 ppm carbon dioxide, Hansen's research team found compelling paleoclimatic evidence that the threshold of safety was only 350 ppm, or even less. The "stunning corollary" of this recalibration of climate sensitivity, he testified, is that "the oft-stated goal of keeping global warming below two degrees Celsius is a recipe for global disaster, not salvation."[6] Indeed, since the current level is about 385 ppm, we may already be past the notorious "tipping point." Hansen has mobilized a Quixotic army of scientists and environmental activists to save the world via an emergency carbon tax, which would reverse greenhouse concentrations to pre-2000 levels by 2015.

I do not have the scientific qualifications to express an opinion on the Hansen controversy, or the proper setting on the planetary thermostat. Anyone, however, who is engaged with the social sciences, or simply pays regular attention to macro-trends, should feel less shy about joining the debate over the other controversial cornerstone of the Fourth Assessment: its socioeconomic projections, and what we might term their "political unconscious." The current scenarios were adopted by the IPCC in 2000 to model future global emissions based on different "storylines" about population growth, as well as technological and economic development. The Panel's major scenarios—the A1 family, the B2, and so on—are well known to policymakers and greenhouse activists, but few outside the research community have actually read the fine print, particularly the IPCC's heroic confidence that greater energy efficiency will be an "automatic" by-product of future economic growth. Indeed, all the scenarios, even the "business as usual" variants, assume that almost 60 percent of future carbon reduction will occur independently of explicit greenhouse-mitigation measures.[7]

The IPCC, in effect, has bet the ranch, or rather the planet, on a market-driven evolution toward a post-carbon world economy: a transition that requires not only international emissions caps and carbon trading, but also voluntary corporate commitments to technologies that hardly exist even in prototype, such as carbon capture, clean coal, hydrogen and advanced transit systems, and cellulosic biofuels. As critics have long pointed out, in many of its "scenarios" the deployment of non-carbon-emitting energy-supply systems "exceeds the size of the global energy system in 1990."[8]

Kyoto-type accords and carbon markets are designed—almost as analogues to Keynesian "pump-priming"—to bridge the shortfall between spontaneous decarbonization and the emissions targets required by each scenario. Although the IPCC never spells it out, its mitigation targets necessarily presume that windfall profits from higher fossil-fuel prices over the next generation will be efficiently recycled into renewable energy technology and not wasted on mile-high skyscrapers, asset bubbles, and mega-payouts to shareholders. Overall, the International Energy Agency estimates that it will cost about $45 trillion to halve greenhouse gas output by 2050.[9] But without the large quotient of "automatic" progress in energy efficiency, the bridge will never be built, and IPCC goals will be unachievable; in the worst case—the straightforward extrapolation of current energy use—carbon emissions could easily triple by midcentury.

Critics have cited the dismal carbon record of the last—lost—decade to demonstrate that the IPCC baseline assumptions about markets and technology are little more than leaps of faith. Despite the EU's much-praised adoption of a cap-and-trade system, European carbon emissions continued to rise, dramatically in some sectors. Likewise, there has been scant evidence in recent years of the automatic progress in energy efficiency that is the *sine qua non* of IPCC scenarios. Much of what the storylines depict as the efficiency of new technology has in fact been the result of the closing down of heavy industries in the United States, Europe, and the ex-Soviet bloc. The relocation of energy-intensive production to East Asia burnishes the carbon balance-sheets of some OECD countries, but deindustrialization should not be confused with spontaneous decarbonization. Most researchers believe that energy intensity has actually risen since 2000—that is, global carbon dioxide emissions have kept pace with, or even grown marginally faster than, energy use.[10]

Return of King Coal

Moreover, the IPCC carbon budget has already been broken. According to the Global Carbon Project, which keeps the accounts, emissions have been rising faster than projected even in the IPCC's worst-case scenario. From 2000 to 2007, carbon dioxide rose by 3.5 percent annually, compared with the 2.7 percent in IPCC projections, or the 0.9 percent recorded during the 1990s.[11] We are already outside the IPCC envelope, in other words, and coal may be largely to blame for this unforeseen acceleration of greenhouse emissions. Coal production has undergone a dramatic renaissance over the last decade, as nightmares of the nineteenth century return to haunt the twenty-first. In China 5 million miners toil under dangerous conditions to extract the dirty mineral that reportedly allows Beijing to open a new coal-fueled power station each week. Coal consumption is also booming in Europe, where fifty new coal-fueled plants are scheduled to open over the next few years,[12] and North America, where 200 plants are planned. A giant plant under construction in West Virginia will generate carbon equivalent to the exhaust of 1 million cars.

In a commanding study titled *The Future of Coal*, MIT engineers concluded that usage would increase under any foreseeable scenario, even in the face of high carbon taxes. Investment in CCS technology—carbon-capture and sequestration—is, moreover, "completely inadequate"; even assuming it is actually practical, CCS would not become a utility-scale alternative until 2030 or later. In the United States, "green energy" legislation has only created a "perverse incentive" for utilities to build more coal-fired plants in the "expectation that emissions from these plants would potentially be 'grandfathered' by the grant of free CO_2 allowances as part of future carbon emission regulations."[13] Meanwhile, a consortium of coal producers, coal-burning utilities, and coal-hauling railroads—calling themselves the American Coalition for Clean Coal Electricity—spent $40 million over the 2008 election cycle to ensure that both presidential candidates sang in unison about the virtues of the dirtiest but cheapest fuel.

Largely because of the popularity of coal, a fossil fuel with a proven 200-year supply, the carbon content per unit of energy may actually rise.[14] Before the American economy collapsed, the U.S. Energy Department was projecting an increase of national energy production by at least 20 percent over the next generation. Globally, the total consumption of fossil fuels is predicted to rise by 55 percent, with international oil exports doubling in volume. The UN Development Programme, which has made its own study of sustainable energy goals, warns that it will require a 50 percent cut in greenhouse gas emissions worldwide by 2050, against 1990 levels, to keep humanity outside the red zone of runaway warming.[15] Yet the International Energy Agency predicts that, in all likelihood, such emissions will actually increase over the next half-century by nearly 100 percent—enough greenhouse gas to propel us past several critical tipping points. The IEA also projects that renewable energy, apart from hydropower, will provide only 4 percent of electricity generation in 2030—up from 1 percent today.[16]

A green recession?

The current world recession—a non-linear event of the kind that IPCC scenarists ignore in their storylines—may provide a temporary respite, particularly if depressed oil prices delay the opening of the Pandora's box of new mega-carbon reservoirs such as tar sands and oil shales. But the slump is unlikely to slow the destruction of the Amazon rainforest, because Brazilian farmers will rationally seek to defend their gross incomes by expanding production. And because electricity demand is less elastic than automobile use, the share of coal in carbon emissions will continue to increase. In the United States, in fact, coal production is one of the few civilian industries that is currently hiring rather than laying off workers. More importantly, falling fossil-fuel prices and tight credit markets are eroding entrepreneurial incentives to develop capital-intensive wind and solar alternatives. On Wall Street, eco-energy stocks have slumped faster than the market as a whole, and investment capital has virtually disappeared, leaving some of the most celebrated clean-energy start-ups, like Tesla Motors and Clear Skies Solar, in danger of sudden crib death. Tax credits, as advocated by Obama, are unlikely to reverse this green depression. As one venture capital manager told the *New York Times*, "natural gas at $6 makes wind look like a questionable idea and solar power unfathomably expensive."[17]

Thus the economic crisis provides a compelling pretext for the groom once again to leave the bride at the altar, as major companies default on their public commitments to renewable energy. In the United States, Texas billionaire T. Boone Pickens has downscaled a scheme to build the world's largest wind farm, while Royal Dutch Shell has dropped its plan to invest in the London Array. Governments and ruling parties have been equally avid to escape their carbon debts. The Canadian Conservative Party, supported by Western oil and coal interests, defeated the Liberals' "Green Shift" agenda based on a national carbon tax in 2007, just as Washington scrapped its major carbon-capture technology initiative.

On the supposedly greener side of the Atlantic, the Berlusconi regime—which is in the process of converting Italy's grid from oil to coal—denounced the EU goal of cutting emissions by 20 percent by 2020 as an "unaffordable sacrifice"; while the German government, in the words of the *Financial Times*, "dealt a severe blow to the proposal to force companies to pay for the carbon dioxide they emit" by backing an almost total exemption for industry. "This crisis changes priorities," explained a sheepish German foreign minister.[18] Pessimism now abounds. Even Yvo de Boer, director of the UN Framework Convention on Climate Change, concedes that, as long as the economic crisis persists, "most sensible governments will be reluctant to impose new costs on [industry] in the form of carbon-emissions caps." So even if invisible hands and interventionist leaders can restart the engines of economic growth, they are unlikely to be able to turn down the global thermostat in time to prevent runaway climate change. Nor should we expect that the G7 or the G20 will be eager to clean up the mess they have made.[19]

Ecological inequalities
Climate diplomacy based on the Kyoto–Copenhagen template assumes that, once the major actors have accepted the consensus

science in the IPCC reports, they will recognize an overriding common interest in gaining control over the greenhouse effect. But global warming is not H. G. Wells's *War of the Worlds*, where invading Martians democratically annihilate humanity without class or ethnic distinction. Climate change, instead, will produce dramatically unequal impacts across regions and social classes, inflicting the greatest damage upon poor countries with the fewest resources for meaningful adaptation. This geographical separation of emission source from environmental consequence undermines proactive solidarity. As the UN Development Programme has emphasized, global warming is above all a threat to the poor and the unborn, the "two constituencies with little or no political voice."[20] Coordinated global action on their behalf thus presupposes either their revolutionary empowerment—a scenario not considered by the IPCC—or the transmutation of the self-interest of rich countries and classes into an enlightened "solidarity" with little precedent in history.

From a rational-actor perspective, the latter outcome only seems realistic if it can be shown that privileged groups possess no preferential "exit" option, that internationalist public opinion drives policymaking in key countries, and that greenhouse gas mitigation can be achieved without major sacrifices in northern-hemispheric standards of living—none of which seem likely. Moreover, there is no shortage of eminent apologists, like Yale economists William Nordhaus and Robert Mendelsohn, ready to explain that it makes more sense to defer abatement until poorer countries become richer and thus more capable of bearing the costs themselves. In other words, instead of galvanizing heroic innovation and international cooperation, growing environmental and socioeconomic turbulence may simply drive elite publics into more frenzied attempts to wall themselves off from the rest of humanity. Global mitigation, in this unexplored but not improbable scenario, would be tacitly abandoned—as, to some extent, it already has been—in favor of accelerated investment in selective adaptation for Earth's first-class passengers. The goal would be the creation of green and gated oases of permanent affluence on an otherwise stricken planet.

Of course, there would still be treaties, carbon credits, famine relief, humanitarian acrobatics, and perhaps the full-scale conversion of some European cities and small countries to alternative energy. But worldwide adaptation to climate change, which presupposes trillions of dollars of investment in the urban and rural infrastructures of poor and medium-income countries, as well as the assisted migration of tens of millions of people from Africa and Asia, would necessarily command a revolution of almost mythic magnitude in the redistribution of income and power. Meanwhile, we are speeding toward a fateful rendezvous around 2030, or even earlier, when the convergent impacts of climate change, peak oil, peak water, and an additional 1.5 billion people on the planet will produce negative synergies probably beyond our imagination.

The fundamental question is whether rich countries will ever actually mobilize the political will and economic resources to achieve IPCC targets, or help poorer countries adapt to the inevitable, already "committed" quotient of global warming. More vividly: Will the electorates of the wealthy nations shed their current bigotry and walled borders to admit refugees from predicted epicenters of drought and desertification—the Maghreb, Mexico, Ethiopia, and Pakistan? Will Americans, the most miserly people when measured by per capita foreign aid, be willing to tax themselves to help relocate the millions likely to be flooded out of densely settled mega-delta regions like Bangladesh? And will North American agribusiness, the likely beneficiary of global warming, voluntarily make world food security, not profit-taking in a seller's market, its highest priority?

Market-oriented optimists, of course, will point to demonstration-scale carbon-offset programs like the Clean Development Mechanism, which, they claim, will ensure green investment in the Third World. But the impact of CDM is thus far negligible; it subsidizes small-scale reforestation and the scrubbing of industrial emissions rather than fundamental investment in domestic and urban use of fossil fuels. Moreover, the standpoint of the developing world is that the North should acknowledge the environmental disaster it has created and take responsibility for cleaning it up. Poor countries rightly rail against the notion that the greatest burden of adjustment to the Anthropocene epoch should fall on those who have contributed least to carbon emissions and drawn the slightest benefits from two centuries of industrial revolution. A recent assessment of the environmental costs of economic globalization since 1961—in deforestation, climate change, overfishing, ozone depletion, mangrove conversion, and agricultural expansion—found that the richest countries had generated 42 percent of environmental degradation across the world, while shouldering only 3 percent of the resulting costs.[21]

The radicals of the South will rightly point to another debt as well. For thirty years, cities in the developing world have grown at breakneck speed without counterpart public investments in infrastructure, housing, or public health. In part this has been the result of foreign debts contracted by dictators, with payments enforced by the IMF, and public spending downsized or redistributed by the World Bank's "structural adjustment" agreements. This planetary deficit of opportunity and social justice is summarized by the fact that more than 1 billion people, according to UN Habitat, currently live in slums, and that their number is expected to double by 2030. An equal number, or more, forage in the so-called informal sector—a first-world euphemism for mass unemployment. Sheer

213

demographic momentum, meanwhile, will increase the world's urban population by 3 billion people over the next forty years, 90 percent of whom will be in poor cities. No one—not the UN, the World Bank, the G20: no one—has a clue how a planet of slums with growing food and energy crises will accommodate their biological survival, much less their aspirations to basic happiness and dignity.

The most sophisticated research to date into the likely impacts of global warming on tropical and semi-tropical agriculture is summarized in William Cline's country-by-country study, which couples climate projections to crop process and neo-Ricardian farm-output models, allowing for various levels of carbon-dioxide fertilization, to look at possible futures for human nutrition. The view is grim. Even in Cline's most optimistic simulations, the agricultural systems of Pakistan (minus 20 percent of current farm output) and Northwestern India (minus 30 percent) are likely devastated, along with much of the Middle East, the Maghreb, the Sahel belt, parts of Southern Africa, the Caribbean, and Mexico. Twenty-nine developing countries, according to Cline, stand to lose 20 percent or more of their current farm output to global warming, while agriculture in the already rich North is likely to receive, on average, an 8 percent boost.[22]

This potential loss of agricultural capacity in the developing world is even more ominous in the context of the UN warning that a doubling of food production will be necessary to sustain the earth's midcentury population. The 2008 food affordability crisis, aggravated by the biofuel boom, is only a modest portent of the chaos that could soon grow from the convergence of resource depletion, intractable inequality, and climate change. In face of these dangers, human solidarity itself may fracture like a West Antarctic ice shelf, and shatter into a thousand shards.

2. OPTIMISM OF THE IMAGINATION

Scholarly research has come late in the day to confront the synergistic possibilities of peak population growth, agricultural collapse, abrupt climate change, peak oil, and, in some regions, peak water, and the accumulated penalties of urban neglect. If investigations by the German government, Pentagon, and CIA into the national-security implications of a multiply determined world crisis in the coming decades have had a Hollywoodish ring, it is hardly surprising. As a 2007/2008 UN Human Development Report observed, "There are no obvious historical analogies for the urgency of the climate change problem."[23] While paleoclimatology can help scientists anticipate the non-linear physics of a warming Earth, there is no historical precedent or vantage point for understanding what will happen in the 2050s, when a peak species population of 9 to 11 billion struggles to adapt to climate chaos and depleted fossil energy. Almost any scenario, from the collapse of civilization to a new golden age of fusion power, can be projected onto the strange screen of our grandchildren's future.

We can be sure, however, that cities will remain the ground zero of convergence. Although forest clearance and export monocultures have played fundamental roles in the transition to a new geological epoch, the prime mover has been the almost exponential increase in the carbon footprints of urban regions in the northern hemisphere. Heating and cooling the urban built environment alone is responsible for an estimated 35–45 percent of current carbon emissions, while urban industries and transportation contribute another 35–40 percent. In a sense, city life is rapidly destroying the ecological niche—Holocene climate stability—which made its evolution into complexity possible.

Yet there is a striking paradox here. What makes urban areas so environmentally unsustainable are precisely those features, even in the largest megacities, that are most anti-urban or sub-urban. First among these is massive horizontal expansion, which combines the degradation of vital natural services—aquifers, watersheds, truck farms, forests, coastal ecosystems—with the high costs of providing infrastructure to sprawl. The result is grotesquely oversized environmental footprints, with a concomitant growth of traffic and air pollution and, most often, the downstream dumping of waste. Where urban forms are dictated by speculators and developers, bypassing democratic controls over planning and resources, the predictable social outcomes are extreme spatial segregation by income or ethnicity, as well as unsafe environments for children, the elderly, and those with special needs; inner-city development is conceived as gentrification through eviction, destroying working-class urban culture in the process. To these we may add the socio-political features of the megalopolis under conditions of capitalist globalization: the growth of peripheral slums and informal employment, the privatization of public space, low-intensity warfare between police and subsistence criminals, and bunkering of the wealthy in sterilized historical centers or walled suburbs.

By contrast, those qualities that are most "classically" urban, even on the scale of small cities and towns, combine to generate a more virtuous circle. Where there are well-defined boundaries between city and countryside, urban growth can preserve open space and vital natural systems, while creating environmental economies of scale in transportation and residential construction. Access to city centers from the periphery becomes affordable, and traffic can be regulated more effectively. Waste is more easily recycled, not exported downstream. In classic urban visions, public luxury replaces privatized consumption through the socialization of desire and identity within collective urban space. Large domains of public or non-profit housing reproduce ethnic and income heterogeneity at fractal scales throughout the city. Egalitarian public services and cityscapes are designed with children, the elderly, and those with special needs in mind. Democratic controls offer powerful capacities for progressive taxation and planning, with high levels of political mobilization and civic participation, the priority of civic memory over proprietary icons, and the spatial integration of work, recreation, and home life.

The city as its own solution

Such sharp demarcations between "good" and "bad" features of city life are redolent of famous twentieth-century attempts to distill a canonical urbanism or anti-urbanism: Lewis Mumford and Jane Jacobs, Frank Lloyd Wright and Walt Disney, Corbusier and the CIAM manifesto, the "New Urbanism" of Andrés Duany and Peter Calthorpe, and so on. But no one needs urban theorists to have eloquent opinions about the virtues and vices of built environments and the kinds of social interactions they foster or discourage. What often goes unnoticed in such moral inventories, however, is the consistent affinity between social and environmental justice, between the communal ethos and a greener urbanism. Their mutual attraction is magnetic, if not inevitable. The conservation of urban green spaces and waterscapes, for example, serves simultaneously to preserve vital natural elements of the urban metabolism while providing leisure and cultural resources for the popular classes. Reducing suburban gridlock with better planning and more public transit turns traffic sewers back into neighborhood streets while reducing greenhouse emissions.

There are innumerable examples like these, and they all point toward a single unifying principle: namely, that the cornerstone of the low-carbon city, far more than any particular green design or technology, is the priority given to public affluence over private wealth. As we all know, several additional Earths would be required to allow all of humanity to live in a suburban house with two cars and a lawn, and this obvious constraint is sometimes evoked to justify the impossibility of reconciling finite resources with rising standards of living. Most contemporary cities, in rich countries or poor, repress the potential environmental efficiencies inherent in human-settlement density. The ecological genius of the city remains a vast, largely hidden power. But there is no planetary shortage of "carrying capacity" if we are willing to make democratic public space, rather than modular, private consumption, the engine of sustainable equality. Public affluence— represented by great urban parks, free museums, libraries, and infinite possibilities for human interaction—represents an alternative route to a rich standard of life based on Earth-friendly sociality. Although seldom noticed by academic urban theorists, university campuses are often little quasi-socialist paradises around rich public spaces for learning, research, performance, and human reproduction.

The utopian ecological critique of the modern city was pioneered by socialists and anarchists, beginning with Guild Socialism's dream—influenced by the bio-regionalist ideas of Kropotkin and later Geddes—of garden cities for re-artisanized English workers, and ending with the bombardment of the Karl Marx-Hof, Red Vienna's great experiment in communal living, during the Austrian Civil War in 1934. In between are the invention of the kibbutz by Russian and Polish socialists, the modernist social housing projects of the Bauhaus, and the extraordinary debate over urbanism conducted in the Soviet Union during the 1920s. This radical urban imagination was a victim of the tragedies of the 1930s and 1940s. Stalinism, on the one hand, veered toward a monumentalism in architecture and art, inhumane in scale and texture, that was little different from the Wagnerian hyperboles of Albert Speer in the Third Reich. Postwar social democracy, on the other hand, abandoned alternative urbanism for a Keynesian mass-housing policy that emphasized economies of scale in high-rise projects on cheap suburban estates, and thereby uprooted traditional working-class urban identities.

Yet the late-nineteenth and early-twentieth-century conversations about the "socialist city" provide invaluable starting points for thinking about the current crisis. Consider, for example, the Constructivists. El Lissitzky, Melnikov, Leonidov, Golosov, the Vesnin brothers, and other brilliant socialist designers—constrained as they were by early Soviet urban misery and a drastic shortage of public investment—proposed to relieve congested apartment life with splendidly designed workers' clubs, people's theaters and sports complexes. They gave urgent priority to the emancipation of proletarian women through the organization of communal kitchens, day nurseries, public baths, and cooperatives of all kinds. Although they envisioned workers' clubs and social centers, linked to vast Fordist factories and eventual high-rise housing, as the "social condensers" of a new proletarian civilization, they were also elaborating a practical strategy for leveraging poor urban workers' standard of living in otherwise austere circumstances.

In the context of global environmental emergency, this Constructivist project could be translated into the proposition that the egalitarian aspects of city life consistently provide the best sociological and physical supports for resource conservation and carbon mitigation. Indeed, there is little hope of mitigating greenhouse emissions or adapting human habitats to the Anthropocene unless the movement to control global warming converges with the struggle to raise living standards and abolish world poverty. And in real life, beyond the IPCC's simplistic scenarios, this means participating in the struggle for democratic control over urban space, capital flows, resource-sheds, and large-scale means of production.

The inner crisis in environmental politics today is precisely the lack of bold concepts that address the challenges of poverty, energy, biodiversity, and climate change within an integrated vision of human progress. At a micro-level, of course, there have been enormous strides in developing alternative technologies and passive-energy housing, but demonstration projects in wealthy communities and rich countries will not save the world. The more affluent, to be sure, can now choose from an abundance of designs for eco-living, but what is the ultimate goal: to allow well-meaning celebrities to brag about their zero-carbon lifestyles or to bring solar energy, toilets, pediatric clinics, and mass transit to poor urban communities?

Beyond the green zone
Tackling the challenge of sustainable urban design for the whole planet, and not just for a few privileged countries or social groups, requires a vast stage for the imagination, such as the arts and sciences inhabited in the May Days of Vkhutemas and the Bauhaus. It presupposes a radical willingness to think beyond the horizon of neoliberal capitalism toward a global revolution that reintegrates the labor of the informal working classes, as well as the rural poor, in the sustainable reconstruction of their built environments and livelihoods. Of course, this is an utterly unrealistic scenario, but one either embarks on a journey of hope, believing that collaborations between architects, engineers, ecologists, and activists can play small but essential roles in making an *alter-monde* more possible, or one submits to a future in which designers are just the hireling imagineers of elite, alternative existences. Planetary "green zones" may offer pharaonic opportunities for the monumentalization of individual visions, but the moral questions of architecture and planning can only be resolved in the tenements and sprawl of the "red zones."

From this perspective, only a return to explicitly utopian thinking can clarify the minimal conditions for the preservation of human solidarity in the face of convergent planetary crises. I think I understand what the Italian Marxist architects Tafuri and Dal Co meant when they cautioned against "a regression to the utopian"; but to raise our imaginations to the challenge of the Anthropocene, we must be able to envision alternative configurations of agents, practices, and social relations, and this requires, in turn, that we suspend the politico-economic assumptions that chain us to the present. But utopianism is not necessarily millenarianism, nor is it confined just to the soapbox or pulpit. One of the most encouraging developments in that emergent intellectual space where researchers and activists discuss the impacts of global warming on development has been a new willingness to advocate the Necessary rather than the merely Practical. A growing chorus of expert voices warn that either we fight for "impossible" solutions to the increasingly entangled crises of urban poverty and climate change, or become ourselves complicit in a de facto triage of humanity.

Thus I think we can be cheered by a 2008 editorial in *Nature*. Explaining that the "challenges of rampant urbanization demand integrated, multidisciplinary approaches and new thinking," the editors urge the rich countries to finance a zero-carbon revolution in the cities of the developing world. "It may seem utopian," they write,

> to promote these innovations in emerging and developing-world megacities, many of whose inhabitants can barely afford a roof over their heads. But those countries have already shown a gift for technological fast-forwarding, for example, by leapfrogging the need for landline infrastructure to embrace mobile phones. And many poorer countries have a rich tradition of adapting buildings to local

practices, environments and climates—a home-grown approach to integrated design that has been all but lost in the West. They now have an opportunity to combine these traditional approaches with modern technologies.[24]

Similarly, the UN Human Development Report warns that the "future of human solidarity" depends upon a massive aid program to help developing countries adapt to climate shocks. The Report calls for removing the "obstacles to the rapid disbursement of the low-carbon technologies needed to avoid dangerous climate change"—"the world's poor cannot be left to sink or swim with their own resources while rich countries protect their citizens behind climate-defence fortifications." "Put bluntly," it continues, "the world's poor and future generations cannot afford the complacency and prevarication that continue to characterize international negotiations on climate change." The refusal to act decisively on behalf of all humanity would be "a moral failure on a scale unparalleled in history."[25] If this sounds like a sentimental call to the barricades, an echo from the classrooms, streets, and studios of forty years ago, then so be it; on the basis of the evidence before us, taking a "realist" view of the human prospect, like seeing Medusa's head, would simply turn us into stone.

Notes

PREFACE

1. Apologies to Larry McMurtry and Walter Benjamin.
2. Hans-Josef Steinberg and Nicholas Jacobs, "Workers' Libraries in Germany before 1914," *History Workshop* 1 (Spring 1976), pp. 175–6.

    Isaac Deutscher used to tell a story about his difficulties as a young Communist in finding an entryway into *Capital*. "I was relieved to hear that Ignacy Daszynski, our famous member of parliament, a pioneer of socialism, an orator on whose lips hung the parliaments of Vienna and Warsaw, admitted that he too found *Das Kapital* too hard a nut. 'I have not read it,' he boasted, 'but Karl Kautsky has read it and has written a popular summary of it. I have not read Kautsky either; but Kelles-Krauz, our party theorist, has read him, and he summarized Kautsky's book. I have not read Kelles-Krauz either, but that clever Jew, Herman Diamond, our financial expert, has read Kelles-Krauz, and has told me all about it." Isaac Deutscher, "Discovering *Das Kapital*," in *Marxism in Our Time* (San Francisco: Ramparts, 1971), p. 257.
3. Boris Nicolaievsky and Otto Maenchen-Helfen, *Karl Marx: Man and Fighter*, expanded edn (London: Allen Lane, 1973 [1933]), p. ix.
4. *Marx and Engels Collected Works* (henceforward *CW*), *Vol. 1* (London: Lawrence & Wishart, 2010), p. 576.
5. Daniel Bensaïd, *Marx for Our Times: Adventures and Misadventures of a Critique* (London: Verso, 2002).

6. The collected works, of course, are not the complete works. The Marx/Engels archives, two-thirds in Amsterdam and one-third in Moscow, contain, in addition to published works, a vast collection of drafts (there are four of *Capital*), articles, newspaper columns, manifestos, fragments, 200 excerpt notebooks, and correspondence with 2,000 individuals. Publication of the whole has been variously estimated to require 130 to 180 printed volumes. Since Austrian Marxists first proposed a collected edition in 1911, moreover, there has been continuous debate over what should be included and how to insulate the editorial apparatus from party ideologies. At times this has been a life-and-death matter: David Riazanov, selected by Lenin in 1921 to lead the Marx-Engels Institute in Moscow, undertook work on the first edition (known as MEGA 1) in 1923, but fell afoul of Stalin, partly because of his opposition to censorship of perceived anti-Russian tracts by Marx and Engels, and was shot in 1938 together with many of his researchers. His work was resumed after 1960 in two different forms: the *Marx-Engels Collected Works* (MECW), which began publication in 1975 and is now finished; and the much more complete and ambitious MEGA II, which, after the collapse of the GDR and the USSR, became a broad international collaboration (the IMES) and remains years from completion. For overviews of this complicated history, see Kevin Anderson, "Uncovering Marx's Yet Unpublished Writings," *Critique* 30/31 (1998); Jurgen Rohan, "Publishing Marx and Engels after 1989: The Fate of the MEGA," *Nature, Society, and Thought* 13: 4 (October 2000); and Amy Wendling, "Comparing Two Editions of Marx-Engels Collected Works," *Socialism and Democracy* 19: 1 (2005). Navigating the shoals and rapids of the MECW is less challenging if one utilizes Hal Draper's splendid chronological guide, *The Marx-Engels Chronicle* (New York: Schocken, 1985).

7. This guesstimate is calculated on the following basis: Russian civil war—1 million Red Army soldiers killed; repression in interwar Europe, including Italy and Spain—150,000; China to 1949—1.5 million; Soviet Union, 1937 purge—150,000 communists; Soviet Union, Second World War (party members and Komsomol only)—3 million; Nazi Europe, including partisans—500,000; Southeast Asia (Indochina, Philippines, Indonesia)—1 million; and Latin America—100,000.

8. Barbara Taylor, *Eve and the New Jerusalem: Socialism and Feminism in the Nineteenth Century* (London: Virago, 1983).

9. "Marxism: Theory of Proletarian Revolution," *New Left Review* I/97 (May–June 1976).

I. OLD GODS, NEW ENIGMAS

1. "History in the 'Age of Extremes': A Conversation with Eric Hobsbawm (1995)," *International Labor and Working-Class History* 83 (March 2013), p. 19.

2. Secondary-sector data from statista.com. The overall growth of the Chinese working class, as the countryside has sent tens of millions of its daughters and sons to labor in the coastal export-processing zones, disguises the simultaneous decline of the state-owned industrial sector and the bitter layoffs of veteran industrial workers. See Ju Li, "From 'Master' to 'Loser': Changing Working-Class Cultural Identity in Contemporary China," *International Labor and Working-Class History* 88 (Fall 2015), pp. 190–208.

3. Erik Brynjolfsson and Andew McAfee, *Race Against the Machine* (Lexington, MA: Digital Frontier, 2011); Simon Head, *Mindless: Why Smarter Machines are Making Dumber Humans* (New York: Basic Books, 2014); and John Peters, "Neoliberal Convergence in North America and Western Europe: Fiscal Austerity, Privatization, and Public Sector Reform," *Review of International Political Economy* 19: 2 (May 2012), pp. 208–35.

4. Shawn Sprague, "What Can Labor Productivity Tell Us About the U.S. Economy?" *BLS: Beyond the Numbers* 3: 12 (May 2014), cited in Martin Ford, *Rise of the Robots: Technology and the Threat of a Jobless Future* (New York: Basic Books, 2015), p. 281.

5. Martin Baily and Barry Bosworth, "U.S. Manufacturing: Understanding Its Past and Its Potential Future," *Journal of Economic Perspectives* 28: 1 (Winter 2014), pp. 3–4.

6. "It is not this abolition we should object to, but its claiming to perpetuate that same work, the norms, dignity and availability of which it is abolishing, as an obligation, as a norm, and as the irreplaceable foundation of the rights and dignity of all." André Gorz, *Reclaiming Work: Beyond the Wage-Based Society* (Cambridge: Polity, 1999 [French 1997]), p. 1.

7. Studies, for example, have contrasted the organized French working class's broadly inclusive sense of "Us," circa 1970s, with the current rage against Muslim immigrants and young unemployed people in general. "Them" is now those "below" the traditional proletariat as well as those "above" it. See Michele Lamont and Nicolas Duvoux, "How Has Neo-liberalism Transformed France's Symbolic Boundaries?" *Culture & Society* 32: 2 (Summer 2014), pp. 57–75;

and Olivier Schwartz, "Vivons-nous encore dans une societé des classes?" September 22, 2009, at laviedesidees.fr.

8. Half of American jobs are estimated to be at risk from automation/computerization in the next twenty years. This is the conclusion of the much-debated report by Carl Frey and Michael Osborne for the Martin School at Oxford University, "The Future of Employment: How Susceptible Are Jobs to Computerisation?" Working Paper, Oxford, September 2013. For a critical response, see Melanie Arntz, Terry Gregory, and Ulrich Zierahn, "The Risk of Automation for Jobs in OECD Countries," OECD Social, Employment and Migration Working Papers No. 189 (Paris: OECD, 2016).

9. See Gregory Woirol, *The Technological Unemployment and Structural Unemployment Debates* (Westport, CT: Greenwood, 1996); J. Jesse Ramirez, "Marcuse Among the Technocrats: America, Automation, Postcapitalist Utopias, 1900–1941," *Amerikastudien/American Studies* 57: 1 (2012), pp. 31–50; Donald Stabile, "Automation, Workers and Union Decline: Ben Seligman's Contribution to the Institutional Economics of Labor," *Labor History* 49: 3 (2008), pp. 275–95; and Daniel Bell, "Government by Commission" (the National Commission on Technology, Automation and Economic Progress, on which Bell served), *The Public Interest* (Spring 1966), pp. 3–9.

10. *Annual Report of the Council of Economic Advisers* (Washington, 2016), pp. 238–9.

11. "Whereas the First Wave laid the foundation for internet infrastructure, and the Second Wave built key applications on top of it (e-commerce, social media, search, etc.), the Third Wave involves embedding these technologies into virtually all non-digital sectors of the economy, such as health care, finance, agriculture, manufacturing, and countless others." Ian Hathaway, "The Third Wave of Digital Technology Meets the Rustbelt," *Brookings: The Avenue*, May 27, 2016.

12. John Markoff, "Skilled Work, Without the Worker," *New York Times*, August 18, 2012. The rate of factory automation is accelerating. Two-thirds of U.S. manufacturers have already adopted 3-D printing technology, while globally the use of industrial robots has doubled since 2013. Daniel Araya and Christopher Sulavik, "Disrupting Manufacturing: Innovation and the Future of Skilled Labor," *Brookings: The Brown Center Chalkboard*, May 6, 2016; and Darrel West, "How Technology Is Changing Manufacturing," *Brookings TechTank*, June 2, 2016.

13. Markoff, "Skilled Work."

14. "Machines Learning," *Economist*, December 3, 2016, p. 53; Commission of the European Communities, "Internet of Things: An Action Plan for Europe," June 18, 2009 (PDF).

15. *World Employment Social Outlook: Trends 2016* (Geneva: ILO, 2016); *Toward Solutions for Youth Employment: A 2015 Baseline Report*, at s4ye.org.

16. There are of course precedents for delinking the triad of urbanization–industrialization–modernization. Trotsky, for instance, characterized Czarist Russia as a case of "industrialization without modernization." See the fascinating discussion in Baruch Knei-Paz, *The Social and Political Thought of Leon Trotsky* (Oxford: OUP, 1978), pp. 94–107.

17. Michael Goldman, "With the Declining Significance of Labor, Who Is Producing Our Global Cities?" *International Labor and Working-Class History* 87 (Spring 2015), pp. 137–64 (on Bangalore); Olu Ajakaiye, Afeikhena T. Jerome, David Nabena and Olufunke A. Alaba, "Understanding the Relationship between Growth and Employment in Nigeria," *Brookings Paper*, May 2016. On the World Economic Forum's concept of the "Fourth Industrial Revolution," see weforum.org.

18. David Neilson and Thomas Stubbs, "Relative Surplus Population and Uneven Development in the Neoliberal Era: Theory and Empirical Application," *Capital and Class* 35: 3 (2011), p. 451.

19. "The Results of the Immediate Process of Production," *CW* 34, p. 204.

20. Schwartz, "Vivons-nous encore dans une societé des classes?" His ethnographic studies of the impact over the last two generations of neoliberalism on the consciousness of miners, bus drivers, and machinists are essential background to any understanding of the successes of Sarkozy and Marine Le Pen.

21. Quoted in David McLellan, *Marxism After Marx* (New York: Houghton Mifflin, 1981), p. 37.

22. Nick Srnicek and Alex Williams, *Inventing the Future: Folk Politics and the Left* (London: Verso, 2015), p. 157.

23. According to the BLS, in the United States currently there are 400,000 machinists, 2.8 million registered nurses, 3.5 million truck drivers, and 3.5 million K-12 teachers. There are also 3.6 million fast food workers and 2.7 million police, prison guards, and security employees.

24. Simon Charlesworth, *A Phenomenology of Working-Class Experience* (Cambridge: CUP, 2000), p. 2. This is an eviscerating account of the human cost of deindustrialization and the destruction of a traditional culture of labor.

25. The complexities of defining and quantifying informality are justly notorious,

but the state-of-the-art discussion is International Labour Office, *Measuring Informality: A Statistical Manual on the Informal Sector and Informal Employment* (Geneva: ILO, 2013).

26. Christian Marazzi, "Money and Financial Capital," *Theory, Culture, Society* 32: 7–8 (2015), p. 42.

27. "A Critique of Hegel's Philosophy of Law: Introduction", *CW* 3, p. 184.

28. A rising class's claim to incarnate general social interest, of course, entails the negation of such claims by older ruling classes. Sieyès, in equating the Third Estate with the nation, simultaneously cast the nobility as the enemies of the nation. "Because their privileges made them idle consumers of wealth instead of active producers, because they insisted on special privileges and exceptions to the laws that governed the rest of the nation, and because they defended these distinctions from other Frenchmen by deliberating in a separate body in the Estates-General, their interests were utterly removed from those of the nation at large." William Sewell, *A Rhetoric of Bourgeois Revolution: The Abbe Sieyès and What Is the Third Estate?* (Chapel Hill, NC: Duke University Press, 1994), p. 5. Although the juridical concept of the Third Estate included all commoners, it was almost entirely represented in the early Revolution by men of property and the professions.

29. See Gil Delannoi, "Review of André Jardin, *Histoire du Libéralisme politique* ... ," *Esprit* 106: 10 (October 1985), p. 105.

30. "Revisionist" accounts of the Revolution (Furet, Ozouf, Maza, and so on) reject any claim that it was authentically "bourgeois" in politics or leadership; indeed, they deny the existence of a French bourgeoisie in 1789. Class in general evaporates in their work. For a succinct overview of the debate and a strong restatement of the case for bourgeois revolution, see Henry Heller, "Marx, the French Revolution, and the Spectre of the Bourgeosie," *Science & Society* 74: 2 (April 2010), pp. 184–214.

31. Eric Hobsbawm, *Echoes of the Marseillaise* (New Brunswick, NJ: Rutgers University Press, 1990), p. 9.

32. Quoted in Warren Breckman, *Marx, the Young Hegelians, and the Origins of Radical Social Theory* (Cambridge: CUP, 1999), p. 301.

33. Stathis Kouvelakis, *Philosophy and Revolution: From Kant to Marx* (London: Verso, 2003), p. 270.

34. See the discussion by François Furet, "Le Jeune Marx et la Revolution Francaise," in Furet, ed., *Marx et la Revolution Francaise* (Paris: Flammarion, 1986), pp. 13–43, especially p. 32. Bouchez and Roux's project explicitly aimed to

counter the bougeoisie's attempt "to confiscate the Revolution for its own benefit." Jeremy Jennings, *Revolution and the Republic: A History of Political Thought in France Since the Eighteenth Century* (Oxford: OUP, 2011), p. 262.

35. Quoted in Jean Bruhat, "La Revolution Française et la Formation de la Pensée de Marx," *Annales historiques de la Revolution francaise* 184 (April-June 1966), p. 127. This was the pioneer investigation on the topic and, in my opinion at least, richer in detail and interpretation that Furet's little book.

36. François Furet, *Marx and the French Revolution* (Chicago: University of Chicago Press, 1988), p. 19.

37. Ibid., p. 23.

38. Breckman, *Marx*, p. 283. Marx was radicalized, like most people, in several stages. Breckman believes that Marx had already made a "moral commitment" to socialism by summer 1843: if this is correct, then his avowed "Jacobin" or revolutionary-democratic period had lasted somewhat less than a year.

39. Lorenz von Stein, *The History of the Social Movement in France, 1789–1850*, ed. and transl. Kaethe Mengelberg (Totowa, NJ: Bedminister, 1964), pp. 264–5. This is a poor, partial translation of the 1850 third edition. I assume that the passage quoted was in the original 1842 edition (titled *Socialism and Communism in Contemporary France*), but a German reader with access to a good library should make the comparison. The fact that Stein was commissioned by the Prussian police to write this report did not at all dampen its popularity amongst young German radicals. David McLellan, *Karl Marx: A Biography* (London: Macmillan, 1973), pp. 45–6. In the 1890s, Franz Mehring and Peter Struve conducted a memorable debate on Stein's influence on Marx.

40. Lloyd Kramer, *Threshold of a New World: Intellectuals and the Exile Experience in Paris, 1830–1848* (Ithaca: Cornell University Press, 1988). p. 144.

41. *CW* 3, pp. 201–2.

42. Neil Davidson, *How Revolutionary Were the Bourgeois Revolutions?* (Chicago: Haymarket, 2012), p. 120. My emphasis.

43. Dorothy Thompson, *The Chartists* (London: Temple Smith, 1984), p. x. Also, "the years 1848 to 1849 witnessed the emergence, for the first time in German history, of a labor movement that stretched over the entire country." The Arbeiterverbruderung (Workers' Brotherhood), "an impressive if loosely-knit network of artisans' and workers' associations" according to Ralf Roth, had affiliates in 400 towns and cities. Ralf Roth, "*Burger* and Workers," in David Barclay and Eric Weitz, eds, *Between Reform and Revolution: German Socialism and Communism from 1840 to 1990* (New York: Berghahn, 1998), p. 114.

44. My figure, compiled from entries in Hal Draper, *The Marx-Engels Chronicle*, vol. 1 of *The Marx-Engels Cyclopedia* (New York: Schocken, 1985).

45. Théodore Dézamy, *Calomnies et Politique de M. Cabet* (Paris: Prévost, 1842), p. 8.

46. Michael Löwy, *The Theory of Revolution in the Young Marx* (Chicago: Haymarket: 2005), pp. 104–5. Emphasis in original.

47. More accurately, Marx embraced a contradiction. He was scathing of utopian socialist or petty producerist schemas that would freeze economic development at a mixed artisanal/industrial stage; yet, from a post-1848 perspective, over-optimistic—to say the least—about the prospects of proletarian leadership of the democratic revolution and its possible "growing over" into social revolution. The relationship between economic stages and the "objective conditions" for revolution is both a constant theme and an internal debate in his work.

48. Karl Marx, "Contribution to the Critique of Hegel's Philosophy of Law, Introduction," *CW* 3, p. 182.

49. "German criticism of Christianity reminded French radicals of Enlightenment-era atheism and materialism, doctrines that such writers as Louis Blanc perceived as the ideology of the bourgeois liberals who triumphed in the French Revolution and who continued to block the creation of a true democratic society. Blanc and others preferred to use a religious model when they wrote about the aims of the French radical party, whereas Marx and the radical Hegelians wanted to eliminate all religious justifications and referents from social criticism and action." Kramer, p. 125.

50. Zinoviev, speaking in 1924, quoted in Lars Lih, *Lenin Rediscovered: What Is to Be Done? in Context* (Leiden: Brill, 2006), p. 30.

51. Daniel Bensaïd, *Marx for Our Time: Adventures and Misadventures of a Critique* (London: Verso, 2002), pp. 99, 103, 107. See also Ellen Wood, *The Retreat from Class: A New "True" Socialism* (London: Verso, 1986), p. 5.

52. Georg Lukács, *History and Class Consciousness: Studies in Marxist Dialectics* (Cambridge, MA: MIT Press, 1971 [1923]), p. 46.

53. When I speak about the "working class of *Capital*," distinguishing it from the proletariat of his earlier philosophical and historical works, I allude to the entire unfinished opus, including the *Grundrisse* and the *1861–63 Economic Manuscripts*.

54. Marcello Musto, "The Rediscovery of Karl Marx," *International Review of Social History* 52 (2007), p. 478.

55. Étienne Balibar, *The Philosophy of Karl Marx*, new edn (London: Verso, 2017), p. 6.

56. Michael Lebowitz, *Beyond Capital: Marx's Political Economy of the Working Class* (London: Macmillan, 1992), pp. 14, 152. See also Roman Rosdolsky, "Appendix 1. The Book on Wage-Labour," in his *The Making of Marx's "Capital,"* (London: Pluto, 1977), pp. 57–61. In his superb recent book on *Capital*, Callinicos argues that "the chapter on the working day [*Volume 1*] is the clearest refutation" of Lebowitz's claim of one-sidedness in *Capital*. Lebowitz, however, specifically acknowledges the inclusion of instances of proletarian praxis in *Volume 1*, but enumerates at length—and quite convincingly in my opinion—the missing elements, especially those from Marx's early writings, that would have formed the content of the *Wage-Labour* volume. Alex Callinicos, *Deciphering Capital: Marx's Capital and Its Destiny* (London: Bookmarks, 2014), p. 309.

57. Werner Sombart, *Why Is There No Socialism in the United States?* (London: Macmillan, 1976). Robert Michels, *Political Parties: A Sociological Study of the Oligarchical Tendencies of Modern Democracy* (New York: Free Press, 1962). The 1915 English translation is also a revision of the original 1911 German book, with an important new chapter on "Party Life in Wartime."

58. These notes might be considered an adventurous expansion of the theses in "The Special Class," Chapter 2 of Hal Draper, *Karl Marx's Theory of Revolution, II: The Politics of Social Classes* (New York: Monthly Review, 1978), pp. 33–48. Draper's trilogy, along with his two-volume *The Marx-Engels Cyclopedia*, is an unsurpassed resource for navigating and understanding Marx's politico-theoretical legacy.

59. David Shaw, "Happy in Our Chains? Agency and Language in the Postmodern Age," *History and Theory* 40 (December 2001), pp. 19, 21.

60. Alex Callinicos, *Making History: Agency, Structure, and Change in Social Theory* (Leiden: Brill, 2005 [1987]). I also skirt important debates in industrial sociology (a vast literature) that touch on class consciousness and agency. In an influential 1984 article, for example, Michael Burawoy proposed that proletarian potentials for militant action and consciousness had to be understood in terms of a "politics of production" that was both internal and external to the factory system. Different *factory regimes*, he argued, were shaped by the interaction of labor processes with family structures, inter-capitalist competition, and state forms. His intricate comparison of the nineteenth-century textile industries in Lancashire, New England, and Russia was a bravura demonstration of the

fertility of this approach, and it illuminated the complexly variable forms of social regulation that could exist in otherwise similar industries. Although Burawoy was faulted for making an unwarranted leap from his textile case studies to large-scale generalizations about the contrasting revolutionary potentials of national working classes, his critics acknowledged that the "politics of production" marked a major conceptual advance over conventional Marxist or institutionalist analyses of the labor process and class consciousness. Michael Burawoy, "Karl Marx and the Satanic Mills: Factory Politics under Early Capitalism in England, the United States, and Russia," *AJS* 90: 2 (1984), pp. 247–82. Buroway expanded his analysis of factory regimes the following year in *The Politics of Production* (London: Verso, 1985).

61. In one of his early London articles ("Review/May to October, 1850"), Marx first argued that the revolutions of 1848 were ignited by the economic crisis of 1847, and that the revolutionary moment ended with the return of prosperity at the end of 1849. He later incorporated this article as Part IV of *Class Struggles in France*.

62. The key texts are Rosa Luxemburg, "Militarism in the Sphere of Capital Accumulation," Chapter 32 of *The Accumulation of Capital* (*Complete Works*, *Volume 2* (London: Verso, 2016), pp. 331–4; and Lenin, "The Impending Catastrophe and How to Combat It" [1917], *CW* 25, pp. 323–69.

63. The Argentinian, Australian, and New Zealand labor movements could easily be added to the list, but not yet the Japanese.

64. In a reply to dogmatic critics, Lukács, citing Franz Mehring's history of the SPD, disputed any simplistic correlation between plant size and class consciousness. While skilled machine workers in large factories were only won to Social Democracy by protracted and arduous organizing, "cigar workers, cobblers, tailors, etc. joined the ranks of the revolutionary movement more swiftly." Georg Lukács, *A Defence of* History and Class Consciousness*: Tailism and the Dialectic* (London: Verso, 2000 [1925/26]), pp. 68–9.

65. See the discussion in Marcel van der Linden and Wayne Thorpe, "The Rise and Fall of Revolutionary Syndicalism," in their edited volume, *Revolutionary Syndicalism: An International Perspective* (Aldershot, UK: Scolar, 1990), pp. 1–25.

66. Bensaïd, *Marx for Our Times*, p. 118.

67. Roger Magraw, "Socialism, Syndicalism and French Labor Before 1914," in Dick Geary, ed., *Labour and Socialist Movements in Europe Before 1914* (Oxford: Berg, 1989), p. 53.

Notes for Pages 28 to 35

68. "At Le Creusot Schneider [the owner] was deputy, lived in a chateau, and had his statue in the town square; his valet brought wedding gifts to loyal employees" (Magraw, p. 63). George Pullman didn't send presents via valet to his resident workers, but instead infiltrated "spotters" to "mingle with them to catch and report to their masters any sign or word expressive of disapproval or criticism of the authorities." Almont Lindsey, *The Pullman Strike* (Chicago: University of Chicago Press, 1942), p. 64.

69. Yavuz Karakisla, "The 1908 Strike Wave in the Ottoman Empire," *Turkish Studies Association Bulletin* 16: 2 (September 1992), p. 155.

70. Kevin Callahan, "The International Socialist Peace Movement on the Eve of World War I Revisited," *Peace & Change* 29: 2 (April 2004), p. 170.

71. Statistic from Yury Polyakove cited in Robert Gerwarth, "The Central European Counter-Revolution: Paramilitary Violence in Germany, Austria and Hungary After the Great War," *Past and Present* 200 (August 2008), p. 181.

72. Charles Maier, *Recasting Bourgeois Europe* (Princeton, NJ: Princeton University Press, 1975), p. 136.

73. "The head of this emancipation is philosophy, its heart is the proletariat. Philosophy cannot be made a reality without the abolition of the proletariat, the proletariat cannot be abolished without philosophy being made a reality." *CW* 4, p. 187.

74. "1844 Introduction," *CW* 3, p. 186.

75. Joachim Singelmann and Peter Singelmann, "Lorenz von Stein and the Paradigmatic Bifurcation of Social Theory in the Nineteenth Century," *British Journal of Sociology* 37: 3 (September 1986), p. 442.

76. *CW* 4, pp. 36–7.

77. Karl Kautsky, *From Handicraft to Capitalism* (London: SPGB, 1907), pp. 14, 15. This is a separate translation of a chapter in *The Class Struggle* ("The Erfurt Program"), 1892.

78. From a petition of Hessian guilds to the Frankfurt Assembly in 1848. P. Noyes, *Organization and Revolution: Working-Class Associations in the German Revolutions of 1848–1849* (Princeton, NJ: Princeton University Press, 1966), p. 25. Christopher Johnson, writing about the popularity of Icarian communism amongst the Lyonnais silk weavers, described them as "the most mature and politically conscious working class on the Continent" circa 1840. Christopher Johnson, "Communism and the Working Class before Marx: The Icarian Experience," *American Historical Review* 76: 3 (June 1971), p. 658.

79. Karl Marx, *Grundrisse* (London: Allen Lane/New Left Review, 1973), p. 604.

233

80. Marc Mulholland, "Marx, the Proletariat, and the 'Will to Socialism,'" *Critique* 37: 3 (2009), pp. 339–40.

81. David Montgomery, "Commentary and Response," *Labor History* 40: 1 (1999), p. 37.

82. Marx, *Grundrisse*, p. 770.

83. See the essays in Maxine Berg, Pat Hudson, and Michael Sonenscher, eds., *Manufacture in Town and Country Before the Factory* (Cambridge: CUP, 1983).

84. Sanford Elwitt, "Politics and Ideology in the French Labor Movement," *Journal of Modern History* 49: 3 (September 1977), p. 470.

85. Ronald Aminzade, "Class Analysis, Politics, and French Labor History," in Lenard Berlanstein, ed., *Rethinking Labor History: Essays on Discourse and Class Analysis* (Urbana, IL: University of Illinois Press, 1993), p. 93.

86. Jacques Rancière, "The Myth of the Artisan: Critical Reflections on a Category of Social History," *International Labor and Working-Class History* 24 (Fall 1983), p. 4.

87. Karl Marx, *Capital Volume I* (London: Penguin, 1976), p. 574. Marx, of course, did believe that *wage workers* as a whole would constitute overwhelming majorities in all advanced industrial societies.

88. Adam Przeworski, "Proletariat into a Class: The Process of Class Formation from Karl Kautsky's *The Class Struggle* to Recent Controversies," *Politics and Society* 7: 4 (1977), pp. 358–9.

89. *Capital Volume I*, pp. 517, 574–5. In pre-revolutionary Russia, according to Barbara Clements, "almost half of all women working for a wage were domestic servants (approximately 10 million)." Barbara Clements, "Working-Class and Peasant Women in the Russian Revolution, 1917–1923," *Signs* 8: 2 (Winter 1982), p. 225.

90. See Leonore Davidoff, "Mastered for Life: Servant and Wife in Victorian and Edwardian England," *Journal of Social History* 7 (1974), pp. 406–28.

91. For the legal history on both sides of the Atlantic, see Part III, "Law, Authority, and the Employment Relationship," in Christopher Tomlins, *Law, Labor, and Ideology in the Early American Republic* (Cambridge: CUP, 1993), pp. 223–94.

92. Mary Nolan, "Economic Crisis, State Policy, and Working-Class Formation in Germany, 1870–1900," in Ira Katznelson and Aristide Zolberg, eds, *Working-Class Formation: Nineteenth-Century Patterns in Western Europe and the United States* (Princeton, NJ: Princeton University Press, 1986), p. 364.

93. Raphael Samuel, "Mechanization and Hand Labour in Industrializing Britain," in Lenard Berlanstein, ed., *The Industrial Revolution and Work in*

Nineteenth-Century Europe (London: Routledge, 1992), p. 38. This is the counter-pressure to the tendency for the introduction of machinery into one branch to bring about its introduction into others. See *Capital Volume I*, p. 393.

94. Gareth Stedman Jones, *Outcast London: A Study in the Relationship Between Classes in Victorian Society* (Oxford: OUP, 1971), p. 107.

95. Marx apparently showed little interest in the early activities of Jewish socialists in London, but after his death Eleanor became a habitué of the Jewish Socialist Club with the enthusiastic support of Engels, who himself was the fiercest foe of anti-Semitism in the ranks of the Second International. See the discussion in Nathan Weinstock, *Le Pain de Misere: Histoire du movement ouvrier juif en Europe. Tome II* (Paris: Le Decouverte, 2002), pp. 92–5.

96. *Capital Volume I*, p. 467.

97. *The Poverty of Philosophy*, *CW* 6, p. 183; *CW* 34, p. 123.

98. "The Results of the Direct Process of Production," *CW* 34, pp. 428–9. In other translations: "the immediate process of production."

99. Étienne Balibar, "On the Basic Concepts of Historical Materialism," in Louis Althusser and Étienne Balibar, *Reading Capital* (London: Verso, 2015), p. 404.

100. "The Results of the Direct Process of Production," *CW* 34, pp. 14–18. This is the unpublished "Part Seven" of *Capital Volume I*.

101. Carlo Vercellone, "From Formal Subsumption to General Intellect: Elements for a Marxist Reading of the Thesis of Cognitive Capitalism," *Historical Materialism* 15 (2007), p. 24.

102. *Capital Volume I*, pp. 423, 510. "It would be possible to write quite a history of the inventions, made since 1830, for the sole purpose of supplying capital with weapons against the revolts of the working-class" (p. 436).

103. *CW* 34, p. 30.

104. Ibid., p. 123. Emphases in original. For a sophisticated treatment of this distinction and its implications for class formation, see David Neilson, "Formal and Real Subordination and the Contemporary Proletariat: Re-coupling Marxist Class Theory and Labour-Process Analysis," *Capital & Class* 31: 1 (Spring 2007), pp. 89–123.

105. Friedrich Lenger, "Beyond Exceptionalism: Notes on the Artisanal Phase of the Labour Movement in France, England, Germany and the United States," *International Review of Social History* 36 (1991), p. 2.

106. See Robert Hoffman, *Revolutionary Justice: The Social and Political Theory of P.-J. Proudhon* (Urbana: University of Illinois Press, 1972), pp. 311–15. One

should not overstate the distinction as it applied to specific struggles. In the 1840s, for example, it was not uncommon for artisans and factory workers to act as a single class. Chartism was an alliance of both groups, and the great revolt of the Silesian weavers in 1844 was immediately accompanied by strikes in Berlin's calico factories as well as amongst railroad workers. P. H. Noyes, *Organization and Revolution: Working-Class Associations in the German Revolutions of 1848–1849* (Princeton, NJ: Princeton University Press, 1966), p. 34.

107. André Gorz, *Strategy for Labor* (Boston: Beacon, 1967), p. 3.

108. Herbert Marcuse, *One-Dimensional Man* (Boston: Beacon, 1964), p. 26 fn 7. Rosdolsky mounts a fierce attack on this nexus of exploitation and immiseration in his *The Making of Marx's "Capital,"* calling it just a "legend" (p. 307). But the careful reader will note that the object of Rosdolsky's scorn is the idea of secular (increasing) impoverishment, what Stalinist dogma called the "law of absolute immiseration," not the destruction of employment and standards of living during depressions and wars.

109. Lebowitz, *Beyond Capital*, Chapter 2. Lebowitz interprets Marx, I think correctly, as asserting that immiseration is *inherent* in capitalism at all times, but that its content—the reproductive minimum—is variable; he also rightly emphasizes that immiseration does not spontaneously generate class consciousness. But at the same time I believe that Marcuse is more accurate in attributing to Marx the belief that impoverishment or its threat has been an empirical requirement of all genuine revolutionary crises.

110. The panic ensued from the Bank of England's refusal to rescue the "shadow banking system" represented by discount houses and bill brokers. The experience led to the modern policy of the Bank as "lender of last resort," according to the principles advocated by Walter Bagehot in his famous book *Lombard Street* (1873). Recent financial disasters have revived interest in the events of 1866. "The analogy with the Fed's refusal to help Lehman in September 2008 and the events that followed is not only tempting: it is legitimate." Marc Flandreau and Stefano Ugolini, "Where It All Began: Lending of Last Resort and the Bank of England during the Overend-Gurney Panic of 1866," *Norge's Bank Working Paper*, 2011, p. 4.

111. *Capital Volume I*, p. 668.

112. Jeffry Frieden, *Global Capitalism: Its Fall and Rise in the Twentieth Century* (New York: W. W. Norton, 2006), p. 121.

113. Marx was arguing that, since unions were powerless to prevent workers from

losing ground in a downturn, it was all the more important for them to fight for higher wages in periods of prosperity when the demand for labor was high. (*CW* 20, p. 143.)

114. Eric Hobsbawm, *The Age of Empire: 1876–1914* (New York: Vintage, 1989), pp. 48–9.

115. In an unpublished draft from 1892, Engels claimed: "The absence of crisis since 1868 [is] attributable to the expansion of the world market, which distributed the excess English and European capital *over the entire world* in transport equipment and the like, and equally in a whole mass of different types of machinery. Thus a crisis due to overspecialization in railways, banks, etc., or in special American equipment or in the Indian trade became impossible, though small crises, like the Argentinian one, [have been] possible for the last three years. But all this goes to show that a gigantic crisis is preparing itself." "On Certain Peculiarities in England's Economic and Political Development," September 12, 1892, *CW* 27, pp. 324–5.

116. Leon Trotsky, *Manifesto of the Communist International to the Workers of the World*, March 6, 1919, in Jane Degras, ed, *The Communist International: Documents, 1919–1943, Volume 1 (1919–1922)* (Oxford: OUP, 1956), p. 40.

117. *CW* 11, p. 187.

118. Eric Hobsbawm, "Class Consciousness in History," in István Mészáros, ed., *Aspects of History and Class Consciousness* (London: Routledge, 1971), p. 9.

119. Constantin Pecqueur, *Économie sociale … sous l'influence des applications de la vapeur* (Paris: Desessart, 1839), pp. xi, 62–3. Pecqueur, the advocate of a rather sinister version of state socialism, has occasionally been celebrated—by French writers—as the "French Marx." See Joseph Marie, *Le socialisme de Pecqueur* (Whitefish, MT: Kessinger, 2010 [1906]), pp. 66–7, 108–10.

120. Katherine Archibald, *Wartime Shipyard: A Study in Social Disunity* (Berkeley, CA: University of California Press, 1947).

121. Ralph Darlington, "Shop Stewards' Leadership, Left-Wing Activism and Collective Workplace Union Organization," *Capital & Class* 76 (2002), p. 99.

122. Sometimes workplace resistance was organized by underground traditions brought into the factory or mine by groups of immigrants. For example, the Molly Maguires of the anthracite belt of Pennsylvania in the 1860s–70s were largely Irish speakers from communities of Donegal with a history of secret organization and counter-violence against landlords. See the remarkable study by Kevin Kenny, *Making Sense of the Molly Maguires* (New York: New York University Press, 1995).

123. Kevin Murphy, *Revolution and Counterrevolution: Class Struggle in a Moscow Metal Factory* (Chicago: Haymarket, 2007), pp. 12, 18.

124. Roger Friedlander, *The Emergence of a UAW Local, 1936–1939: A Study in Class and Culture* (Pittsburgh: University of Pittsburgh Press, 1977).

125. *CW* 4, p. 511.

126. *CW* 6, p. 211.

127. Gerald Friedman, *State-Making and Labor Movements: France and the United States, 1876–1914* (Ithaca, NY: Cornell University Press, 1998), pp. 50–1.

128. Nick Salvatore, *Eugene V. Debs: Citizen and Socialist* (Urbana, IL: University of Illinois Press, 1992), p. 138.

129. Michelle Perrot, "1914: Great Feminist Expectations," in Helmut Gruber and Pamela Graves, eds, *Women and Socialism, Socialism and Women: Europe Between the Two World Wars* (New York: Berghahn, 1998), p. 27.

130. *Capital Volume I*, p. 553.

131. Sidney Pollard, "Factory Discipline in the Industrial Revolution," *The Economic History Review* (new series) 16: 2 (1963), p. 260.

132. Kathleen Canning, "Gender and the Politics of Class Formation: Rethinking German Labor History," *American Historical Review* 97: 3 (June 1992), p. 757.

133. Barrington Moore, Jr, *Injustice: The Social Bases of Obedience and Revolt* (White Plains, NY: M. E. Sharpe, 1978), p. 268.

134. The wrath of the workers was directed especially against the glass manufacturer Eugene Baudoux, who had introduced a new technology that deskilled artisan glass-blowers. Both his factory, the most modern in Europe, and his chateau were burned to the ground. Gita Deneckere, "The Transforming Impact of Collective Action: Belgium, 1886," *International Review of Social History* 38 (1993), pp. 350–2.

135. Moore, *Injustice*, p. 253.

136. Abraham Ascher, *The Revolution of 1905: Russia in Disarray* (Palo Alto, CA: Stanford University Press, 1988), pp. 140–1.

137. Pioneer management consultant Mary Parker Follett, quoted in Wallace Hopp and Mark Spearman, *Factory Physics: Foundations of Manufacturing Management* (Chicago, IL: Irwin, 1996), p. 40.

138. Marcel van der Linden and Wayne Thorpe, "The Rise and Fall of Revolutionary Syndicalism," in van der Linden and Thorpe, *Revolutionary Syndicalism*, p. 11.

139. Alain Cottereau, "The Distinctiveness of Working-Class Cultures in France, 1848–1900," in Ira Katznelson and Aristide Zolberg, *Working-Class Formation:*

Nineteenth-Century Patterns in Western Europe and the United States (New Haven, NJ: Princeton, 1986), pp. 131–3, 140.

140. Ibid., pp. 146–7.

141. Leon Trotsky, *The History of the Russian Revolution* (three volumes in one) (New York: Simon & Schuster, 1937), p. 11. Following the bloody clashes between workers and armed police in Petersburg's shipyards and engineering works during May Day 1901, General Ratnik, the director of the Baltic Works, circulated an insightful study of the composition of the metallurgical work-force. About one-fifth of the workers, mostly skilled and literate, belonged to Trotsky's "hereditary proletarian" stratum and were both the most able workers and the most dangerous activists. Their families, for the most part, had artisanal or petty-bourgeois roots or, if originally from the countryside, had long lived in the city. But the vast majority of the workforce, especially those who worked in the "hot shops," were newly recruited peasants, about half of whom maintained their rural allotments and village bonds. General Ratnik acknowledged that they were the most deferential to traditional authority, but at the same time the least equipped to deal with the demands of technol-ogy or work productively. The battle for efficiency, he concluded, rested on management's ability to win the modern workers away from radical groups and make them allies in reorganizing production along "American lines" (i.e. Taylorism). See Heather Hogan, "Scientific Management and the Changing Nature of Work in the St Petersburg Metalworking Industry, 1900–1914," in Leopold Haimson and Charles Tilly, eds, *Strikes, Wars and Revolutions in an International Perspective* (Cambridge: CUP, 1989), pp. 356–79.

142. Charters Wynn, *Workers, Strikes, and Pogroms: The Donbass–Dnepr Bend in Late Imperial Russia, 1870–1905* (Princeton, NJ: Princeton University Press, 1992), pp. 4–8.

143. Introduction to Karl Marx's *The Class Struggles in France, 1848 to 1850* (1895), *CW* 27, p. 128

144. Ibid., p. 516.

145. Ibid., p. 522.

146. Hilferding, from the left of the SPD, also embraced the general strike as the ultimate weapon to defend universal suffrage and a socialist majority, but added that its use would require "the will to decisive battle." Kautsky simply proposed a study of the tactic. See Carl Schorske, *German Social Democracy, 1905–1917: The Development of the Great Schism* (Cambridge: Harvard University Press, 1955), pp. 35–6.

147. Phil Goodstein, *The Theory of the General Strike from the French Revolution to Poland*, Eastern European Monographs (New York: Columbia University Press, 1984), pp. 134–5.

148. Janet Polasky, "A Revolution for Socialist Reforms: The Belgian General Strike for Universal Suffrage," *Journal of Contemporary History* 27: 3 (July 1992), p. 463.

149. Jesper Hamark and Christer Thornqvist, "Docks and Defeat: The 1909 General Strike in Sweden and the Role of Port Labour," *Historical Studies in Industrial Relations* 34 (2013), pp. 22–3. They argue that the month-long general strike ultimately collapsed because the government and employers were able to keep the docks open.

150. Georges Sorel, *Reflections on Violence* (Glencoe, IL: Free Press, 1950), p. 145.

151. Rosa Luxemburg, "The Mass Strike [1906]," in Helen Scott, ed., *The Essential Rosa Luxemburg* (Chicago: Haymarket, 2008), pp. 141, 147; and Shorske, *German Social Democracy*, pp. 57–8. For Trotsky's well-known critique of "spontaneousness," see Leon Trotsky, "Who Led the February Insurrection?"—Chapter VIII of *The History of the Russian Revolution* (three volumes in one), Volume 1, pp. 142–52. In addition to the revolution in the Russian empire, 1 million workers demonstrated in the Austrian realm and Saxony. "It was estimated that 250,000 demonstrated in Vienna alone." See Christoph Nonn, "Putting Radicalism to the Test: German Social Democracy and the 1905 Suffrage Demonstrations in Dresden," *International Review of Social History* 41 (1996), p. 186.

152. Lenin, "The Reorganization of the Party" (1905), *CW* 10, p. 32; Goodstein, *Theory of the General Strike*, p. 153. Lenin, of course, had argued four years earlier in "What Is to Be Done?" that trade unionism was the spontaneous consciousness of the proletariat.

153. Philip Foner, *The Industrial Workers of the World, 1905–1917* (vol. 4 of *The History of the Labor Movement in the United States*) (New York: International Publishers, 1980), pp. 281–94.

154. Pierre Broué, *The German Revolution, 1917–1923* (Chicago: Haymarket, 2006 [1971]), p. 68.

155. Patrick Cunninghame, "For an Analysis of Autonomia: An Interview with Sergio Bologna" (conducted in June 1995), *Left History* 7: 2 (2000), pp. 92–3.

156. *CW* 6, p. 354.

157. *CW* 34, p. 34. In giving an account of the evolution of the steam-powered

factory in *Capital* (an account that draws heavily upon Andrew Ure's 1835 *Philosophy of Manufactures*), Marx describes the "superior class of workers … whose occupation it is to look after the whole of machinery and repair it from time to time, composed of engineers, mechanics, joiners etc.," as "numerically unimportant"(*Capital Volume I*, p. 545).

158. *CW* 20, p. 11. Similarly, there is a fascinating, if surprising discussion in *Capital Volume III* of how the credit system has created ownership forms that anticipate a socialist economy: "Capitalist joint-stock companies as much as cooperative factories should be viewed as transition forms from the capitalist mode of production to the associated one, simply that in one case the opposition is abolished in a negative way, and in the other, in a positive way." Karl Marx, *Capital Volume III* (London: Penguin, 1991), p. 572.

159. *Capital Volume I,* pp. 384–5.

160. A near consensus exists amongst British labor historians that "skilled workers managed to keep intact their occupational communities and to form strong and stable craft unions that were able to resist local employers and authorities, and to engage in collective bargaining to an extent that far exceeded unions on the continent." Flemming Mikkelsen, "Working-Class Formation in Europe and Forms of Integration: History and Theory," *Labor History* 46: 3 (August 2005), p. 288.

161. John Foster, in his well-known study of the decline of radical labor after 1845 and the rise of a mid-Victorian aristocracy of labor in Britain, offers a detailed account of the "piecemaster" system in Oldham's crucial textile-machinery industry, and the "pacemaker" elite in its large cotton industry. John Foster, *Class Struggle and the Industrial Revolution* (London: Weidenfeld & Nicholson, 1974), pp. 224–34.

162. James Hinton, *The First Shop Stewards' Movement* (London: Allen & Unwin, 1973), p. 57.

163. In the United States, of course, scientific management and "fordism" were not just heavy weapons deployed against the point-of-production power of craft unionism, but also strategies for utilizing unskilled immigrants as "human fuel" in industry. Similarly, in the early Soviet Union, Taylorism was seen— reasonably—as a progressive technique for industrially integrating a young, largely peasant working class, the proletariat of 1917 having either died during the Civil War or been drafted into state administration.

164. The "disappearance of the polyvalent skilled worker," Gorz claims, "has also entailed the disappearance of the class able to take charge of the socialist project

and translate it into reality. Fundamentally, the degeneration of socialist theory and practice has its origins here" (Gorz, *Farewell*, p. 66).

165. In the United States, the immigrant Cornish, who brought ancient skills as hard-rock miners as well as strong union traditions, were quickly promoted en masse as a managerial elite in U.S. mines, usually in conflict with the Irish laborers who worked under them. The 4th of July was notorious in the copper capital of Butte, Montana, where the two groups held separate parades that often ended in brawls or riots.

166. Eric Hobsbawm, *The Age of Capital: 1848–1875* (London: Weidenfeld & Nicolson, 1975), p. 225.

167. Victoria Bonnell, *Roots of Rebellion: Workers' Politics and Organizations in St Petersburg and Moscow, 1900–1914* (Berkeley, CA: University of California Press, 1983), p. 159.

168. See Jeffrey Haydu, *Between Craft and Class: Skilled Workers and Factory Politics in the United States and Britain, 1890–1922* (Berkeley, CA: University of California Press, 1988).

169. "The 1897 dispute was the greatest head-on clash which had ever occurred in British Industry on the prerogatives of management within the workplace." The rationalization of production within the metal-working sector was driven by increasing competition with U.S. and German exporters. R. Clarke, "The Dispute in the British Engineering Industry 1897–98: An Evaluation," *Economica* (May 1957), pp. 128–9.

170. Michelle Perrot, "Introduction: From the Mechanic to the Metallo," in Leopold Haimson and Charles Tilly, eds, *Strikes, Wars, and Revolutions in an International Perspective: Strike Waves in the Late Nineteenth and Early Twentieth Centuries* (Cambridge: CUP, 1989), p. 266; and Elisabeth Domansky, "The Rationalization of Class Struggle: Strikes and Strike Strategy of the German Metalworkers' Union, 1891–1922," in Haimson and Tilly, *Strikes, Wars, and Revolutions*, pp. 345–8.

171. Haimson argues that there were in fact two distinct younger strata in the big factories: first-generation hereditary workers and a new influx from the countryside. The first group "constituted the intermediary link between the leading circles of the Bolshevik Party and the laboring masses [the second group]," and "in the spring and summer of 1913, these green youths ... had begun to flow from the [ad hoc] strike committees into the open trade unions and had seized their leadership from the older generation of Menshevik trade unionists." Leopold Haimson, "The Problem of Social Stability in Urban

Russia, 1905–1917 (Part One)," *Slavic Review* 23: 4 (December 1964), pp. 633–6.

172. Chris Wrigley, "Introduction," in Wrigley, ed., *Challenges of Labour: Central and Western Europe, 1917–1920* (London: Routledge, 1993), pp. 4–5.

173. Domansky, "Rationalization of Class Struggle," p. 350.

174. Thierry Bonzon, "The Labour Market and Industrial Mobilization, 1915–1917," in Jay Winter and Jean-Louis Robert, eds, *Capital Cities at War: Paris, London, Berlin: 1914–1919* (Cambridge: CUP, 1997), p. 180.

175. Ibid., p. 188.

176. Moore, *Injustice*, p. 256.

177. Chris Fuller, "The Mass Strike in the First World War," *International Socialism* 145 (posted January 5, 2015), at isj.org.uk.

178. Eric Hobsbawm, *Uncommon People: Resistance, Rebellion and Jazz* (New York: New Press, 1998), p. 88.

179. I have not seen a comprehensive typology in the literature. Some councils were completely autonomous of plant unions, while others overlapped with unions or were more radical versions of the plant committees. Others were city-wide strike committees in a proto-Bolshevik configuration, or ad hoc municipal governments that included sailors and soldiers. In Russia Lenin initially endorsed the factory committees and their demands for workers' control against the often-Menshevik-controlled unions, but then, after the Mensheviks resigned, he switched his support back to the unions—and eventually, with the disintegration of production during the Civil War, to one-man management of the factories. Barbara Allen, *Alexander Shlyapnikov: 1885–1937* (Chicago: Haymarket, 2016), pp. 111–12.

180. Steve Smith, "Craft Consciousness, Class Consciousness: Petrograd 1917," *History Workshop* 11 (Spring 1981), p. 39.

181. Ibid., pp. 39–40.

182. Raimund Loew, "The Politics of Austro-Marxism," *New Left Review* I/118 (November–December 1979).

183. Ralf Hoffrogge, *Working-Class Politics in the German Revolution* (Chicago: Haymarket, 2015), p. 110.

184. Antonio Gramsci, "The Turin Workers' Councils," in Robin Blackburn, ed., *Revolution and Class Struggle: A Reader in Marxist Politics* (London: Fontana/Collins, 1977), p. 380.

185. Gramsci's "factory council," of course, was a strategic asymptope not a fully realized vision. As Carl Boggs points out, 'the factory councils that actually

appeared in Piedmont during the *Ordine Nuovo* years never approximated the theoretical prescription formulated by Gramsci. Of the hundreds that did emerge, most evolved out of the old union-affiliated internal commissions, and these moved only gropingly toward real democratic involvement among all workers." Moreover the banks and financial system remained under bourgeois control. Carl Boggs, "Gramsci's Theory of the Factory Councils: Nucleus of the Socialist State," *Berkeley Journal of Sociology* 19 (1974–75), p. 180.

186. Stephen Marcus regards this chapter as "the best single thing Engels ever wrote," and attaches particular importance to his decision to begin his account with urbanization rather than the mechanized factory. Stephen Marcus, *Engels, Manchester, and the Working Class* (New York: Random House, 1974), pp. 144–5.

187. Friedrich Engels, *The Condition of the Working-Class in England*, *CW* 4, p. 418. "The early labour movements," Lenger claims, "were above all urban phenomena. Since many early factory workers did not live in the larger cities this urban concentration of labour activists suggests that the artisanal dominance was even stronger than the occupational structure would suggest" (Lenger, *Beyond Exceptionalism*, p. 4). Obviously, some of the most classical industrial centers, such as the Ruhr and South Wales, constituted a different geographical model: networks of pit and mill villages linked closely with one another and to small and medium-sized industrial cities such as Newport, Swansea, Bochum, and Essen.

188. Engels, *Condition of the Working-Class in England*, p. 421.

189. See Chapter 1 ("Berlin") of Hugh McLeod, *Piety and Poverty: Working-Class Religion in Berlin, London and New York, 1870–1914* (New York: Holmes & Meier, 1996). In Wedding, for instance, barely 3 percent of the population were considered communicants (p. 11).

190. Eric Hobsbawm, "Labour in the Great City," *New Left Review* I/166 (November–December 1987), p. 45.

191. Ibid., p. 47.

192. Michelle Perrot, "On the Formation of the French Working Class," in Ira Katznelson and Aristide Zolberg, eds, *Working-Class Formation: Nineteenth-Century Patterns in Western Europe and the United States* (Princeton, NJ: Princeton University Press, 1986), p. 102.

193. Thierry Bonzon, "The Labour Market and Industrial Mobilization, 1915–1917," in Jay Winter and Jean-Louis Robert, eds, *Capital Cities at War: Paris, London, Berlin, 1914–1919* (Cambridge: CUP, 1997), p. 191.

194. Tyler Stovall, *Paris and the Spirit of 1919* (Cambridge: CUP, 2012), p. 265. "The idea that the suburbs threatened the well-being and civilization of the urban center, representing the barbarians at the gate, has a long history in France. At the same time, as the uprisings of November 2005 have demonstrated, new associations of the suburbs with multiculturalism, disaffected youth, and Islamic fundamentalism have revived the idea of the urban frontier as a zone of political danger, indeed insurrection" (pp. 264–5).

195. Shelton Stromquist, "'Thinking Globally; Acting Locally': Municipal Labour and Socialist Activism in Comparative Perspective, 1890–1920," *Labour History Review* 74: 3 (2009), p. 576. This is a fascinating and much recommended essay.

196. Not everywhere, of course, was municipal politics a practical terrain for the labor movement. In Europe some cities did not have elected local governments, or, as in Germany, had councils elected by plural suffrage that gave exorbitant power to the middle classes.

197. Christopher Ansell and Arthur Burris, "Bosses of the City Unite! Labor Politics and Political Machine Consolidation, 1870–1910," *Studies in American Political Development* 11: 1 (April 1997), p. 27.

198. William Kenefick, *Red Scotland! The Rise and Fall of the Radical Left, c. 1872 to 1932* (Edinburgh: Edinburgh University Press, 2007), pp. 12–13.

199. Steven Lewis, *Reassessing Syndicalism: The* Bourses du Travail *and the Origins of French Labor Politics*, Working Paper Series #39 (Cambridge, MA: Harvard Center for European Studies, 1992), pp. 2, 8–10.

200. Carl Levy, "Currents of Italian Syndicalism before 1926," *International Review of Social History* 45 (2000), p. 230.

201. Gwyn Williams, *Proletarian Order: Antonio Gramsci, Factory Councils and the Origins of Italian Communism, 1911–1921* (London: Pluto, 1975), p. 24.

202. For a justly celebrated account of the original nexus of feminism and socialism, broken after 1848, see Barbara Taylor, *Eve and the New Jerusalem: Socialism and Feminism in the Nineteenth Century* (London: Virago, 1983).

203. The SPD might well have taken the same patriarchal attitude as the Austrian party if not for the fierce agitation of the redoubtable Clara Zetkin. For a valuable overview, see Ellen DuBois, "Woman Suffrage and the Left: An International Socialist-Feminist Perspective," *New Left Review* I/186 (July–August 1991), pp. 20–45. For the interwar period, see Gruber and Graves, *Women and Socialism*.

204. David Montgomery, *The Fall of the House of Labor* (New York: CUP, 1987),

p. 1. Speaking of the work of Susan Porter Benson: "Her findings underscore the crucial role of mutual support and reciprocity in working-class households and neighborhoods. She argues that such reciprocity existed mostly among women, while men figured primarily as contributors of greater or lesser portions of their wages." David Montgomery, "Class, Gender, and Reciprocity: An Afterword," in Susan Porter Benson, *Household Accounts: Working-Class Family Economies in the Interwar United States* (Ithaca, NY: Cornell University Press, 2007), p. 194.

205. Temma Kaplan, "Female Consciousness and Collective Action: The Case of Barcelona, 1910–1918," *Signs* 7: 3 (Spring 1982), pp. 555–6. Kaplan argues that, in addition to class consciousness, historians must recognize the existence of a militant, neighborhood-based "female consciousness" growing out of women's traditional responsibilities for household health and nutrition. The radicalization of this consciousness, she suggests, was a necessary condition for urban revolution, too often ignored by historians.

206. Harold Benenson, "Victorian Sexual Ideology and Marx's Theory of the Working Class," *International Labor and Working-Class History* 25 (Spring 1984), p. 6.

207. Marcel Streng, "The Food Riot Revisited: New Dimensions in the History of 'Contentious Food Politics' in Germany before the First World War," *European Review of History* 20: 6 (2013), pp. 1,081–3.

208. Karen Hunt, "The Politics of Food and Women's Neighborhood Activism in First World War Britain," *International Labor and Working-Class History* 77 (Spring 2010), p. 8.

209. Ralf Hoffrogee tantalizes us with a brief portrait of Clare Casper, the only female member of the Berlin Shop Stewards' Action Committee and a comrade of Luxemburg and Liebknecht. Ralf Hoffrogee, *Working-Class Politics in the German Revolution: Richard Muller, the Revolutionary Shop Stewards and the Origins of the Council Movement* (Chicago: Haymarket, 2015), p. 107.

210. Kaplan, "Female Consciousness and Collective Action," pp. 561–3.

211. Geoff Eley, *Forging Democracy: The History of the Left in Europe, 1850–2000* (Oxford: Oxford Univesity Press, 2002), p. 58.

212. See Michael Gordon, "The Labor Boycott in New York City, 1880–1886," *Labor History* 16: 2 (1975), pp. 184–229; and Ernest Spedden, *The Trade Union Label* (Baltimore, MD: Johns Hopkins University Press, 1910).

213. Van Ginderachter and M. Kamphuis, "The Transnational Dimensions of the Early Socialist Pillars in Belgium and the Netherlands," *Revue belge de*

philology et d'histoire 90: 4 (2012), p. 1,328. See also the fascinating website vooruit.be; and Peter Scholliers, "The Social-Democratic World of Consumption: The Path-Breaking Case of the Ghent Cooperative Vooruit Prior to 1914," *International Labor and Working-Class History* 55 (Spring 1999), pp. 71–91.

214. Tyler Stovall, *The Rise of the Paris Red Belt* (Berkeley, CA: University of California Press, 1990), p. 24. The Parisian working class was unsurpassed in its caustic repertoire of anti-bourgeois songs and doggerel, but nothing sharpened its mental guillotine more than the hatred of rack-renting landlords.

215. See Chris Ealham, "An Imagined Geography: Ideology, Urban Space, and Protest in the Creation of Barcelona's 'Chinatown,' c. 1835–1936," *International Review of Social History* 50 (2005), pp. 373–97.

216. Friedrich Engels, *The Housing Question* (1872), *CW* 23, p. 319.

217. Engels saw homeownership, not as a panacea, as did Proudhon, but as shackles around the ankles of the worker. He quotes a letter that Eleanor Marx wrote during their visit to the United States about how American workers were being "chained" to their homes. "The workers must shoulder heavy mortgage debts in order to obtain even these dwellings, and now become the slaves of their employers for fair. They are tied to their houses, they cannot go away, and must put up with whatever working conditions are offered them" (ibid., p. 330 fn).

218. Robert Fogelson, *The Great Rent Wars: New York, 1917–1929* (New Haven: Yale University Press, 2013), p. 59.

219. Stovall, *Paris and the Spirit of 1919*, pp. 46–7.

220. Fogelson, *The Great Rent Wars*, p. 61.

221. James Baer, "Tenant Mobilization and the 1907 Rent Strike in Buenos Aires," *Americas* 49: 3 (January 1993), pp. 343–63.

222. B. Moorehouse, M. Wilson, and C. Chamberlain, "Rent Strikes, Direct Action and the Working Class," *Socialist Register 1972* (London: Merlin, 1972), pp. 135–6; and Hinton, *First Shop Stewards' Movement*, pp. 126–7.

223. Fogelson, *The Great Rent Wars*, pp. 1–2.

224. Ibid., p. 86; Andrew Wood and James Baer, "Strength in Numbers: Urban Rent Strikes and Political Transformation in the Americas, 1904–1925," *Journal of Urban History* 32: 6 (September 2006), pp. 862–84; and Ronald Lawson, "Origins and Evolution of a Social Movement Strategy: The Rent Strike in New York City, 1904–1980," *Urban Affairs Quarterly* 18: 3 (March 1983), pp. 371–95.

225. The United States, with its diverse and divided working class, became the seedbed of the mass-consumption culture industries and their cheap thrills and spectacles, often aimed at immigrant audiences who knew little English. Although historical research confirms that communal recreations organized through unions and socialist ethnic federations were relatively common in the early twentieth century, leisure time in general was privatized in modes that would not become common in much of Europe until the 1930s or even the 1950s.

226. In some histories, this organized sphere is conflated with "worker culture" per se, which of course it was not. The life-world of the industrial working class in 1900 also included the informal society of the pub, employer-sponsored recreation, weekend public spaces, and commercialized popular entertainment and spectacle. In early Soviet Russia, moreover, "cultured leisure" took second place in workers' clubs to dancing and the cinema, the Charleston and Douglas Fairbanks. See Diane Koenker, *Republic of Labor: Russian Printers and Soviet Socialism, 1918–1930* (Ithaca, NY: Cornell University Press, 2005), pp. 187, 279–80.

227. Toni Offermann, "The Lassallean Labor Movement in Germany: Organization, Social Structure, and Associational Life in the 1860s," in David Barclay and Eric Weitz, *Between Reform and Revolution: German Socialism and Communism from 1840 to 1990* (New York: Berghahn, 1998), p. 105.

228. Vernon Lidtke, *The Alternative Culture: Socialist Labor in Imperial Germany* (New York: OUP, 1985), pp. 7–8.

229. Ibid., p. 194. Helmut Gruber portrays a Viennese socialism in the 1920s magnificently devoted to the cultivation of culture and proletarian identity but unprepared to face its ruthless enemies. "The preparatory cultural strategy, which legitimated the whole Viennese experiment, had no real links to the process of coming to power in the future. Nor was the relationship made clear between cultural hegemony through *Bildung* and the laws of capitalist development." Helmut Gruber, *Red Vienna: Experiment in Working-Class Culture, 1919–1934* (Oxford: OUP, 1991), p. 39.

230. Kurt Shell, *The Transformation of Austrian Socialism* (New York: SUNY Press, 1962), pp. 10–11.

231. Gerald Brenan, *The Spanish Labyrinth: The Social and Political Background of the Spanish Civil War* (Cambridge: CUP, 1943), p. 218.

232. Chris Ealham, *Class, Culture and Conflict in Barcelona, 1898–1937* (London: Routledge, 2005), p. 36.

233. Brenan, *Spanish Labyrinth*, p. 145. See also Lily Litvak, *Musa libertaria: Arte, literature y vida cultural del anarquismo español (1880–1913)* (Madrid: FELAL, 2001); and Eduard Masjuan, *La ecologia humana en el anarquismo iberico* (Madrid: Icaria, 2000)—a fascinating discussion of anarchist urbanism.

234. To what extent was proletarian pub life or its functional equivalents (cafés, social clubs, and so on) open to working-class women? A simple question that probably has complex and diverse answers, but awaits further research into working-class leisure and family life.

235. Pamela Swett, *Neighbors and Enemies: The Culture of Radicalism in Berlin, 1929–1933* (Cambridge: CUP, 2004), pp. 97–9.

236. Nolan, "Economic Crisis," pp. 128–9.

237. Peter Nettle, "The German Social Democratic Party 1890–1914 as a Political Model," *Past and Present* 30 (April 1965), pp. 76–7. See also Klaus Ensslen, "German-American Working-Class Saloons in Chicago," in Hartmut Keil, *German Workers' Culture in the United States, 1850 to 1920* (Washington, D.C.: Smithsonian Institute, 1988), pp. 157–80.

238. Tom Goyens, *Beer and Revolution: The German Anarchist Movement in New York City, 1880–1914* (Urbana, IL: University of Illinois Press, 2007).

239. Melvyn Dubofsky, *We Shall Be All: A History of the IWW* (New York: Quadrangle, 1969), p. 174.

240. Margaret Kohn, "The Power of Place: The House of the People as Counterpublic," *Polity* 33: 4 (Summer 2001), p. 513.

241. For short architectural biographies of the most famous examples, see *Maisons du Peuple* (Brussels: Archives d'Architecture Moderne, 1984).

242. The expression was Turati's. See Earlene Craver, "The Third Generation: The Young Socialists in Italy, 1907–1915," *Canadian Journal of History* 31 (August 1966), p. 203.

243. On the hardbitten "realism" of younger workers, see Nolan, "Economic Crisis," pp. 122–3.

244. Engels, Introduction to Sigismund Borkheim's pamphlet, *In Memory of the German Blood-and-Thunder Patriots, 1806–1807, CW XXVI*, p. 451.

245. Karl Marx, "The Belgian Massacres: To the Workmen of Europe and the United States" (leaflet issued by First International, May 5, 1869), *CW* 21, p. 47.

246. See Karl Liebknecht, *Militarism and Anti-Militarism* (1907) at marxists.org.

247. Carl Schorske, *German Social Democracy, 1905–1917* (Cambridge, MA: Harvard University Press, 1955), p. 99.

248. Nettle, "German Social Democratic Party," p. 73.

249. Schorske, *German Social Democracy*, p. 108.

250. Williams, *Proletarian Order*, pp. 36–7.

251. Isabel Tirado, *Young Guard! The Communist Youth League, Petrograd 1917–1920* (New York: Greenwood, 1988), p. 14.

252. Matthias Neumann, *The Communist Youth League and the Transformation of the Soviet Union, 1917–1932* (London: Routledge, 2012), pp. 21–2.

253. Anne Gorsuch, *Youth in Revolutionary Russia: Enthusiasts, Bohemians, Delinquents* (Bloomington, IN: Indiana University Press, 2000), pp. 16, 42.

254. Fritz Wildung, SPD sports spokesman, quoted in David Steinberg, "The Workers' Sport Internationals, 1920–28," *Journal of Contemporary History* 13 (1978), p. 233.

255. Michael Kruger, "The German Workers' Sport Movement between Socialism, Workers' Culture, Middle-Class Gymnastics and Sport for All," *International Journal of the History of Sport* 31: 9 (2014), p. 1,100.

256. Robert Wheeler, "Organized Sport and Organized Labour: The Workers' Sports Movement," *Journal of Contemporary History* 13: 2 (April 1978), p. 192.

257. After the First World War, socialism and the bicycle resumed their love affair, especially in Germany and France. "The [German] Workers Cycling Association (ARS) not only boasted 320,000 members (1929)—the largest cycling organization in the world—but also maintained a cooperative bicycle factory" (Wheeler, p. 198).

258. After the war, it was reorganized as the Socialist Workers' Sport International (1920), but now competed with the Sportintern (1921), the Comintern's sports international. On the latter, see Barbara Keys, "Soviet Sport and Transnational Mass Culture in the 1930s," *Journal of Contemporary History* 38: 3 (2003), pp. 413–34.

259. James Riordan, "The Worker Sports Movement," in James Riordan and Arnd Kruger, *The International Politics of Sport in the 20th Century* (London: Spon, 1999), p. 105.

260. Steinberg, "Workers' Sport Internationals," p. 233. Veterans of 1848 brought the Turners to the United States, and the Socialistic Turnerbund of North America, with other anti-slavery *Turnverein*, furnished bodyguards for Abolitionist leaders, and most famously for Lincoln at his first Inauguration. Turners also provided the cores of many of the best Union regiments. Annette Hofmann, "The Turners' Loyalty for Their New Home Country: Their Engagement in the American Civil War," *International Journal of the History of Sport* 12: 3 (1995), p. 156.

261. Lidtke, *Alternative Culture*, pp. 7–8, 17. In his chapter on songs and *Lieder-bücher*, Lidtke gives wonderful examples of socialists satirizing war-making and mocking patriotism in the "burlesque" style that Brecht later transferred to the theater.

262. Richard Evans, *The Third Reich in Power, 1933–1939* (New York: Penguin, 2005), p. 272.

263. Jonathan Rose, *The Intellectual Life of the British Working Classes* (New Haven: Yale University Press, 2008), p. 8. See also Dennis Sweeney, "Cultural Practice and Utopian Desire in German Social Democracy: Reading Adolf Levenstein's *Arbeiterfrage* (1912)," *Social History* 28: 2 (2003), pp. 174–99.

264. By 1850, three-quarters of adult French males and half of French women could read, as could two-thirds of the British population. Asaf Shamis, "The 'Industrialists of Philosophy': Karl Marx, Friedrich Engels, and the 'Discourse Network of 1840,'" *Media History* 22: 1 (2016), p. 71.

265. Thompson, *The Chartists*, p. 6.

266. Gregory Vargo, "'Outworks of the Citadel of Corruption': The Chartist Press Reports the Empire," *Victorian Studies* 54: 2 (Winter 2012), p. 231. See also Stephen Coltham, "English Working-Class Newspapers in 1867," *Victorian Studies* 13: 2 (December 1969).

267. Karl Marx, *Economic Manuscripts of 1861–63, CW* 34, p. 101 ("Relative Surplus Value").

268. In Germany, Alex Hall argues, "official news" was a reaction to the success of the SPD press, rather than vice versa: "The government had begun to respond in a variety of different ways, both to the pressure put upon it to counteract the propaganda of the SPD, as well as to the need to reflect its own position more adequately than hitherto … In the short-term, the basic requirement was to provide a virtually daily system of government-inspired news items and ministerial press releases, which would expose the hollowness of socialist claims and foster support for government policies." Alex Hall, "The War of Words: Anti-Socialist Offensives and Counter-Propaganda in Wilhelmine Germany, 1890–1914," *Journal of Contemporary History* 11: 2–3 (July 1976), p. 15.

269. In 1912 there were three English-language Socialist daily newspapers in the United States: the *New York Call*, the *Chicago Daily Socialist*, and the *Milwaukee Leader*. In addition, German speakers could read the daily *New Yorker Volkszeitung*, while Yiddish socialists relished Abraham Cahan's daily *Forverts*, which had a national circulation of 275,000.

270. This is an alternative translation (thanks to my nephew Juan Pablo Gonzales) to the one that appears in Engels, "Marx and the *Neue Rheinische Zeitung* (1848–49)," *CW 26*, p. 122.

271. John Reed, *Ten Days That Shook the World* (New York: Boni & Liveright, 1919), p. 24.

272. Gerhard Ritter, "Workers' Culture in Imperial Germany," *Journal of Contemporary History* 13 (1978), p. 166. In *The Class Struggle [The Erfurt Program—1892]*, Kautsky wrote: "One of the most remarkable phenomena of modern society is the thirst for knowledge displayed by the proletariat … It is among the despised and ignorant proletariat that the philosophical spirit of the brilliant members of the Athenian aristocracy is revived." *The Cooperative Commonwealth*, adapted from Kautsky, *Class Struggle* for the *New York People* by Daniel DeLeon, *Labour Library #9* (New York: Labour Library, 1898), p. 37.

273. "The union of these two polar opposites of modern society, science and the workingman—when these two join forces they will crush all obstacles to cultural advance with an iron hand, and it is to this union that I have resolved to devote my life so long as there is breath in my body." Ferdinand Lassalle, *Science and the Workingman* (New York: International Library, 1900 [1863]), pp. 44–5.

274. Martyn Walker, "'Encouragement of Sound Education amongst the Industrial Classes': Mechanics Institutes and Working-Class Membership, 1838–1881," *Educational Studies* 39: 2 (2013), p. 142. Walker debunks the claim that the institutes were dominated by the middle classes: instead, he argues, they represented a "convergence of class interests." "Working-class radicals aligned themselves with middle-class sympathisers in relation to politics and self-help" (p. 145).

275. Quoted in Ed Block, "T. H. Huxley's Rhetoric and the Popularization of Victorian Scientific Ideas: 1854–1874," *Victorian Studies* 29: 3 (Spring 1986), p. 369.

276. Ralph Colp, "The Contacts Between Karl Marx and Charles Darwin," *Journal of the History of Ideas* 35: 2 (1974), pp. 329–38; and Jenny Marx, "Letter to Johann Becker (29 January 1866)," *CW 42*, p. 568.

277. E. P. Thompson, "Eighteenth-Century English Society: Class Struggle Without Class?" *Social History* 3: 2 (May 1978), p. 148.

278. Chapter 24 ("Conflict Over the Labor Contract") of Rudolf Hilferding, *Finance Capital: A Study of the Latest Phase of Capitalist Development* (Routledge: London, 1981); Schorske, *German Social Democracy*, pp. 29–30.

279. Leopold Haimson, "The Historical Setting in Russia and the West," in Haimson and Tilly, *Strikes, Wars, and Revolutions*, p. 24.

280. Hobsbawm, *Age of Empire*, p. 123.

281. For American examples, see Chapter 4 ("Workers Organize Capitalists") of John Bowman, *Capitalist Collective Action: Competition, Cooperation and Conflict in the Coal Industry* (Cambridge: CUP, 1989); and Chapter 3 ("Workers Organizing Capitalists") of Colin Gordon, *New Deals: Business, Labor and Politics in America, 1920–1935* (Cambridge: CUP, 1994).

282. Joshua Cole, "The Transition to Peace, 1918–1919," in Winter and Robert, *Capital Cities at War*, p. 222.

283. Quoted and discussed in Steve Wright, *Storming Heaven: Class Composition and Struggle in Italian Autonomist Marxism* (London: Pluto, 2002), pp. 36–7.

284. Hobsbawm, *The Age of Extremes* (London: Michael Joseph, 1994), pp. 7–8.

285. Göran Therborn, "The Rule of Capital and the Rise of Democracy," *New Left Review* I/103 (May–June 1977), pp. 23–4.

286. Luxemburg, "Mass Strike," p. 145. In a statistical study of strikes during the 1905 Revolution, Lenin empirically vindicated Luxemburg's analysis (*CW* 16, pp. 393–422).

287. Eric Hobsbawm, "Mass-Producing Traditions: Europe, 1870–1914," in David Boswell and Jessica Evans, eds, *Representing the Nation: A Reader* (London: Routledge, 1999), p. 62.

288. Hagen Koo, *Korean Workers: The Culture and Politics of Class Formation* (Ithaca, NY: Cornell University Press, 2001), pp. 18–19.

289. The wording is Marx's. "Instructions for the Delegates of the Provisional General Council. The Different Questions" (August 1866), *CW* 20, p. 187.

290. Sidney Fine, "The Eight-Hour Day Movement in the United States, 1888–1891," *Mississippi Valley Historical Review* 40: 3 (December 1953), p. 444.

291. See *New York Times*, May 2–4, 1890.

292. Gary Cross, *Quest for Time: The Reduction of Work in Britain and France, 1840–1940* (Berkeley: University of California Press, 1989), pp. 134–5; Gary Cross, "The Quest for Leisure: Reassessing the Eight-Hour Day in France," *Journal of Social History* 18: 2 (Winter 1984), p. 200.

293. Perry Anderson, "The Antinomies of Antonio Gramsci," *New Left Review* I/100 (November 1976–January 1977), p. 15.

294. Haimson, "Historical Setting," pp. 27–8.

295. Arno Mayer, *The Persistence of the Old Regime: Europe to the Great War* (New York: Pantheon, 1981), pp. 23–34. "In all respects, including numbers and

wealth, the agrarians continued to surpass the magnates of business and the liberal professions." In England and elsewhere, moreover, rural elites were often the largest urban landlords as well (pp. 24–5).

296. Aminzade, "Class Analysis," pp. 93–4.

297. Friedrich Engels, "The Peasant Question in France and Germany," (1894), *CW* 27, pp. 484, 498.

298. Athar Hussain and Keith Tribe, *Marxism and the Agrarian Question*, 2nd edn (London: Macmillan, 1983), p. 26.

299. "Engels was emphatic that promises to save the small peasant would simply degrade the party to the level of the Anti-Semites, transforming a workers' party into an ordinary *Volkspartei*." Kautsky, in *The Agrarian Question* (1899), was more nuanced about the fate of the peasantry, but nonetheless asserted that they would soon be outstripped by the growth of the agricultural proletariat. Jairus Banaji, "Review Article: Illusions About the Peasantry: Karl Kautsky and the Agrarian Question," *Journal of Peasant Studies* 17: 2 (1990), p. 290.

300. Bruno Schonlank at the Frankfurt Congress. Massimo Salvadori, *Karl Kautsky and the Socialist Revolution, 1880–1938* (London: New Left Books, 1979), p. 50.

301. See Chapter 4 ("The Radomir Rebellion") of Joseph Rothschild, *The Communist Party of Bulgaria: Origins and Development, 1883–1936* (New York: Columbia University Press, 1959).

302. Ivan Berend, *Decades of Crisis: Central and Eastern Europe Before World War II* (Berkeley, CA: University of California Press, 1998), p. 82.

303. There is also a Dutch exception to the SPD model. "The main organizational base of the SDAP [Social Democratic Labor Party] was among the tenant farmers and landless laborers of rural Friesland who had been politicized during the prolonged economic crisis of the 1880s." The party's initial urban labor base was confined to the Diamond Workers Union in Amsterdam. John Gerber, *Anton Pannekoek and the Socialism of Workers' Self-Emancipation, 1873–1960* (Dordrecht: Kluwer, 1989), p. 4.

304. Tony Judt, *Socialism in Provence, 1871–1914* (Cambridge: CUP, 1979), pp. 6–7.

305. In "The Social Base of Nineteenth-Century Andalusian Anarchism in Jerez de la Frontera," Temma Kaplan demonstrates the breadth of the movement and the important roles of craftsmen, teachers, and smallholders, in addition to the mass of day laborers. *Journal of Interdisciplinary History* 6: 1 (Summer 1975), pp. 47–70.

306. Frank Snowden, "The City of the Sun: Red Cerignola, 1900–15," in Martin

Blinkhorn and Ralph Gibson, *Landownership and Power in Modern Europe* (London: HarperCollins, 1991), p. 203.

307. "[Agricultural workers] often contributed one-fourth to one-third of the total number of strikers and days lost per year, and their contribution was especially crucial in almost every strike wave (when they accounted for up to 50 percent of the aggregate strike activity)." Lorenzo Bordogna, Gian Primo Cella, and Giancarlo Provasi, "Labor Conflicts in Italy Before the Rise of Fascism, 1881–1923: A Quantitative Analysis," in Haimson and Tilly, *Strikes, Wars and Revolutions*, p. 229.

308. Thomas Sykes, "Revolutionary Syndicalism in the Italian Labor Movement: The Agrarian Strikes of 1907–08 in the Province of Parma," *International Review of Social History* 21: 2 (1976), p. 176.

309. Anthony Cardoza, "Commercial Agriculture and the Crisis of Landed Power: Bologna, 1880–1930," in Blinkhorn and Gibson, *Landownership and Power*, p. 194.

310. Matti Alestalo and Stein Kuhnle, "The Scandinavian Route: Economic, Social, Political Developments in Denmark, Finland, Norway, and Sweden," *International Journal of Sociology* 16: 3–4 (Fall 1986–Winter 1987), p. 24. See also Timothy Tilton, "The Social Origins of Liberal Democracy: The Swedish Case," *American Political Science Review* 68: 2 (June 1974), pp. 561–71.

311. Stefano Bartolini, *The Political Mobilization of the European Left, 1860–1980: The Class Cleavage (Cambridge Studies in Comparative Politics)* (Cambridge: CUP, 2007), p. 481.

312. Esther Kingston-Mann, "A Strategy for Marxist Bourgeois Revolution: Lenin and the Peasantry, 1907–1916," *Journal of Peasant Studies* 7: 2 (1998), p. 135.

313. See Robert Linhart, *Lénine, les Paysans, Taylor*, 2nd edn (Paris: Seuil, 2010).

314. D. A. Longley, "Officers and Men: A Study of the Development of Political Attitudes Among the Sailors of the Baltic Fleet in 1917," *Soviet Studies* 25: 1 (1973), pp. 28–50.

315. Pierre Broué, *The German Revolution, 1917–1923* (Chicago: Haymarket, 2006), p. 97.

316. Ibid., p. 100.

317. Marx, *Poverty of Philosophy*, *CW* 6, p. 176.

318. Lukács, *History and Class Consciousness*, pp. 63, 66. Emphasis in original.

319. Ibid., pp. 69, 76–7.

320. Stephen Perkins, *Marxism and the Proletariat: A Lukácsian Perspective* (London: Pluto, 1993), p. 171.

321. Lukács, *History and Class Consciousness*, pp. 74, 80.

322. Lenin, "The Tasks of the Revolution" (October 1917), *CW* 26, p. 60.

323. Alexander Rabinowitch, *The Bolsheviks Come to Power: The Revolution of 1917 in Petrograd* (Chicago: Haymarket, 2004), pp. 311–12.

324. W. A. Preobrazhensky, "The Average Communist," in *The Preobrazhensky Papers, Volume 1: 1886–1920* (Chicago: Haymarket, 2015), p. 557.

325. Between 50 million and 55 million Europeans are estimated to have emigrated overseas in the nineteenth and early twentieth centuries. Dirk Hoerder, *Cultures in Contact: World Migrations in the Second Millennium* (Durham, NC: Duke University Press, 2002), pp. 331–2.

326. Speech of George Julian Harney reprinted in Friedrich Engels, "The Festival of Nations in London," *CW* 6, p. 11.

327. Jacques Grandjonc, "Les etrangers a Paris sous la monarchie de Juillet et la seconde Republique," *Population* (French edn) 29 (March 1974), p. 84. Stanley Nadel, noting that "the average journeyman stayed in Paris for only a limited period, perfecting his trade and then moving on," calculated "that somewhere between 100,000 and a half million veterans of the Paris workshops had returned to Germany before the end of the decade [1840s]." Stanley Nadel, "From the Barricades of Paris to the Sidewalks of New York: German Artisans and the European Roots of American Labor Radicalism," *Labor History* 30: 1 (Winter 1989), pp. 49–50.

328. Yvonne Kapp, *Eleanor Marx*, vol. 2 (New York: Pantheon, 1976), p. 161.

329. In "Principles of Communism," a rough draft for the *Manifesto*, Engels proclaimed: "So long as it is not possible to produce so much that not only is there enough for all, but also a surplus for the increase of social capital and for the further development of the productive forces, so long must there *always* be a ruling class disposing of the productive forces of society, and a poor, oppressed class" (*CW* 6, p. 349).

330. Marx, *Grundrisse*, pp. 704–8. Conversely, the suppression of free time and its conversion into disciplined toil was seen by the bourgeoisie as the very foundation of industry, if not civilization. Marx quotes the early economist Cunningham (1770): "There is a very great consumption of luxuries among the laboring poor of this kingdom; particularly among the manufacturing populace, *which they also consume their time, the most fatal of all their consumptions*" (*CW* 34, p. 294).

331. "The problem as he sees it is not a redistribution, more just or more equal of existing wealth. For Marx, communism is the creation of new wealth, of new

needs and of the conditions for their satisfaction." Shlomo Avineri, *The Social and Political Thought of Karl Marx* (Cambridge: CUP, 1968), p. 64.

332. Michael Lebowitz, "Review: Heller on Marx's Concept of Needs," *Science and Society* 43: 3 (Fall 1979), pp. 349–50; and Agnes Heller, *The Theory of Need in Marx* (London: Allison & Busby, 1976).

333. Marx and Engels distinguished between the Fourierist phalansteries and Owenite colonies, which set themselves apart from the class struggle, and cooperative institutions that were integral parts of the workers' movements.

334. Karl Marx, *The Civil War in France*, *CW* 22, p. 335.

335. "[Under capitalism] the labourer looks at the social nature of his labour, at its combination with the labour of others for a common purpose as he would at an alien power … The situation is quite different in factories owned by the labourers themselves, as in Rochdale, for instance." *Capital Volume II* (Moscow: Progress, 1962), p. 85.

336. Massimo Salvadori, *Karl Kautsky and the Socialist Revolution, 1880–1938* (London: Verso, 1979), p. 14.

337. Kendall Bailes, *Origins of the Soviet Technical Intelligentsia, 1917–1941* (Princeton, NJ: Princeton University Press, 1978).

338. The famed Hungarian economist János Kornai, a former Marxist reformer, singles out the dismal state of the "telephone under socialism" as a prime example of a planned economy's inability to innovate or develop revolutionary new products. János Kornai, *Dynamism, Rivalry and the Surplus Economy* (Oxford: OUP, 2014), pp. 57–60.

339. Pekka Sutela and Vladimir Mau, "Economics Under Socialism: The Russian Case," in Hans-Jürgen Wagener, *Economic Thought in Communist and Post-Communist Europe* (London: Routledge, 1998), p. 43.

340. Eden Medina, *Cybernetic Revolutionaries: Technology and Politics in Allende's Chile* (Cambridge, MA: MIT Press, 2011), p. 159.

341. In the field of production planning, for example, a hugely complex problem that would have required eighty-two years of computer time to solve in 1982, by 2003 "could be solved in about a minute—an improvement by a factor of around *43 million*" (Ford, *Rise of the Robots*, p. 71).

342. Leon Trotsky, "Report on the World Economic Crisis," Third Congress of the Communist International, atwsws.org.

2. MARX'S LOST THEORY

1. Rogers Brubaker, "Ethnicity, Race, and Nationalism," *Annual Review of Sociology* 35 (2009), p. 22; J. G. A. Pocock, "Review of *British Identities Before Nationalism* by Colin Kidd," *Scottish Historical Review* 79: 2 (October 2000), p. 262.

2. Anthony D. Smith, *Nationalism* (Cambridge: Polity, 2010), p. 3.

3. Clifford Geertz, ed., *Old Societies and New States* (New York: Free Press, 1963), p. 107.

4. Erica Benner, *Really Existing Nationalisms: A Post-Communist View from Marx and Engels* (Oxford: Clarendon, 1995), p. 222.

5. In more than a dozen books published between 1933 and 1967, Kohn examined nationalism in "the East," and the USSR, as well as in Switzerland, England, Germany, the United States, and France. A disenchanted Zionist who became a leading advocate of a bi-national state in Palestine, Kohn argued nonetheless that the "ethical nationalism" of the Jews offered the first proof that universality could be combined with nationality—an ideal subsequently incarnated in Anglo-American and Dutch liberalism and French republicanism. During the Cold War, Kohn abandoned his vestigial sympathies (ardent in the early 1920s) for the Soviet Union to become a propagandist for the Free World. In *American Nationalism: An Interpretative Essay* (1957), he celebrated U.S. history as the irresistible flowering of English liberalism and French rationalism in the soil of unprecedented economic opportunity. Although published the same year that mobs and bayonets were blocking the court-ordered integration of Little Rock's Central High, his book extolled America's "civic nationalism" as the global ideal for nation-building.

6. Quotes from Rogers Brubaker: "The Manichean Myth: Rethinking the Distinction between 'Civic' and 'Ethnic' Nationalism," in Hanspeter Kriesi, Klaus Armington, Andreas Wimmer, and Hannes Siegrist, eds, *Nation and National Identity* (Zurich: Verlag Rüeger, 1999), p. 69; Brubaker, "Ethnicity, Race and Nationalism," pp. 13, 30; Rogers Brubaker, *Nationalism Reframed: Nationhood and the National Question in the New Europe* (Cambridge: CUP, 1996), p. 16.

7. Brubaker, *Nationalism Reframed,* pp. 7, 15–17, 21.

8. Siniša Malešević, "The Chimera of National Identity," *Nations and Nationalism* 17: 2 (2011), pp. 272–3.

9. Siniša Malešević, *Identity as Ideology: Understanding Ethnicity and Nationalism* (New York: Palgrave Macmillan, 2006), p. 7.

10. Siniša Malešević, *The Sociology of Ethnicity* (London: Sage, 2004), p. 4. Malešević reminds his peers that Weber was also a non-essentialist who believed that ethnicity should be conceptualized as "a potential social attribute and not as an actual group characteristic" (p. 10).

11. Malešević, *Identity as Ideology*, p. 28.

12. Ernst Haas, *Beyond the Nation-State: Functionalism and International Organization* (Stanford: Stanford University Press, 1964), p. 455; Malešević, *Nation-States and Nationalisms* (Cambridge: Wiley, 2013), p. 15.

13. Anthony D. Smith, *Chosen Peoples: Sacred Sources of National Identity* (Oxford: OUP, 2003); Régis Debray, *Critique of Political Reason* (London/New York: Verso, 1983).

14. Siniša Malešević, "'Divine *Ethnies*' and 'Sacred Nations': Anthony D. Smith and the Neo-Durkheimian Theory of Nationalism," *Nationalism and Ethnic Politics* 10: 4 (2004), pp. 561, 587. For Debray's view of Durkheim's circular reasoning, see *Critique of Political Reason*, pp. 172–3.

15. Using both ethnographic and sociological tools, Malešević and Brubaker have independently explored these solidarities in the field. Brubaker, along with local colleagues, has conducted an ambitious parallel study of nationalist politics and "everyday ethnicity" in the Transylvanian city of Cluj-Napoca, where "intense and intractable elite-level ethno-political conflict," earlier spurred by the Ceaus-escu dictatorship, continues today. One of their most interesting discoveries in this city where Magyars and Romanians have coexisted for centuries is a dramatic difference in the nationalist temperature inside the chauvinistic political sphere and outside, in daily life, where people are much more concerned about the economic malaise than the hegemony of their respective national cultures. Similarly, Malešević, in several ingenious case studies, has demonstrated that ethno-national hatreds in the former Yugoslavia did not so much erupt from below as they were stirred from the top down by intense fearmongering in the warlord-controlled media.

16. Benner, *Really Existing Nationalisms*, p. 98 n. 4.

17. Franz Borkenau, *World Communism* (New York: W. W. Norton, 1939), p. 94.

18. Tom Nairn, "The Modern Janus," *New Left Review* I/94 (November–December 1975), p. 3; Ernesto Laclau, "Introduction" in Ephraim Nimni, *Marxism and Nationalism: Theoretical Origins of a Political Crisis* (London: Pluto, 1991), p. vi.

19. Régis Debray, "Marxism and the National Question," *New Left Review* I/105 (September–October 1977), pp. 26, 31, 32.

20. Erica Benner, *Machiavelli's Prince: A New Reading* (Oxford: OUP, 2013); and *Machiavelli's Ethics* (Princeton, NJ: Princeton University Press, 2009).

21. Benner, *Really Existing Nationalisms*, pp. 9, 50, 228. My emphasis.

22. This debate unfortunately has too often been conducted through the method of selective quotation, elliptical reasoning, and undisciplined speculation. Authors routinely fail to acknowledge the dramatic evolution of Marx's views, not least through passionate engagement with contemporary politics; quotes from 1844 can be cited side-by-side with those from 1870, as if they had comparable authority. For this reason, Solomon Frank Bloom's *The World of Nations: A Study of the National Implications in the Work of Karl Marx* (New York: Columbia University Press, 1941) remains the best English-language starting-point for understanding the development of Marx's thinking about nationalism. Although long out of print and rarely cited, this elegantly written book is an eye-opener, especially for those who think that Marx was purely an anti-nationalist or that he believed in the automatic disappearance of the nation under socialism. Bloom, who read in German virtually all of the Marx then available, interprets texts with scrupulous attention to their historical moment as well as to the later revisions of their ideas. He is, therefore, an almost indispensable companion to reading Benner.

23. Before the 1860s, Marx and Engels evaluated international politics by the dual standard of the interests of the working class as a whole and the socioeconomic progress of humanity in general, therefore "no consistent attitude toward national aspirations was possible everywhere and at all times ... the same sort of international reckoning might smile upon the independence of some nations but frown upon that of others" (Bloom, *World of Nations*, p. 7). However, the American Civil War, the Polish revolt, and the Fenian plots created a new strategic problematic, in which Marx began to conceive racial equality and colonial liberation as preconditions for revolutionary consciousness amongst white American and English workers. This was followed in the 1870s by his reconsideration of the role of agrarian class struggle in the potential internal collapse of Czardom. Engels, while courageously supportive of the Irish, retained until his death a "Great German" in his attitudes toward the rights of smaller Slav nationalities, often shockingly expressed: see the impressively doc-umented discussion of all these topics in Kevin Anderson, *Marx at the Margins: On Nationalism, Ethnicity, and Non-Western Societies* (Chicago: University of Chicago Press, 2010).

24. Friedrich Engels, "The Debate on Poland in the Frankfurt Assembly," in Karl

Marx, *The Revolutions of 1848: Political Writings, Volume 1* (London/New York: Verso, 2010), p. 152.

25. Terrell Carver, "Marx's *Eighteenth Brumaire of Louis Bonaparte*: Eliding 150 Years," *Strategies* 16: 1 (2003), p. 9.

26. Jeffrey Mehlman, *Revolution and Repetition: Marx/Hugo/Balzac* (Berkeley: University of California Press, 1977), p. 82.

27. Maurice Agulhon, *The Republican Experiment, 1848–1852* (Cambridge: CUP, 1983), pp. 115, 196–7.

28. Karl Marx, *The Eighteenth Brumaire of Louis Bonaparte*, in Karl Marx, *CW Vol. 11*, pp. 112–13. Emphasis in original.

29. Marx, *Eighteenth Brumaire*, p. 190; Bloom, *World of Nations*, p. 76; Marx, *Eighteenth Brumaire*, p. 192.

30. Benner, *Really Existing Nationalisms*, p. 103.

31. Ibid., p. 52.

32. The *Brumaire's* methodology shows the influence of the intensive research that Marx conducted in late 1843 and early 1844 (the so-called *Kreuznach Notebooks*) for a proposed but never written history of the French Convention. The *Memoirs* of the deputy to the Convention, the Jacobin René Levasseur de la Sarthe, was a paticularly rich source as the young Marx attempted to reconstruct the intricate and constantly changing alignments of factions and the social forces that impelled them. See *CW* 3, pp. 361–74.

33. Karl Marx and Friedrich Engels, *The German Ideology*, in *CW Vol. 5*, p. 77.

34. The events of 1848–51 in France, like those in any revolution, were complicated because of the entry and exit of so many actors, as well as the constantly changing balance of forces, but, as Bob Jessop has emphasized, Marx's analysis is not a conventional linear narrative: "Marx's text presents a complex periodization of contemporary history rather than a simple chronology. This makes it a model of political analysis that has inspired many subsequent Marxist analyses and also won the respect of many orthodox historians for its theoretical power and empirical insight. He distinguishes three successive periods, the first of brief duration, the second and third having three phases each, and the third phase of the third period having four steps ... Marx offers three interpretations of each period. In distinguishing the periods, he refers first to their immediate conjunctural significance, then to the primary institutional site in and around which the political drama unfolds. In addition, each period (and its phases, where these are distinguished) is discussed in terms of its past, its present, and, as far as it was already on the public record or Marx deemed it knowable,

its future significance." Bob Jessop, "The Political Scene and the Politics of Representation: Periodizing Class Struggle and the State in *The Eighteenth Brumaire*," preprint and unpaginated version of his "The Politics of Representation and *The Eighteenth Brumaire*," in Mark Cowling and James Martin, eds, *The Eighteenth Brumaire Today: (Post)Modern Interpretations* (London: Pluto, 2002).

35. In some key respects, the failure of the Second Republic anticipated that of the first German Republic as described by David Abraham: "The crisis of the last years of the Weimar Republic stemmed in part from the inability of the state to organize the interests of the dominant classes in an autonomous fashion beyond partial interests. The Republic was unable to safeguard existing social relations, not because of any revolutionary threat, but because of the conflicts and contradictions within the bloc of dominant classes, together with the results of the policy indeterminacy of the preceding years." David Abraham, *The Collapse of the Weimar Republic: Political Economy and Crisis* (New York: Lynne Rienner, 1986), pp. 2–3.

36. Engels's characterization of Bismarck is discussed in Hal Draper, *Karl Marx's Theory of Revolution, Volume 1: State and Bureaucracy* (New York: Monthly Review, 1977), pp. 385–590. For Thalheimer, see Martin Kitchen, "August Thalheimer's Theory of Fascism," *Journal of the History of Ideas* 34: 1 (January–March 1973); V. I. Lenin, "The Beginning of Bonapartism," *CW Vol. 25*; Leon Trotsky, "German Bonapartism" (October 30, 1932), in Leon Trotsky, *The Struggle Against Fascism in Germany* (New York: Pathfinder, 1971). Less convincing is Trotsky's comparison of the kleptocratic dimensions of the Second Empire and Stalinism in "The Bonapartist Philosophy of the State," *New International* 5: 6 (June 1939).

37. Sergio Bologna, "Money and Crisis: Marx as Correspondent of the *New York Daily Tribune*, 1856–57" (1973), transl. Ed Emery in *Common Sense* 13 (January 1993).

38. Karl Marx, "The Economic Crisis in Europe," *CW Vol. 15*, p. 109.

39. Karl Marx, "The French Crédit Mobilier, III," *CW Vol. 15*, p. 21.

40. For the quote, see Marx to Engels, December 26, 1865, *CW Vol. 42*, p. 206.

41. Sudir Hazareesingh, *The Saint-Napoléon: Celebrations of Sovereignty in Nineteenth-Century France* (Cambridge, MA: Harvard University Press, 2004), pp. 22–3, 31. Bastille Day was officially established in 1880.

42. Karl Marx, *The Class Struggles in France*, *CW Vol. 10*, p. 58.

43. Friedrich Engels, *Briefwechsel*, IV, pp. 339–40: translated and quoted in Bloom, *World of Nations*, pp. 146–7.

44. Friedrich Engels, *The Magyar Struggle* (January 1849), and letter to August Bebel (September 29, 1891), *CW Vol. 49*, p. 246. My emphasis.
45. Debray, "Marxism and the National Question," p. 31.
46. Ronald Aminzade, *Ballots and Barricades: Class Formation and Republican Politics in France, 1830–1871* (Princeton, NJ: Princeton University Press, 1993), p. 9.
47. Marx, *Class Struggles in France*, pp. 57, 50. My emphasis.
48. Ibid., pp. 122, 100, 80. Emphasis in original.
49. Charles Beard, *An Economic Interpretation of the Constitution of the United States* (New York: Macmillan, 1913), pp. 14–16. A superb interpretation of Beard's ideas is Clyde Barrow, *More Than a Historian: The Political and Economic Thought of Charles A. Beard* (New Brunswick, NJ: Routledge, 2000).
50. James Madison, "The Federalist 10," in Alexander Hamilton, John Jay, and James Madison, *The Federalist Papers* (Createspace, 2018).
51. Jessop, "Politics of Representation."

3. THE COMING DESERT

1. "It was assumed that for all practical purposes and decisions, climate could be considered constant." Hubert Lamb, *Climate, History and the Modern World* (London: Routledge, 1995), p. 2.
2. George Woodcock and Ivan Avakumovic, *The Anarchist Prince: The Biography of Prince Peter Kropotkin* (London: T. V. Boardman, 1950), p. 71.
3. Prince Kropotkin, "The Orography of Asia," *Geographical Review* 23: 2–3 (February–March 1904).
4. Woodcock and Avakumovic, *Anarchist Prince*, pp. 61–86. On his recognition of the plateau as a fundamental landform, see Alexander Vucinich, *Science in Russian Culture: 1861–1917* (Palo Alto, CA: Stanford University Press, 1970), p. 88.
5. Woodcock and Avakumovic, *Anarchist Prince*, p. 73. In later years, there would be fierce debate over historical fluctuations in the level and aerial expanse of the Caspian, but the controversy, like so many others, was unresolvable in the absence of any technique for dating land features. From midcentury, however, the hypothesis of creeping desertification in Central Asia was familiar to the educated public: for an example, see Friedrich Engels, *The Dialectics of Nature* (New York: International, 1940 [1883]), p. 235.

6. Tobias Kruger, *Discovering the Ice Ages: International Reception and Consequences for a Historical Understanding of Climate* (Leiden: Brill, 2013), pp. 348–51.

7. "The desiccation I speak of is not due to a diminishing rainfall. It is due to the thawing and disappearance of that immense stock of frozen water which had accumulated on the surface of our Eurasian continent during the tens of thousands of years that the glacial period had been lasting. Diminishing rainfall (where such a diminution took place) is thus a consequence, not a cause of that desiccation." Kropotkin, "On the Desiccation of Eurasia and Some General Aspects of Desiccation," *Geographical Journal* 43: 4 (April 1914). See also Peter Kropotkin, *Memoirs of a Revolutionist* (Garden City, NY: Doubleday, 1962 [1899]), pp. 156–7.

8. His brother Alexander oversaw the publication of the first volume, 828 pages in length: *Issledovanie o lednikovom periode* ("Researches on the Glacial Period") (St. Petersburg: zap.imp.russk.geogr.vol. 1, 1876). A short review appeared in *Nature* on June 23, 1877. An incomplete draft of the second volume was seized by the secret police and not published until 1998. See Tatiana Ivanova and Vyacheslav Markin, "Piotr Alekseevich Kropotkin and His Monograph *Researches on the Glacial Period* (1876)," in Rodney Grapes, David Oldroyd, and Algimantas Grigelis, eds., *History of Geomorphology and Quaternary Geology* (London: Geological Society, 2008), p. 18.

9. The famed Californian Josiah Whitney (after whom the peak is named) had also been advocating a concept of progressive desiccation since at least the early 1870s. He dismissed the popular idea that deforestation was responsible for climate change, instead proposing that the Earth had been simultaneously drying and cooling for several million years. This theory put him in the odd position of arguing that the modern climate of the American West was colder than during the Ice Age—a contradiction he resolved by rejecting evidence for the existence of continental ice sheets. In his view, Agassiz and others had confused the strictly local phenomena of glacial advance with global refrigeration. See J. D. Whitney, *The Climatic Changes of Later Geological Times: A Discussion Based on Observations Made in the Cordilleras of North America* (Cambridge: University Press, John Wilson & Son, 1882), p. 394.

10. Theophrastus of Eresus, *Sources for His Life, Writings, Thought and Influence: Commentary Vol. 3.1, Sources on Physics (Texts 137–233)* (Leiden: Brill, 1998), p. 212.

11. Already by the mid-eighteenth century, colonial officials were crusading for the establishment of forest reserves to prevent desiccation of the rich plantation

islands of Tobago and Mauritius. Richard Grove, the historian who has done most to establish the colonial origins of environmentalism, cites the example of Pierre Poivre, *commissaire-intendant* of Mauritius. Poivre gave a major speech in Lyon in 1763 on the climatic dangers of deforestation: "This speech may go down in history as one of the first environmentalist texts to be based explicitly on a fear of widespread climate change." Richard Grove, "The Evolution of the Colonial Discourse on Deforestation and Climate Change, 1500–1940," in Richard Grove, *Ecology, Climate and Empire* (Cambridge: White Horse, 1997), p. 11. Seventy years later, July Monarchy propagandists invoked the desertification of North Africa by the Arabs as an excuse for the conquest of Algeria. The French promised to change the climate and push back the desert by massive afforestation. Diana Davis, *Resurrecting the Granary of Rome: Environmental History and French Colonial Expansion in North Africa* (Athens, OH: Ohio University Press, 2007), pp. 4–5, 77.

12. Buffon believed that land clearance changed temperature as well as rainfall. Since Paris and Quebec City were at the same latitude, he suggested that the most likely explanation for their different climates was the warming that resulted from draining the wetlands and cutting down the forests around Paris. Clarence Glacken, *Traces on the Rhodian Shore* (Berkeley: University of California Press, 1976), p. 699.

13. Jérôme-Adolphe Blanqui quoted in George Perkins Marsh, *Man and Nature* (Cambridge, MA: Harvard University Press, 1965 [1864]), pp. 160ff, 209–13.

14. Michael Williams, *Deforesting the Earth: From Prehistory to Global Crisis* (Chicago: University of Chicago Press, 2003), p. 431.

15. Karl Fraas, *Klima und Pflanzenwelt in der Zeit: ein Beitrag zur Geschichte Beider* ("Climate and Plant World Over Time: A Contribution to History") (Landshut: J. G. Wölfe, 1847). Fraas was an important influence on Perkins Marsh, and his famous thesis in *Man and Nature* that humanity was catastrophically reshaping nature on a global scale.

16. Marx to Engels, March 25, 1868, in *CW Vol. 42*, pp. 558–9.

17. Friedrich Engels, "The Part Played by Labour in the Transition from Ape to Man," in *Dialectics of Nature*, pp. 291–2. Even in the case of contemporary industrial civilization, he wrote, "we find that there still exists here a colossal disproportion between the proposed aims and the results arrived at, that unforeseen effects predominate, and that the uncontrolled forces are far more powerful than those set into motion according to plan" (p. 19).

18. *CW Vol. 25*, p. 511.

19. Both Newton and Halley believed in "a succession of earths, a series of creations and purgations. Historical periods were punctuated by cometary catastrophes, with comets serving as divine agents to reconstitute the entire solar system, to prepare sites for new creations and to usher in the millennium." Sara Genuth, "The Teleological Role of Comets," in Norman Thrower, ed., *Standing on the Shoulders of Giants: A Longer View of Newton and Halley* (Berkeley, CA: University of California Press, 1990), p. 302.

20. Anne O'Connor, *Finding Time for the Old Stone Age: A History of Palaeolithic Archaeology and Quaternary Geology in Britain, 1860–1960* (Oxford: OUP, 2007), pp. 28–30.

21. Kruger, *Discovering the Ice Ages*, p. 475. In the early twentieth century, varve (annual lake-sediment layers) and tree-ring chronologies began to be used to calculate the age of deglaciation events, but it was not until the refinement of carbon-14 analysis in the postwar period that reliable dating became possible.

22. James Fleming, *Historical Perspectives on Climate Change* (Oxford: OUP, 1998), pp. 52–3.

23. For an overview of the century-long controversy about desiccation in Central Asia, see David Moon, "The Debate over Climate Change in the Steppe Region in Nineteenth-Century Russia," *Russian Review* 69 (2010). Contemporary perspectives include François Herbette, "Le problème du dessèchement de l'Asie intérieure," *Annales de Geographie*, 23: 127 (1914); and John Gregory, "Is the Earth Drying Up?" *Geographical Journal* 43: 2 (March 1914).

24. Peter Kropotkin, "The Desiccation of Eur-Asia," *Geographical Journal*, 23: 6 (June 1904).

25. Kropotkin, *Memoirs of a Revolutionist*, p. 239.

26. Desiccation, of course, is a geomorphological fact in many landscapes, but the impressionistic archaeology of European explorers neither proved causal relationships between ruins and desertification, nor established a comparative chronology. Petra, for instance, is an oft-cited example of catastrophic climate change, but the city-state's decline was actually the result of changing trade routes and a 333 AD earthquake that destroyed its elaborate water-supply system.

27. David Moon, *The Plough that Broke the Steppes: Agriculture and Environment on Russia's Grasslands, 1700–1914* (Oxford: OUP, 2013), pp. 91–2, 130–3.

28. Eduard Brückner, *Klimaschwankungen seit 1700* (Vienna: Hölzel, 1890), p. 324.

29. Nico Stehr and Hans von Storch, "Eduard Brückner's Ideas: Relevant in His

Time and Today," in Stehr and von Storch, eds, *Eduard Brückner: The Sources and Consequences of Climate Change and Climate Variability in Historical Times* (Dordrecht: Springer, 2000), pp. 9, 17.

30. Robert Cromie, *A Plunge into Space* (London: Frederick Warne & Co., 1890).

31. "To talk of Martian beings is not to mean Martian men. Just as the probabilities point to the one, so do they point away from the other. Even on this Earth man is of the nature of an accident. He is the survival of by no means the highest physical organism. He is not even a high form of mammal. Mind has been his making. For aught we can see, some lizard or batrachian might just as well have popped into his place early in the race, and been now the dominant creature of this Earth. Under different physical conditions, he would have been certain to do so. Amid the surroundings that exist on Mars, surroundings so different from our own, we may be practically sure other organisms have been evolved of which we have no cognizance." Percival Lowell, *Mars* (Boston: Houghton Mifflin, 1895), p. 211.

32. Alfred Russel Wallace, *Is Mars Habitable?* (London: Macmillan, 1907).

33. Percival Lowell, *Mars and Its Canals* (New York: Macmillan, 1906), pp. 153, 384. I have been unable to ascertain Kropotkin's opinion of Lowell's thesis. By scientific temperament he was more likely to have agreed with his friend Wallace.

34. Percival Lowell, *Mars as Abode of Life* (New York: Macmillan, 1908), pp. 122, 124, 142–3.

35. Gabriele Gramelsberger, "Conceiving Processes in Atmospheric Models," *Studies in the History and Philosophy of Modern Physics* 41: 3 (September 2010).

36. Nils Ekholm, "On the Origins of the Climate of the Geological and Historical Past and Their Causes," *Quarterly Journal of the Royal Meteorological Society* XXVII: 117 (January 1901).

37. Curzon's comments described in Sidney Burrard, "Correspondence," *Geographical Journal* 43: 6 (June 1914). Curzon was speaking in defense of his friend Sir Thomas Holdich of the Royal Engineers, who became a convinced desiccationist after a lifetime surveying the Northwest Frontier of India.

38. When the workers on the family estates occupied the land during the Biennio Rosso, Caetani abdicated his titles to his younger brother and emigrated to Vernon, a town at the foot of the magnificent Selkirk mountains in British Columbia, where in his younger days he had once hunted grizzly bears. After his death in 1935, his wife and daughter, an accomplished artist, became

legendary recluses. See Sveva Caetani, *Recapitulation: A Journey* (Vernon, BC: Coldstream, 1995); "Sveva Caetani: A Fairy Tale Life," available online at en.copian.ca.

39. See Premysl Kubat, "The Desiccation Theory Revisited," *Les carnets de l'ifpo* (Institute français du Proche-Orient), April 18, 2011, at www.ifpo.hypotheses. org; Nimrod Hurvitz, "Muhibb ad-Din al-Khatib's Semitic Wave Theory and Pan-Arabism," *Middle Eastern Studies* 29: 1 (January 1993).

40. Ellsworth Huntington, "The Rivers of Chinese Turkestan and the Desiccation of Asia," *Geographical Journal* 28: 4 (October 1906).

41. Geoffrey Martin, *Ellsworth Huntington: His Life and Thought* (Hamden, CT: Shoe String Press, 1973), pp. 92–3.

42. Douglas (1867–1962) had been Lowell's principal assistant in the "mapping" of the Martian canals, before becoming interested in the possible relationship between sunspot activity and rainfall. He refined the use of ring-width in trees as a proxy for weather, an endeavour properly called dendroclimatology. But his techniques also opened the possibility of dating ancient trees or, for that matter, wooden beams in *pueblo* ruins. In the beginning, only a floating (relative) chronology was possible, but in 1929 Douglas discovered "HH–39," a beam from an Arizona ruin that allowed him to tie together a continuous series of measurements from 700 AD to the present, and thus permit the first calendrical dating of a prehistoric archaeological site.

43. Ellsworth Huntington, *The Pulse of Asia* (Boston: Houghton, Mifflin & Co., 1907), p. 385. For his original endorsement of Kropotkin's ideas, and his subsequent modification of them, see Huntington, "Climatic Changes," *Geographical Journal* 44: 2 (August 1914).

44. Owen Lattimore, "The Geographical Factor in Mongol History" (1938), in Lattimore, *Studies in Frontier History: Collected Papers, 1928–1958* (Oxford: OUP, 1962).

45. Toynbee wrote an appreciative foreword to Geoffrey Martin's biography of Huntington.

46. Philippe Fôret, "Climate Change: A Challenge to the Geographers of Colonial Asia," *Perspectives* 9 (Spring 2013). In his 1914 book on Russian Central Asia, Aleksandr Voeikov described Huntington's "pulse of Asia" theory as "an inanity." Aleksandr Voeikov, *Le Turkestan Russe* (Paris: Colin, 1914), p. 360.

47. Martin, *Ellsworth Huntington*, p. 86.

48. Ibid., p. 86.

49. Transcript of his lecture in *Physics Today*, October 1989, p. 43.

50. Emmanuel Le Roy Ladurie, *Histoire du climat depuis l'an mil* (Paris: Flammarion, 1967), p. 17.

51. Charles Brooks, *Climate Through the Ages: A Study of the Climate Factors and Their Variations*, rev. edn (New York: McGraw Hill, 1949 [1926]), p. 327.

52. Rhoads Murphey, "The Decline of North Africa since the Roman Occupation: Climatic or Human?" *Annals of the Association of American Geographers* 41: 2 (1951).

53. Martin, *Ellsworth Huntington*, pp. 102–3, 111.

54. Fleming, *Historical Perspectives on Climate Change*, p. 100. He adds: "Although Huntington's thought was indeed influential in its time, since then his racial bias and crude determinism have been largely rejected. Nonetheless, his categorical errors seem destined to be repeated by those who make overly dramatic claims for weather and climatic influences" (p. 95).

55. It was published in Russian in 1998. An English-language anthology of Kropotkin's scientific writings—on geography, glaciology, ecology, and evolution—is long overdue.

56. See "Appendix A: The Published Works of Ellsworth Huntington," in Martin, *Ellsworth Huntington*.

57. Martin, pp. 249–50.

58. David Blackbourn, *The Conquest of Nature: Water, Landscape, and the Making of Modern Germany* (New York: Pimlico, 2006), pp. 278, 285–6.

59. Sir Gilbert Walker, "Climatic Cycles: Discussion," *Geographical Journal* 89: 3 (March 1937).

60. Stehr and von Storch, "Eduard Brückner's Ideas," p. 12.

61. Aaron Putnam et al., "Little Ice Age Wetting of Interior Asian Deserts and the Rise of the Mongol Empire," *Quaternary Science Reviews* 131 (2016), pp. 333–4, 340–1. One of the co-authors is the Lamont-Doherty Earth Observatory's "pope," Wallace Broecker, who first proposed the theory of the meridional overturning circulation in the North Atlantic—the famed "conveyor belt."

62. Colin P. Kelley, Shahrzad Mohtadi, Mark A. Cane, Richard Seager, and Yochanan Kushnir, "Climate Change in the Fertile Crescent and Implications of the Recent Syrian Drought," *Proceedings of the National Academy of Sciences* 112: 11 (March 17, 2015).

63. Akio Kitoh, Akiyo Yatagai, and Pinhas Alpert, "First Super-High-Resolution Model Projection that the Ancient 'Fertile Crescent' Will Disappear in This Century," *Hydrological Research Letters* 2 (2008).

4. WHO WILL BUILD THE ARK?

1. This paper was given as a talk at the UCLA Center for Social Theory and Comparative History in January 2009.
2. The Cato Institute's execrable Patrick Michaels, in the *Washington Times*, February 12, 2005.
3. Jan Zalasiewicz et al., "Are We Now Living in the Anthropocene?" *GSA Today* 18: 2 (February 2008).
4. Ibid.
5. Indeed, three leading contributors to Working Group 1 charged that the Report deliberately understated the risks of sea-level rise and ignored new research on instability in the Greenland and West Antarctic ice sheets. See the debate in "Letters," *Science* 319 (January 25, 2008), pp. 409–10.
6. James Hansen, "Global Warming Twenty Years Later: Tipping Point Near," testimony before Congress, June 23, 2008.
7. Scientific Committee on Problems of the Environment (SCOPE), *The Global Carbon Cycle* (Washington, DC: SCOPE, 2004), pp. 77–82; IPCC, *Climate Change 2007: Mitigation of Climate Change: Contribution of Working Group III to the Fourth Assessment Report* (Cambridge: IPCC, 2007), pp. 172, 218–24.
8. SCOPE, *Global Carbon Cycle*, p. 82.
9. International Energy Agency, *Energy Technology Perspectives: In Support of the G8 Plan of Action—Executive Summary* (Paris: IEA, 2008), p. 3.
10. Josep Canadell et al., "Contributions to Accelerating Atmospheric CO_2 Growth," *Proceedings of the National Academy of Sciences* 104: 20 (November 2007), pp. 18, 866–70.
11. Global Carbon Project, *Carbon Budget 2007*, at globalcarbonproject.org, p. 10.
12. Elisabeth Rosenthal, "Europe Turns Back to Coal, Raising Climate Fears," *New York Times*, April 23, 2008.
13. Stephen Ansolabehere et al., *The Future of Coal* (Cambridge, MA: MIT Press, 2007), p. xiv.
14. Pew Center on Global Climate Change, quoted in Matthew Wald, "Coal, a Tough Habit to Kick," *New York Times*, September 25, 2008.
15. UN *Human Development Report 2007/2008: Fighting Climate Change: Human Solidarity in a Divided World*, p. 7.
16. IEA report quoted in *Wall Street Journal*, November 7, 2008.
17. Clifford Krauss, "Alternative Energy Suddenly Faces Headwinds," *New York Times*, October 21, 2008.

18. Peggy Hollinger, "EU Needs Stable Energy Policy, EDF Warns," *Financial Times*, October 5, 2008.

19. The shameful charade in Copenhagen, crowned by Obama's desperate deceit of an agreement, exposed less the political gulf between nations than the moral abyss between governments and humanity. In the meantime, the famous 2° C of additional warming, which president and premier have vowed to prevent, is already working its way through the world ocean: a future that will happen even if all carbon emissions ceased tomorrow. On "committed" warming and the underlying illusion of Copenhagen, see the harrowing if awkwardly titled article by Scripps Institution researchers V. Ramanathan and Y. Feng, "On Avoiding Dangerous Anthropogenic Interference with the Climate System: Formidable Challenges Ahead," *Proceedings of the National Academy of Science* 105 (September 23, 2008), pp. 14,245–50.

20. UN *Human Development Report 2007/2008*, p. 6.

21. U. Srinivasan et al., "The Debt of Nations and the Distribution of Ecological Impacts from Human Activities," *Proceedings of the National Academy of Science* 105 (February 5, 2008), pp. 1,768–73.

22. William Cline, *Global Warming and Agriculture: Impact Estimates by Country* (Washington, DC: Center for Global Development, 2007), pp. 67–71, 77–8.

23. UN *Human Development Report 2007/2008*, p. 6.

24. "Turning Blight into Bloom," *Nature* 455 (September 11, 2008), p. 137.

25. UN *Human Development Report 2007/2008*, p. 2.

Index

Index

Index

Index

Index

Elwitt, Sanford, 37
emancipatory agency, 16
employers' organizations, 116
Engels, Friedrich, xiv, 7–78, 13, 14, 15,
    49, 60–1, 69, 90–1, 92, 112, 119,
    130, 144, 147, 161, 169, 171, 172,
    184, 235n95, 244n186, 257n330,
    261n23
environmentalism, 265–6n11
environmental politics, 220
episodic immiseration, 45
equality
    economic equality, 86
    gender equality, 51, 52
    racial equality, 261n23
Erfurt Program, 28, 35, 86–7, 148–9
Evans, Oliver, 114
existential condition, and essence of
    proletariat, 35
exploitation, xix, 2, 19, 33, 38, 41, 44,
    47, 49, 51, 54, 73, 114, 119, 164, 165,
    175, 176, 178, 236n108
extinctions, 203, 204

Fabian Society, 82
factories, and unions, 47–59
factory committees, 76, 107, 243–4n179
factory council movement, 74, 244n185
factory labor, 36, 71
factory occupations, 65–6
factory regimes, 232n60
factory workers, 24, 26, 38, 43,
    236n106, 244–8n187
family wage, 51–2
Faraday, Michael, 114
Federación Obrera Regional Argentina
    (FORA), 93
"Federalist Paper Number 10"
    (Madison), 176–7
Fédération Sportive Socialiste

Internationale, 110
Federterra, 86, 133
female consciousness, 246n205
feminism, xvi, 51, 246n202
Ferrer, Francisco, 145
Ferry, Jules, 122
festival culture, 96
Festival Hall (Ghent), 103
FGS, 107
Finance Capital (Hilferding), 116
financial/tertiary economies, as ideal-
    typical economy, 7
Fine, Sidney, 124
First International, 20, 27, 105, 124,
    144
Fitzpatrick, John, 84
Fleming, James, 196
Fogelson, Robert, 92–3
Foner, Philip, 66–7
football codes, 109–10
Ford, Henry, 55
fordism, 242n163
formal proletariat, 24
Foster, John Bellamy, xiii, 241–2n161
Foster, William Z., 77
Fourierist phalansteries, 257n334
Fourth Assessment Report (IPCC),
    204, 205
Foxconn, 4
Fraas, Karl, 183, 266n15
free speech, 75, 101
free time, 102, 146, 147, 257n331. *See
    also* leisure time
Free Trade Unions, 116
Free Unions, 29, 61, 84, 96
Frey, Carl, 226n8
Frieden, Jeffry, 45
Friedlander, Peter, 48–9
Fucik, Julius, xi
Fuller, Chris, 73

Index

Index

Index

Index

Index

Müller, Richard, 73–4, 77
multiculturalism, 245n194
Mumford, Lewis, 217
municipalism, 82
"munitionettes," 73
Murphey, Rhoads, 195
Murphy, Kevin, 48
Mussolini, Benito, 107, 134
Musto, Marcello, 19
Myrdal, Gunnar, 153–4

Nadel, Stanley, 249n328
Nairn, Tom, 160–1
Narrow Socialists, 131
National Commission on Technology,
   Automation and Economic
   Progress, 3
national identity, 158
nationalism
   according to Borkenau, 160
   calculating interests, 173–8
   classes and, 165–72
   Marx and Engels on, 161, 162
   Marx on, 260–1n22
   politics of in 1848, 155–78
   secret power of, 158
   without the nation, 156–60
Nationalism Reframed (Brubaker), 157
National Labor Union, 124
natural climate change, xx, 182, 187,
   196
natural selection, theory of, 185, 189
Nature, 221
navies, and attempt at revolution,
   136–40
Nazis, 197
Neilson, David, 5
Nettle, Peter, 100, 106
Neue Rheinische Zeitung, 16, 162, 163
Neue Zeit, 61, 106

Neukölln (Berlin), 79
newspapers, role of, 112
Newton, Isaac, 185, 267n19
New Unionism, 28, 50
New Urbanism, 217
New Woman and Man, 97
New York Call, 110
New York Tribune, xiv, 169
Nicolaus, Martin, xii
1905 Revolution (Russia), 54, 120–1
Nolan, Mary, 100
non-labour of the few, 147
"non-linear" proletarianization, 57
Nordhaus, William, 211
Northern Star, 111–2
Notes from the Gallows (Fucik), xi

October Revolution, 118–19, 126
Offermann, Toni, 96
old working class, 6
open-air free speech, 101
open shop, 117
Operai e Capitale (Tronti), 118
oppression, 39, 119, 144, 158, 160, 167
organizational capacity, as one of three
   crucial elements of revolutionary
   agency, 18
organizing campaigns, 49, 84
The Origin of Species (Darwin), 115,
   179
Osborne, Michael, 224n8
Outcast London (Jones), 40
overdeterminations, 21
Owenite experiments, 74, 261n334
ownership and control, centralization
   of, 118

Packingtown (Chicago), 79
Paine, Tom, 144
paleo-proletariat, 24

286

Index

Index

Index

Index

von Haussman, Baron, 91
von Hayek, Friedrich, 152
von Humboldt, Alexander, 183
von Mises, Ludwig, 150, 152
von Ranke, Leopold, 9
von Schirach, Baldur, 111
von Stein, Lorenz, 11, 12, 34, 35, 197
Vooruit coop (Ghent), 89–90, 112,
  247n213

Wage (Marx), x
wage depression, 45
wage-labor, 36, 43, 52, 119, 133
wages system, 36
Wahre Jakob, 112
Walker, Gilbert, 197
Walker, Martyn, 253n274
walkouts, 32, 50, 76–7, 118, 124
Wallace, Alfred Russell, 114, 189
Waltham-Lowell system, 54–5
warming, 260n19. *See also* global
  warming
*Wartime Shipyard: A Study in Social
  Disunity* (Archibald), 47–8
Weber, Eugen, 167
Weber, Max, 150, 159, 259n10
Wheeler, Robert, 109–10
white supremacy, as true Achilles' heel
  of labor movement, 51
Whitney, Josiah, 265n9
"Who Led the February Insurrection?"
  (Trotsky), 240–1n151
*Why There Is No Socialism in the United
  States* (Sombart), 21
Wiener, Norbert, 3
Williams, Alex, 6
Williams, Gwyn, 86, 107
Williams, Michael, 183
Winckler, Hugo, 192
Wisconsin school of labor history, 83–4

Wobblies, 101
women
  as essential to capitalist production,
    52
  openness of pub life and
    equivalents to, 249n234
women's suffrage, 86–7, 147
Women's War, 88
Wood, Ellen, 8
work, according to Gorz, 2
workers and soldiers' councils
  (*Arbetier-und Soldatenrate* and
  soviets), 74–5
workers' control, mass strikes and,
  59–77
Workers Cycling Association (ARS),
  250–1n257
workers' movement
  in 1880s, 82
  and agrarian question, 127–36,
    254n299, 255n307
  assembling of historic bloc of allied
    oppressed groups by, 127
  cooperative institutions as integral
    parts of, 257n334
  creation of leisure time by, 95
  as following tracks of
    revolutionary democracy, 144
  as needing to break military
    monopoly of bourgeois state
    from inside, 136
  as needing to confront power of
    capital in every aspect of social
    life, 119
  as needing to speak not only
    language of scientific socialism
    but also dialects of past popular
    struggles, 121
  young workers' movement, 107
Workers' Palaces, 101–2

293